LIVE Intentionally

65 Challenges for a Healthier, Happier Life

Cara Sue Achterberg

This publication contains the opinions and ideas of its author. It is intended to provide helpful and informative material on the subjects addressed in the publication. It is sold with the understanding that the author and publisher are not engaged in rendering medical, health, psychological, or any other kind of personal professional services in the book. If the reader requires personal, medical, health or other assistance or advice, a competent professional should be consulted.

The author and publisher specifically disclaim all responsibility for any liability, loss, or risk, personal or otherwise, that is incurred as a consequence, directly or indirectly, of the use and application of any of the contents of this book.

The recipes in this book have been carefully tested. To the best of our knowledge, they are safe and nutritious for ordinary use and users. For those people with food or other allergies, or who have special food requirements or health issues, please read the suggested content of each recipe carefully and determine whether or not they may create a problem for you. All recipes are used at the risk of the consumer. We cannot be responsible for any hazards, loss or damage that may occur as a result of any recipe use. For those with special needs, allergies, requirements or health problems, in the event of any doubt, please contact your medical adviser prior to the use of any recipe.

Cover design by Joan Snyder of Pippi's Pen Shoppe, York, PA

For my favorite children, Brady, Adelaide, and Ian. Thank you for being my test subjects, my biggest fans, my best teachers, and my heart's motivation.

Contents

Introduction

I'm not a detail person. I hate to read directions. Do-It-Yourself books usually sit unused on my shelf. So why would I write a blog and a book full of DIY platitudes and instructions? I did it because learning to live intentionally saved my family's health and changed our lives for the better. That was information I just couldn't keep to myself.

I came to intentional eating kicking and screaming. I used to be a Diet Coke girl. I drank it like water. And those barbeque flavored baked Lays? Loved them dipped in fat-free sour cream. When I got my first kitchen, I bought a case of Kraft Macaroni and Cheese and alternated meals comprised of an entire box of mac-n-cheese with cans of SpaghettiOs and sugar-free Jell-O in any flavor. Suffice it to say, I was awash in artificial flavors, colors, and ingredients.

When I began cooking for a family, my habits improved only slightly. I went with what was easy and kept everyone happy – frozen lasagnas, hot dogs, and burgers supplemented by plenty of takeout Chinese food and pizza. The cabinets were full of chips, cookies, and cereal; the fridge full of ice cream, soda, and lunch meats.

We were a busy family going in five different directions at once. Stress was the name of the game. I assumed this was simply part of raising a family in today's society, until my family's health began to fall apart. My husband's cholesterol was hovering near the danger zone and two of my kids were diagnosed with ADHD and prescribed drugs with frightening side-effects. My oldest son was on three meds for asthma and I suffered from near-constant allergies. Then, over the course of one month, my four-year-old son's soft, gorgeous, red curls all fell out, leaving him bald from an auto-immune condition called alopecia areata.

Something had to give. I jumped in with everything I had. It was time to clean up our act. I began by removing the chemicals from our lives and our diet. The cleaning closet was emptied, the pantry cleared out. I read everything I could, talked to experts, and listened to fanatics. I learned how to grow, can, freeze, and create all of our food. I changed our patterns, limiting screens, encouraging exercise and creativity, and getting rid of mountains of stuff we didn't need. I cleared the air in our house of toxic chemicals and began to see us as citizens of this earth rather than visitors to the planet. This book is the story of the past eight years.

As I said at the outset, I'm not one for complicated directions so this book breaks down the changes we made in our lives in simple, clear directions, along with some hopefully entertaining stories of our journey. There are recipes, ideas, and inspiration for creating your own Intentional Life your way. I invite you to take what you can use, and recycle the rest.

You can plow through it all at once or take it in bite size pieces. Each chapter is designed to stand alone. As I dreamed up this book, I envisioned groups of people reading the book and sharing their own adventures in intentional living on a weekly basis, complete with field trips! I even wrote a group guide to help you structure your meetings.

While this book is written from my point of view as a mom of three kids, you don't need to be a mom (or have kids living with you presently) to embrace the ideas presented in this book. We all need to live intentionally – with or without kids.

Each chapter ends with three challenges – choose the one that works for you. I promise you that making even one small change will move you toward a healthier, happier, more Intentional Life. Once you get a taste of that, you'll want more.

And my family? Well, my husband is no longer flirting with cholesterol drugs, none of my children are on any prescription meds, and I rarely even get a cold anymore. We are all healthier than we've ever been. We are still busy people, but we are making time to connect as a family. Our house no longer harbors any toxic chemicals and our gardens grow larger each year. We know our neighbors, patronize our local store owners, and spend our money and time on the things that matter. In short, we are living intentionally. You can, too.

What Does an Intentional Life Look Like?

An Intentional Life is a life that is real. One that can be trusted.

It means more than healthier eating, it means knowing your food – where it came from, how it was prepared, and what it can do for you. It's learning to make more of your own food from scratch enabling you to eat well affordably. For many, that means discovering the joy and satisfaction of gardening, too.

Living intentionally means feeling good about how you spend your time and how your children spend their time. It's taking care of your body and teaching your children to do the same. It's exploring your own creativity and abilities and not being a stand-by passenger in this life.

An Intentional Life will lead you to get to know your neighbors, the farmers who grow your food, and other people who wrestle with the same desire to change their lives. It will motivate you to learn more about nutrition, our food system, our government, and your community. You will find yourself reading labels and surfing the internet for information and recipes.

An Intentional Life is unplugged. It's not dependent on screens or the latest gadget. It means considering how much stuff you have and how much you need. Living intentionally requires that you weigh the cost/benefits of adding that new game system or the latest fashions. It will mean sharing more and wanting less.

Intentional lives are not dictated by convenience. Sometimes living intentionally requires a bigger effort and a little more time. Sometimes it doesn't. It's a life not governed by the bottom-line or time-saved, but that's not to say it doesn't value both of those goals.

Living Intentionally will lead you to buy locally, make your own food, and parent your children in ways that may not, at first, be easy.

An Intentional Life can sometimes make you feel out of step with the masses.

Living Intentionally is about common sense. Think about what you are eating. Think about what you are doing. Think about how you are affecting the planet, your neighbors, and your community. Think about how you are parenting. Be intentional.

An Intentional Life is a life you feel good about – **down to your core.** It's knowing you are doing the best you can for your health, your family, and your world. It requires no excuses.

Challenges

At used book sales, I'm drawn to the self-help books. I don't know if this is because I'm curious about what other people need help with or because I've found gold there in those hills before. I cart home armloads of self-help books. I start and promptly put down most of them after ten or twenty pages. But some I read and even re-read and underline. Inevitably these are the books that offer not just a new idea or way of looking at my problem/goal/need, but the ones that offer something I can do about it. I squirm with pleasure when I come across a list of resources, exercises, plans, and most especially challenges. I love a good challenge.

Someone asked me in the early edits of this book, why *challenges?* Why not *suggestions?* I thought about that question. Suggestions are gentle and helpful, but they are always perceived as *optional.* Many of the best suggestions get lost in our good intentions. A challenge forces you to action – *am I going to do this or not?* You won't change your life unless you do something different – unless you make a decision to change. Taking on a challenge gives you a vehicle for change.

At the end of each chapter in this book, I've included some challenges. And because I am sensitive to the fact that not everyone is as enamored as I am with big challenges, I offer challenges on a sliding scale. There is a *basic challenge* that just about anyone can do, a *serious challenge* for someone who's up for a little more, and then there is the *extreme challenge* for the crazy people out there. The people like me. You can pick and choose your challenge on a chapter by chapter basis, depending on how much energy you have left over after picking up all the dirty socks lying about and whether you have to clean for company this week. See, I'm flexible.

A Word About Resistant Kids and Reluctant Husbands

Most people resist change. They like things the way they are. They like things they know, kids especially, which is somewhat amusing to me because they are the first ones to line up for the cheese curls when they find out the new formula will turn your tongue blue. Maybe the resistance is in the way we approach it. Kids (and some husbands) hear *healthy* and think *bad-tasting*. My kids say the word organic with the same inflection they might use for the words brussel sprouts. When a parent says- *We're going to do something different* - kids immediately brace themselves for less fun or more responsibilities. And family meetings strike fear in the hearts of children and husbands alike. It doesn't have to be that way.

I find the best way to begin doing something new or different is to simply do it. Sometimes the less fuss we make about a new food, habit, or experience, the better. Take a page from Nike's book and *Just do it*. They'll follow; you'll see.

I'm not going to tell you that it was easy and now my kids are true believers. It took a long time. In certain instances we still haven't moved beyond the initial, *Yuck!* There are plenty of moments when I throw up my hands in exasperation after I've served a meal that cost a fortune and tastes fabulous, yet they refuse to even try it. I do find myself all alone hanging clothes on the line and we have frequent stand-offs involving dirty dishes and clothes that have not been put in drawers. That said, for many of our changes, my kids enthusiastically lead the way.

The two big things you need when trying to convert your children to a healthier lifestyle are persistence and compromise. You have to keep putting things out there -particularly as it pertains to food, but you also have to be reasonable. My kids had a few non-negotiables. They weren't willing to give up their pancake syrup or their Cheez-its. So we compromised. I buy the imitation flavored, artificially colored syrup they love on special occasions and birthdays, and one box of Cheez-its each week.

I doubt that any of my children remember what ultra-pasteurized milk in a plastic jug tastes like. They don't pine for their Peter Pan peanut butter. By consistently offering healthier alternatives, they've adapted. They even seem a little proud that we eat so healthy when they explain the menu to guests.

When I pulled out the reusable fabric bags to replace the plastic baggies and threw out their favorite plastic water bottles, they bristled. But the tussle soon blew over and I doubt they remember the plastic of their childhood. We celebrate Earth Hour every spring, just like Valentine's Day or Easter. My husband always refers to *when you changed the way we do things*, but nowadays he is just as likely as I to come up with an idea for making our house and family healthier and happier.

I think it comes down to what a lot of things come down to in parenting – holding your ground. You have to draw your line and then stick to it. *This is the way we do things now.* I don't tell them where their new clothes came from or offer to stop at McDonalds. When I make a change, if a question arises, I tell them it's because this new way or food or idea is healthier for us and for the earth. Enough said. This is the way we do things now. Forever. It won't change. You can't waffle. Kids will run right over a waffler.

The bottom line is that organic, local, healthy food tastes better. Doing the right thing for the earth feels right. Sharing the responsibility for our house and our pets builds self-worth. It's a different way of approaching life. Your kids will figure this out, too. Sometimes it takes a while, but they'll come around. And they won't starve meanwhile – honest.

Husbands can occasionally put up more of a fight. After all, they've been living the way they've been living much longer than your children who are relatively new to this earth. If your husband doesn't jump on board with changes you want to make for your family, it can be tough. Hopefully, if you sit him down and explain how important this is to you, he's the kind of guy who will support you. If not, all you can do is set the example and remind him that he's an adult, and as such, he can buy/cook/eat/clean/live the way he wants to, just without your assistance.

For the first few years of our newly Intentional Life, my husband still ate lunch at Burger King almost every day. He made snarky remarks and drifted towards the kids' camp when I put flaxseed in his granola and cooked his eggs in coconut oil. He was more accepting of the compost bin and the chickens. Although he rolled his eyes every weekend when I announced our next project, he still offered his support, an open mind, and his carpentry skills. Nowadays he's a convert and no longer spends his lunch money on Burger King. He feels better, his cholesterol is down, and he enjoys our healthy lifestyle.

I have friends whose husbands have not been as accepting of changes to the family's lifestyle. My best advice is to set the example. Don't let a spouse's resistance be an excuse not to change your own life. If you are in charge of the kitchen, you don't have to announce every change you make. If your spouse is in charge of the purse strings, you have to be frugal and careful, but you don't have to buy junk. Rome wasn't built in a day, sometimes you have to start with baby steps.

One more thing – and this is important - you cannot push your eating preferences on other parents. When my kids go to friends' houses, I never question what they will eat. They can and should eat whatever is served. It's important to teach your kids that manners matter, and everyone makes their own decisions about how and what they eat – and we respect that. No judgment. I don't run for the hills when someone pulls out the Styrofoam plates or the Fritos, although sometimes I do collect the plastic water bottles to recycle after a public event.

Common Protests

I have no time!

Believe me, I hear ya. Here's the thing – none of us has the time. If it's important, you will *make* the time. I tell this to my husband when he says he has no time to work out, yet hits the snooze button at least three times each morning – that's 27 minutes! If someone in your family had a life-threatening condition and it required you to eat healthy and remove the toxins from your house, you'd find the time. The way many of us are eating and living these days *is* a life-threatening condition. So, I don't accept the excuse *I haven't got the time*. You don't have to change everything today; it took me at least a year to feel we had truly changed our lifestyle. You begin by making little changes and gradually you'll find you're doing things a whole new way. As a dear friend says to me whenever I'm overwhelmed – "Baby steps."

I don't know where to start!

The first step is always the most intimidating. Do what works for you and don't judge yourself. Any improvement you make in the quality of the food you eat and the life you lead is better than none. You can work your way through this book chapter by chapter, making a change a week or you can skip around and make the changes that work for you. The important thing is that you're moving forward!

What's so bad about processed foods?

I've been around horses most of my life. Colic is the biggest killer of horses. Colic is really just a symptom – intestinal pain. The reason you can have intestinal pain and feel better in 24 hours, yet it kills horses, is simple. Horses' systems only work in one direction. Horses can't throw up. So if they eat something their body can't process, it will kill them. Happens all the time.

Most of us don't think too much about what happens to our food once it gets past our taste buds. We don't consider that our bodies are machines that require certain nutrients. When we eat processed foods, we are giving our body things it doesn't need and was never meant to process.

If you put the wrong gas or oil in a machine and try to run it, it may run, but not well. Do this long enough and the entire engine might seize up. When we force our bodies to process things we are not meant to process, it weakens our health and can cause our systems to break down.

Are you telling me that I have to become "organic"?

An Intentional Life is about healthy, responsible living. This does lean towards organic, because I believe that's how all food should be grown. That said, I don't believe it's necessary to eat only organic food. I believe in local, responsibly grown, and/or manufactured products first, organic if I can get them. It would be incredibly expensive, and in my opinion limiting, to buy only certified organic items. Many farmers who would like to be certified organic point out the difficulty and cost of getting that rating. I live in Amish country, and while most Amish farms are truly organic and have been for centuries, none of them are certified organic.

Labels can be confusing, but sometimes they are all we have. Choose products with clear, simple ingredients lists with or without the little green and white *certified organic* circle. Knowing exactly what ingredients are in your food and how they were grown is key. If you don't recognize an ingredient on a label – look it up. Is it something you want to put in your body? This is about eating smart. A generation or two ago, everyone lived organically. Somewhere along the line we let big business tell us what to eat, instead of our bodies.

I don't know if I can do this. It seems too hard.

Not knowing if you can do this is no reason not to try. Some ideas might be hard, but others will be easy. Maybe you can't do everything in this book, but you can make some changes. You can move yourself closer to the life you want to live. This is not a competition or a race. Some of the ideas presented in this book may live as seeds in your heart until you have the time, energy, and resources to take them on. Making just one change may empower you to make another and another.

Now is not a good time.

I've stalled on plenty of big projects. This book has been rumbling around my mind and heart for over five years. I kept telling myself I'd write it when I finally knew enough. I'd write it when I finally became a "writer." I'd write it after the kids were all in college. And then one day I realized that there would always be an excuse. Excuses are easy to find, especially when you're a mom with busy kids and a life of her own. I'll leave you with the quote that finally got me moving – *Do not wait until the conditions are perfect to begin. Beginning makes the conditions perfect.* (Adam Cohen)

GETTING
STARTED

1

What If

One Sunday I was talking with a group of teenagers about a Habitat for Humanity project we were thinking of taking on the next summer. We weren't completely sure what we were getting into, and some of us were nervous. We pondered many angles to questions that began with, *What if....?* What if we did this? What if we could raise the money? What if we learned how to use power tools? What if we could make a difference in one community? One family? The questions created exciting possibilities.

Too often we get bogged down in the *What Is*. Adults are especially guilty of this. The younger a soul is the more they seem able to indulge the *What Ifs*. My kids are full of *What Ifs*. What if I made a house by gluing together six thousand Popsicle sticks – would it be big enough for me to live in? What if I shut the cat in the hamper and rolled it down the steps? What if I put a marshmallow in the microwave? What if I jump off the deck holding an umbrella? The *What Ifs* of children are endless.

Adults can easily get stuck in *What Is*. What is the point in recycling? There's so much waste already. What's the difference if I buy a greener car? There's already a million gas guzzlers on the road. What's the matter with a few diet sodas? They aren't going to kill me.

Or maybe our *What Is* revolves around somebody else taking care of it. The government is working on that problem. It's the school's job to teach my kids. The media is everywhere; what's one more hour in front of the television? All kids watch TV. They all have cell phones. They all eat processed food. Besides I'm no cook. We don't have any extra money right now. I'm too busy. They're too picky. We hide behind *What Is*. But it doesn't have to be that way.

What if we turned off our TVs? What if the stupid thing broke and we never replaced it? What if you read a book with your kid (even if that kid can read it for themselves)? What if you wrote a book together? What if you tried canning food? What if you learned to bake bread? What if you taught your kids to eat healthy? What if you started a garden, or a window box, or even a pot of basil? Sure, you don't have time or money or your kids' interest – that's *What Is*. But if you want to change your life, you have to start asking *What If*. What if I took that course? What if I volunteered to help? What if I got involved in local politics? What if my kids and I start a project together? What if I eliminated just one processed food from my diet? What if I started making one basic staple of our diet – bread, yogurt, ice cream, granola, whatever. What if we did something differently or tried something new?

I don't know what will happen if you change a habit or try something new, but I can tell you one thing, it won't be a *What Is* anymore. The only way this world or our lives will change is if we start to think in terms of *What Ifs* and we don't let the *What Is* get in the way. What if more people shopped with their conscience? What if we gave our time, money, and ideas more freely? What if consumers demanded organic produce and supported local farmers? What if we cut our trash output in half?

I read somewhere that when a butterfly on the far reaches of the earth flaps its wings, there are consequences worldwide. Any small change you make will affect the planet, your community, and the people around you. Even if you're only making a tiny dent in your health, your carbon footprint, or your children's education, your actions might be an example others follow. And then there's that whole snowball effect.

What Ifs are risky. They can be embarrassing, painful, time-consuming, and frustrating. They can even be dangerous. But they make life so much more exciting. And they give us the opportunity to make a difference. People who change the world or their community or even their lives, are people who ask *What if?*

Challenges

Basic: Write *What If* at the top of a piece of paper and finish the sentence 15 times. Ask your spouse/friend/kids to do the same.

Serious: Make a pledge to read this book and accept at least the basic challenge of every chapter.

Extreme: Ask some friends, or your family, to read this book with you and commit to reading a chapter and accepting a challenge each week. Keep each other accountable and cheer each other on.

2

Affording a Healthier Diet

Yesterday I made my monthly trek to my favorite natural food grocery store. As I made my selections, I was well aware that some of the food I was choosing cost significantly more than similar versions in the grocery store. The food I selected was pesticide free, hormone free, additive free, preservative free, and in many cases certified organic. Good healthy food costs more. I'm going to share with you ways you can spend less through your own efforts, resourcefulness, gardens, and preserving, but the bottom line is it may cost you more, especially in the beginning.

Cost should not be a deterrent because this is life or death we're talking about. Feeding your family healthy food will protect them for a lifetime. There is no cost too high for avoiding things like cancer, heart disease, autoimmune disorders, and diabetes. And you'll never know if you dodged these bullets because you ate and lived well or because you're lucky. Science has yet to connect all the dots, but we cannot afford to wait. Trust your instincts and common sense. It's best not to take chances on your health.

So how do you afford it? You take a long hard look at your budget and figure out how to save in other areas. When I confessed to my mother-in-law that I was shopping at Goodwill for our clothes, she said, "It makes sense to spend more on the things you put *in* your body than *on* your body."

Choosing to live a healthier, more planet conscious life costs more in some ways and less in others. You can save money by making and growing much of your own food and by cleaning with simple inexpensive products. There is no way around buying some things that cost a premium. It's a balance you have to find with your own budget and your own life. It may be "cheaper" for you to pay the high cost of an organic item versus making it yourself. Your time is worth money, too. I'm certain as more people demand organic products, the cost of organics will go down and the options will increase.

One easy way to save money on a healthier diet is to stock up. I once received an e-mail from a friend with an attachment from Johns Hopkins concerning what to do if a pandemic strikes. It said to stay home. Easy enough. It also said to have 16 days' worth of food stockpiled. Not a problem. I've become quite the believer in stocking up. That wasn't always the case.

I used to make frequent trips to the market and buy *only what I needed* in the firm belief that this was better for our budget. The problem with that logic was that I was often running to the store for *just this one thing* and coming home with a cartload of stuff. Let me be clear here – the less you go to the store the less you spend. It doesn't take a rocket scientist to figure that out.

Stock up. Keep your pantry and freezer well stocked. It stands to reason if you know you eat pasta at least once a week, you can buy all the pasta you need months in advance (it keeps). Stocking up on staples like pasta, pasta sauce, chicken broth, ketchup, syrup, cereal, jelly, peanut butter, beans and other items that will store well saves you a last minute trip to the grocery store with cranky kids in tow that not only costs money, but time. Fill your freezer with staples like bread (even if you make your own), butter (you need this for nearly everything), flour (keeps fresher, longer in the freezer as do nuts), veggies and fruit. We'll talk later about filling your freezer with a cow!

Preserve in-season fruits and vegetables by freezing or canning. For this a large stand-alone freezer is essential. If you hope to grow and harvest your own fruits and vegetables, or even if you plan to buy from a Farmers' Market, being able to store them saves you money. Many foods can be purchased less expensively in bulk, but without some way of storing them, they will go to waste. A freezer also allows you to stock up when products go on sale.

Don't feel you must go out and buy a brand new freezer. Although the newer versions are better energy-wise, there are lots of cheap and even free freezers to be found. We got our commercial freezer at no cost from a friend who was downsizing. People discard freezers for lots of reasons and unless you've ever tried to get rid of one, you can't appreciate how difficult it is. You can't put your unwanted freezer out for the trash and hauling one to the dump is a sizable task. Ask around – you may be surprised to find one right under your nose. Two other good sources for inexpensive freezers are Freecycle.org or Craigslist.com. You might also have a local community paper that places ads for free – check for someone looking to unload a freezer or add your own *WANTED* listing.

There is enough controversy surrounding plastic that for leftovers and storing bulk dry items, I stick to glass. It's been around forever and so far, no bad press. I think glass keeps food fresher and I know it looks better. Plus, glass can be put in the dishwasher without breaking down or discoloring or getting that funny warped shape that keeps the lid from ever properly sealing again. Glass storage containers last longer and come in all sizes and shapes. I make laminated labels for my jars and get a strange thrill when I see them all lined up in my drawer. It makes me feel very Martha Stewart-ish. I store dried fruit, sugars, baking powder, corn meal, salt, spices, pasta, oatmeal, rice, and pretty much anything I buy in bulk in glass containers. Plus leftovers, veggies prepped for future use, and home baked treats.

Freezer storage is another story. For this, plastic is fine. I'm admitting right up front that I have a container fetish. Ask my husband or check out my basement. Even though you can now recycle almost anything, I still hang on to all useful containers. This has come in very handy for me, not only saving us money, but making my life simpler. Small medicine bottles are great for storing the wealth of dried herbs we grow and large yogurt containers are perfect for freezing applesauce, pureed pumpkin, tomato sauce, and chicken broth. Having various containers on hand has been a lifesaver when packing for a picnic, taking food to a friend in need, or sending food to school or church for an event.

Find a place to store plastic containers and you will be helping yourself and the planet. I wish I had a handy tip for storing miscellaneous plastic containers. I put like-size containers nested together in large plastic bins and shelve them. I use the drawers of an old desk for the little containers, but there's no easy answer.

If you don't have enough containers already hoarded, you'll need freezer bags in varying sizes, plus a sharpie marker to label everything. It's critical that you label everything you freeze. You think you'll remember what they are – but you won't. Strawberry sauce and spaghetti sauce look awfully alike after they've been frozen a few months (so do applesauce and chicken broth). That isn't a pleasant lesson to learn the hard way – take it from me.

Before bagging fruits or vegetables to freeze, be sure they are as air dry as possible. You can use a salad spinner to help with this. Always remove all the extra air to help prevent freezer burn. After you've filled your bag, shift the ingredients around until they're as flat as can be and freeze the bag in this position. After it is completely frozen, you can stack your bags up like bricks in the freezer and they take up less room (and look neat and organized).

Shop less. Before you rush off to the store to get one crucial ingredient, do two things. First, if it stores well, add it to your list of things to keep in stock. Second – think of something else you can serve instead. I'm telling you – flexibility will save you hundreds of dollars. It's really nice and supremely organized to have the week's menu made up ahead of time and posted primly on the fridge, but if you haven't got exactly what you need to follow the plan, improvise or serve something else before you run to the store to get the missing ingredient. Always have a Plan B.

Centralize your shopping list. My list is a pad of paper on the side of the fridge. Everyone knows that if you open the last of anything (jelly, ketchup, olive oil), you must write it on the list or Mommy may wig out on you. If I kept the list in my purse or on my phone, others would not have access (since those two objects have a way of going missing). This system works for us, but it did take a little enforced guilt/natural consequences in the beginning to get everyone with the program. A central list works because then it's not up to me to inventory the kitchen or rely on my ever-decomposing memory to remember all the things we might need each time I go to the store.

Shop alone. Under no circumstance should you take kids to the grocery store. (Unless maybe you're doing math homework that requires it.) I'm usually all for teaching the children by example, but I know if I take my kids to the grocery store, I leave stressed out and laden with things I didn't go there to buy (like Cheezits in every flavor). Plus, I almost always arrive home missing at least one item I planned to buy but left behind in the interest of my children's safety and my sanity. There will be time to teach them about shopping for groceries (like when they come home from college).

Organize your cupboards. Clean them out. Knowing what you have saves you money. We have a pantry that is so deep I must stand on a high bar stool to see the back of the top shelf. Things can and do get lost back there. It's important to know what you already have before you end up buying yet another package of cornmeal (we currently have three). This is a case of do what I say, not what I do (a line that never works on my kids). I know how happy I've felt on the few occasions when my pantry was organized. Most times it was because the house was for sale (face all the labels out – it will make your cabinet look organized, even if it isn't). It takes time to organize. You need to have a garbage can, a recycling bin, and a give-away box handy.

Ultimately, we find ways to afford the things that are really important to us. It comes down to priorities, and maybe a little creative bookkeeping. I shop at Goodwill, swap books with friends or use the library, and wait for movies to hit the $2 movie house. I also stock up on the food I know my family will eat. This means my family eats grass-fed beef, locally ground grains, and organic pesticide-free strawberries. Seems like a fair trade to me.

Challenges:

Basic: Figure out what your family spends on food, clothing, entertainment, and travel by keeping a log for a month. Inventory your pantry. Donate what you won't use. Use what you will. Make a list of the items your family eats regularly so that you can stock up on these foods.

Serious: Develop a dream budget and a practical budget. Create a system for your shopping list. Make sure everyone knows the system. Come up with a plan for shopping without kids. Consider swapping children with a friend who might also benefit from shopping alone.

Extreme: Decide where you will cut back so that you can afford to buy better food. Consider your clothing, cable, and eating out expenses. Try going without a few things (Starbucks coffee, movie rental, fast food stop, dry cleaning) for one month and see if you miss them. Reconsider your current pantry space. Is there another closet/cabinet available for overflow? Could you add a shelf somewhere? Buy/acquire an extra freezer and fill it with staples.

3

Don't Be a Blind Consumer

I've thought a lot about how far removed we are from our food. What triggered these thoughts originally was the blind chicken living in her own personal custom-built hutch attached to our garage. When this hen survived the attack by the other chickens that took her eyes out, my first thought was – *Sunday dinner!*

I'm sure you're shuddering. But really, we had 31 other perfectly good chickens and this one was now one more chore waiting to happen. Why shouldn't we butcher it? My children gave impassioned arguments in favor of saving the life of "Kernel" (named after the ill-fated Popcorn who was carried off by a hawk), none of which amounted to anything more than - *how could you?*

When I mentioned my idea to friends, they asked, "Could you really kill it?" I don't know. Maybe? I'd never had the opportunity. But it seemed to me that if I was going to eat meat, I really should be able to kill the animal that supplied it. We all should. Don't get me wrong – I know it would be hard. I was certain I would have nightmares afterward and shed plenty of tears in the process, but I also thought that morally I shouldn't be eating meat if I couldn't do the deed.

Not that long ago, everyone killed the animals that supplied the meat for their dinner. My father-in-law likes to horrify us by demonstrating with a windmilling arm how he snapped the neck of the chickens he killed for dinner back in his day.

After watching the movie, *Food Inc.,* I was convinced that we needed to raise our own chickens for meat. I explained to the kids that our chickens would be much better off than the chickens in the film. They would live happy, carefree lives right up until the moment we butchered them. No dice. When the kids petitioned to let our two broody hens hatch the eggs they had to be pried off of each night, I offered to make them a deal. I would let the hens hatch some of their eggs, but we would raise the boy chicks for meat. They quickly decided that the joy of watching the hens hatch chicks would not offset the final end for some of those precious chicks.

How many of us really know what we're eating? We've become so far removed from creating our own food that most of us have to look up how to hard boil an egg or make a pie crust. Our grandparents could do these things in their sleep. I can't help but wonder how the waistlines of Americans might be effected if they had to make all their own foods. If we ate only what we created with our own hands from ingredients purchased whole or grown ourselves, I bet we'd lose some serious weight. Maybe I should create a diet called *Made (and Lost) From Scratch.*

There's a quiz that occasionally makes the rounds of the internet and serves as a distressing reminder of how unaware we are of what we eat. It lists the ingredients in the average breakfast cereal, cracker, cookie, and bread. Then it asks the reader to identify which is which. It's impossible. In fact, you wouldn't even recognize the group of ingredients as any food because most of the lengthy list is impossible to even pronounce.

"If you are what you eat and you don't know what you're eating, do you know who you are?" (Anonymous) It's funny, but it's also a very poignant comment on the state of the average person's diet.

The next time you're shopping, pick up your favorite box of crackers or cereal and take a look at the ingredients. Do you know recognize anything? If you don't, you're gambling your health (and possibly your life) on the trustworthiness of some huge manufacturer whose main consideration is how much you'll pay for said product.

You're also banking your life on our government's ability to regulate the food industry. They wouldn't allow companies to sell something that would endanger your health, right? Of course not, just like they wouldn't allow you to have a mortgage you can't afford or allow an oil company to drill miles deep in the ocean with no safety net.

Our blind chicken survived the winter, and in the spring we began letting her out for short periods. She was happiest pecking for her own food rather than being cooped up in a cage. Problem was, the neighbor's dog knew exactly what was in his dog food.

Be smart and remember, we truly are what we eat.

Challenges

Basic: Start reading labels. Try to buy only food with ingredients you recognize.

Serious: Declare a *Homemade Week* and eat only food you make yourself or purchase from someone who made the food themselves (in other words, you have to buy from the hands that created it).

Extreme: Take the serious challenge one step further and incorporate this rule into your family's life. Learn to make your most commonly eaten foods. There are lots of recipes in this book and in the book, *Bake the Bread, Buy the Butter* by Jennifer Reese.

Super Extreme: Volunteer to help on butchering day at a local organic or grass-fed farm.

4

Shop Locally

A few years ago, I committed myself (and, by default, my family) to a little experiment. I'd written a column for our local paper entitled, *Shop Like a Pennsylvanian*. While researching that column I found study after study that concluded buying from locally owned stores was better for the local economy. At least fifty percent of the money you spend in local establishments stays in your local community, as opposed to shopping at large retailers and big-box stores, which contribute far less to the local economy. Since we live in a relatively rural area that leans towards the backwards (no offense, I kind of like it that way), I wondered if it were really possible to exclusively shop local. So I decided to test the theory. It was my Gone Local challenge. Here is what I proclaimed on my blog:

I believe that my family and my community benefit when I shop from locally owned enterprises. Therefore, I will shop exclusively from stores owned and operated locally, preferably from stores where I can meet the owner, even better if the owner is operating the store.

It was time to put my money where my mouth, or my computer keys, were.

My other motivation came from an experience I had the first time I ventured to downtown York. Being a natural country bumpkin, I tend to stay as close to home as possible. Cities are not my thing. I ventured to York in search of a tea store reputed to have hundreds of loose teas. There was nothing like this near my little hillside, so I went exploring. I found the tea shop as well as a downtown farmers market and all sorts of one-of-a-kind shops. One adorably pink and sparkly shop offered handmade gifts and pottery. The owner was behind the counter as I made my purchase and I complimented her on such a lovely little store. She said she was glad I liked it but she was closing at the end of the month after nearly ten years in business. She just wasn't making it. Her last comment to me was, "Locals don't shop downtown, it's only the tourists." Her words had echoed in my heart ever since.

When purchasing food, I always tried to "buy local," purchasing produce that has been grown right here. But what about everything else? Why did I go to Wal-Mart, Target or Giant for the things I needed? Why did I do most of my gift shopping online?

Honest answer? It was cheaper and easier. I didn't have to move my butt out of my chair to make the purchase. Anything I wanted was only a mouse click away. I even bought shampoo and toothpaste online. I had a sick love affair with Drugstore.com. Instead of standing in the shampoo aisle weighing the benefits of shiny versus full-bodied, I could collect opinions from perfect strangers who took the time to write reviews. Never mind the generalizations that could be made about the kind of people who take the time to write a 500 word review of a shampoo or toothpaste. And the shipping was free! What's not to love?

But like so many other "conveniences," I hadn't thought through the long-term consequences of my shopping habits. Who was getting my money? My best guess? One of the "one percent."

So instead of carping on this any longer, I decided to see if I could change my ways. I'd never been good at doing things half-way, so I decided to go cold turkey. No more Wal-Mart, no more Giant, no more Amazon (sharp intake of breath noted), and no Drugstore.com. Could I do this? More importantly, could my family and my budget survive this decision?

I didn't know, but I committed three months to finding out.

I worried about the sacrifices. Would there be any decent local wine? Where would I buy my expensive, super-soft toilet paper? Would my kids survive the absence of Cheezits? And just how much was I willing to spend on cat food? I was certain that hair care products could very well be my breaking point.

In the beginning we all thought this was going to be a hardship, each for our own reasons. My kids worried a Cheezit would never pass their lips again and I'd feed them a steady diet of kale and whole wheat noodles. My husband worried I'd spend all the money hidden under our mattresses. I mostly worried that I'd have to eat my words.

Aside from a handful of slip-ups in regards to hair products and auto repair, for the most part we survived on the goods sold by locally owned businesses exclusively for three months. Once more, we more than survived, we thrived.

We saved money, time, and gas by shopping at stores that were family owned right here in our little town instead of trekking 20 or 30 miles to the mall. We saved even more money by purposefully planning all our purchases, and we realized that there were many *needs* we didn't need. We made new friends by getting to know local shopkeepers in our downtown and the family-owned businesses in our township. We ate better both in terms of taste and health because we paid the extra few dollars to buy locally sourced and produced food. We had a lot of fun figuring out where we could buy the things we needed. I didn't miss the big stores, chain restaurants, or online retailers one bit.

People had varying reactions when I shared my experience. There were some who were skeptical and suggested that I was going overboard in my efforts. I never did figure out why they seemed threatened by my experiment. I also met plenty of people who loved the idea and offered ideas, local sources, and their own experiences.

The coolest part was meeting store owners who appreciated my efforts and talking with friends who vowed to try to buy more locally themselves. My brother out in New Mexico e-mailed me during our Gone Local months to tell me that he and his beautiful wife, after reading one of the posts on my blog, had gone out for dinner in a locally owned downtown establishment.

My experiment officially ended after three months, but the new shopping habits I developed did not. I have continued to buy nearly exclusively from locally owned businesses. I couldn't go back to wasting money at Wal-Mart and running to Giant every time I ran out of something. Buying locally feels right. Some things cost more, but the savings continue because I buy intentionally. I've continued to plan my shopping excursions carefully and found new local venues to explore. The biggest change is that now I am deliberate about every purchase I make.

Reflecting on the impact of buying locally for three months made me even more convinced that we have the power to heal our own communities. There's no need to wait for the government to take action or the economy to bounce back, we have the power to help our friends, neighbors, and ourselves by simply thinking before we shop. If everyone made a conscientious effort to buy from locally owned businesses, even if it isn't convenient or familiar, it would only be a matter of time before things began to turn around. Cash is, after all, the grease that spins the wheel of our local economy.

The argument most vehemently made to me about my quest during our experiment had been cost in terms of cash and time. By consolidating my trips and doing without a few things, I easily saved time. The slight dent in the cleanliness of my house is a testament to that fact. And without a doubt we saved literally hundreds of dollars by shopping intentionally and only buying what we needed.

These are selfish reasons to shop locally. The bigger reason, the reason that should weigh on all our hearts, is the fact that shopping locally is what's best for our community. We all recognize that obligation, even if it's buried beneath years of apathy. To paraphrase JFK, "Ask not what your community can do for you, but what you can do for your community." Don't do it just for yourself, even though you will benefit tremendously, shop locally to help the people you call neighbors and friends.

Challenges

Basic: Pay attention to who owns the stores you patronize and who makes/grows the products you buy.

Serious: Explore locally owned stores and change some of your shopping habits to include them. Visit a downtown area.

Extreme: Pledge to shop locally for a week or a month.

5

The To-Do, Should-Do, and Could-Do Lists

I love mornings. I know I'm in the minority on this one. Starting my day with a run, some good reading, and tinkering in the garden while the horses are eating is my favorite way to begin my day. Without this time to center myself, I feel scattered. I try to do all this before anyone else in the house has rolled out of bed. This means my days begin about 5:30am. I hear you groaning.

Many people I encounter tell me that they'd like to do the homemade-organic-healthy food thing but there just isn't the time. Perhaps. Or perhaps it's a matter of organizing the time you have. When you have a free moment – what do you do? In those rare free hours I sometimes find myself feeling like a deer in the headlights – my brain fragmenting in every direction, overwhelmed by the myriad of things I should be doing. To overcome this I depend on my lists.

It's taken a while and my system is always evolving but I depend on three lists - *To-do*, *Should-Do*, and *Could-Do*. I'd like to tell you that I keep these lists in a nice leather bound journal with tabbed sections and highlight flags, but in reality sometimes these lists are on scraps of paper and junk mail envelopes on my counter.

My *Could-Do* list is a list of all the things I'd like to do someday if I had all the time in the world. It's things like *replace the door to the playroom* (the one with the gauges put there by an angry locked-out child) or *Strip the weed-filled bank near the mailbox and plant lilies.* It even has items like *learn to do yoga* and *create a wine cellar in the basement.* Just putting these plans in writing means they might happen someday. I keep this list on my smartphone so that I can survey it while waiting for appointments, children, or the oven timer to sound.

The *Should-Do* list is a list of all the things I'd like to get done this week. It may have as many as 15 things on it and is composed sometime between Sunday afternoon and Tuesday morning when I realize I haven't made one yet. It lists things like *make brownies for the band competition* and *pick up the dry cleaning.* I keep it on my desk or under a stack of papers, somewhere it won't harangue me, but where I can find it when I need it.

The critical list is the daily *To-do* list. I write it out each morning while I'm having my tea. I try not to place more than four or five things on this list. I've come to realize that I can only be sure of getting four, maybe five things done on a given day, even less if there are needy children, animals, or heaven forbid, housework that distract me. If I get everything on my daily list done, it's a banner day and I'll look to my weekly *Should-Do* list. The items on the *Should-Do* list slowly migrate to the daily list. The items on the *Could-Do* list eventually move to the daily *To-do* or weekly *Should-Do* lists or they continue to nag at me electronically for months until they seem irrelevant and I delete them.

Here's an example of one of my daily *To-do* lists: *make bread, cut herbs to dry, clean the kitchen, find someone to give my son a ride on Thursday, and finish researching article.* Those are the things I will get done no matter what. That list is manageable. Sure, I know there are about a million other things that need to get done, but I'm only one person. Life seems more manageable when I can cross off everything on my *To-do* list.

It has taken time to become realistic about the *To-do* list. For many years the list was pages long and I lamented all the things left undone at the end of the day. I wasted plenty of time stressing about what I needed to do and beating myself up for not doing it all.

This system is kinder to my soul. It works for me. Find a system that works for you. But have a manageable plan. If we want to start living intentionally, we have to be intentional about how we spend our time and that means planning ahead and not trying to do more than can humanly be done. Some of the changes I write about in this book can be overwhelming. You don't have to do them all at once, but don't skip them all together because you don't have time *today*. Break it down in to manageable pieces. Keep the tyranny of the urgent from ruling your days. Use your time intentionally.

Challenges:

Basic: Make a *To-do* list daily.

Serious: Make *To-do, Should-do*, and *Could-do* lists. Try using them for one month.

Extreme: Share your system with your spouse and/or kids and challenge them to create their own *To-do, Should-do*, and *Could-do* lists. Make a *Want-to-do-this-lifetime* list, kind of like a Bucket List.

6

10 Tips for Getting A Million Things Done in One Day

I am frequently confronted with a million things to do in one day. Sure, I'm exaggerating, but the feeling of overwhelmedness is real and it might as well be a million things because there is nearly always more to-do's on my to-do list than is humanly possible. Thankfully, as I've gotten older, I've become more efficient. I still don't get a million things done in one day, but I spend less time wandering through the house muttering to myself and eat less chocolate in an attempt to calm my panicked soul. Below is my ever-changing advice for getting a million things done in a day.

1. *Have a list/s.* Keep lists handy of what MUST be done and what COULD be done. Update these regularly. Don't let the tyranny of the urgent control your day. Focus.

2. *If you can take care of something in less than a minute, do it now,* don't put it off. You know you won't do it later and it will nag at your soul each time you see it. For instance – filing something,

putting shoes away, depositing a dish in the dishwasher, hanging a coat in the closet.

3. ***Never go upstairs or downstairs empty-handed.*** Most of us have piles waiting to be put away on a different floor or our house – don't travel so lightly.

4. ***Handle mail only once.*** File it, recycle it, respond to it, but don't leave it lying on the counter clogging up the works.

5. ***Return messages when you get them.*** E-mail, text, phone. Don't waste time trying to remember to get back to someone – do it now.

6. ***Do what needs to be done.*** You may not "feel" like doing it now, but odds are you won't feel like doing it later. Tackle that chore. Have that conversation or pick up the phone. Make the decision hanging over your head. Get it done now instead of letting the guilt of not doing it burden you.

7. ***Bundle your errands.*** If possible save them all for the same day. Don't run out for one thing – make do. Most likely you don't NEED whatever item you're longing for, so save it until it's convenient and make do without it.

8. ***Don't nag your kids.*** Post a list of what needs to be done and follow through on consequences when jobs aren't done. Be very clear on the importance of their work. (HINT: you need serious consequences like no ride to wherever it is they want to go, shutting down the computer, etc.)

9. ***Get up when you wake up.*** Most of us (who aren't teenagers) wake up with the sun, we glance at the clock and roll over to go back to sleep. Your body wakes when it's finished sleeping. The rest that follows is many times fitful and consumed by weird dreams. Get up and get moving when your body wakes up and you'll discover hours of time you never knew you had.

10. ***Log on to e-mail and social media only once (twice if you must) a day.*** It's the biggest time-suck there is and you know it.

Challenges

Basic: Resolve to handle mail only once. Place a recycling basket near wherever it is you sort your mail.

Serious: Tackle a nagging task that has been hanging over your head for months. Embrace the less-that-a-minute habit.

Extreme: Take this list to heart and apply the ideas that will help you be more efficient. Add your own ideas to this list.

7

Train Your Kids to Eat Healthy

My kids, like most kids, would like all their food to be familiar, something they've eaten before and preferably not touching any other food. They rarely try anything new, even when I insist that they ate it when they were toddlers. All odd-looking food is suspect – asparagus, rattlesnake beans, even lobster. This eliminates all manner of exotic food, casseroles, and stir-fries. It seemed like a milestone recently when all three of my kids ate squid while dining out at a restaurant.

Until this point, their only experience with squid was when my oldest son did a school project on the Giant Squid. One of the amazing facts about children is they grow up, so do their taste buds and their minds. Never mind that the calamari was deep fried to oblivion and could just as easily have been fried squirrel for all anyone knew. The older two smothered theirs in ketchup and can now say that they've eaten squid, but the youngest had seconds and thirds with no ketchup!

How do we get our kids to eat new foods? Or more importantly, how do we get them to eat healthy foods? That's one of the biggest challenges parents have, and sadly, most of us are not up to it. For many of us it's much easier to order the nuggets and fries, or cook spaghetti again. I'm with ya, I feel your frustration. Sometimes it's not the fight, it's the menu that gets to me. It's exhausting trying to figure out what to feed them. You have to factor in nutritional needs, work involved, ingredients on hand, and what they'll actually eat.

I believe persistence is the backbone of good parenting. We are the only ones without an agenda trying to influence our children's food choices. We must keep trying. We can't give up. If we give up, they may spend the rest of their lives eating at McDonalds or warming up the leftover pizza. So we have to persist. I know it's exhausting, but we have to do it. Besides, as older parents often tell me – it'll be over before you know it.

So what can you do to expand your child's culinary horizons?

Make it easily available. If my kids walk through the kitchen and say they're hungry, I might suggest an apple and they'll make a face. But if my kids walk through the kitchen and see a big bowl of beautiful apples on the table, they'll pick one up. They might not even have been thinking of a snack, but the apple is so easily accessible and red and shiny - it's irresistible. This works for all kinds of snacks. If you suggest an orange, your child thinks of the labor involved in peeling an orange, but if the orange is already sliced up and waiting on a plate to be eaten – that's a whole other story. Especially when you smile at them with a slice in your own mouth substituting as teeth. They might roll their eyes at you, but they'll be pulling the same orange grin on their sibling. So instead of suggesting a healthy snack, prepare it and they will come. Just like the Kevin Costner movie.

Trust me. It's all about availability. **And pretty much right up there with availability is presentation.** Your kids will eat lots of things you never imagined they'd eat, if it's presented right. (And served with a toothpick.) An overripe banana may taste wonderful, but it looks horrible so don't serve it – mash it up and make banana bread or a smoothie. Get creative with your presentation. I know, I know, I don't want to work that hard either, but back to my earlier point – who else will? I'll tell you who – the snack food companies! Why do you think kids love those lunchables (aside from the sugar and salt and fat)? Presentation! All those cute little compartments and bright packaging. If you don't make eating healthy exciting, who will?

We are a society of snackers. I'm not sure what happened to the rule of three square meals a day, but my children would complain of starvation if we returned to those days. They can't seem to make it from one meal to the next without at least one, sometimes two, snacks. Sometimes I wonder if they've ever felt true hunger.

If your kids are anything like mine, many days they make a meal of their snacks and a snack of their meals. Finding healthy snacks for ourselves and our families is critical to our health. Dreaming up creative healthy snacks will take more time and effort than simply opening a bag of chips. It's worth that effort.

Just keep serving it. A year ago, my daughter would never even consider eating a grilled chicken breast. A chicken nugget? Sure, pass the ketchup. But a marinated chicken breast grilled to perfection? No thank you. We served it weekly for many moons before she finally gave in and ate it. Now she asks for seconds on a regular basis. How many pieces of chicken did the dog have in the interim? Too many to count. Plan a healthy meal and serve it up. Don't consider who will eat what. Just serve it up.

Plan healthy meals and do it again and again. They'll come around. Either that or they'll eventually move out. Don't sacrifice your own healthy eating for your kids' pickiness.

> *Menu Options*
>
> *1. Take It.*
>
> *2. Leave It.*

Involve your kids in the growing, picking, and cooking. There are chapters to come about getting kids involved in the garden, but getting your kids in the kitchen is just as important. It is easier to do it yourself, but taking the time to involve your kids will give them incentive to eat what they cook. Start with the things you know they like – cookies, bread, macaroni and cheese- and move on to things they don't necessarily enjoy yet. Most kids love to cook – it's messy, smelly, exciting, kind of like a science experiment. Embrace the mess ahead of time, knowing that it may not turn out just like the picture.

There's so much to teach them in the kitchen. You might not think you're much of a cook, but get a 10-year-old behind the apron and she'll look to you as the expert. You know how to crack an egg, measure a liquid, preheat an oven –such skill! Share it. Find out what they'd like to make and learn how to cook it together. Bagels are fun to make, pretzels, too. You can't really mess up scrambled eggs and they make a great snack. Another great snack (and an assumed cooking ability) is hard-boiled eggs. If you don't teach them now, they'll be frantically searching the internet someday when their own children want to color Easter eggs.

Let the kids plan the menu. Tell them they need to balance the meal and include things like protein, veggies, fruit, dairy, and whole grains. Get them thinking. Everyone is more enthusiastic when it's their own idea.

Feeding kids healthy food and getting them to try new things sounds easy, but I do know it's not. I struggle too. Maybe challenging your kids to eat squid isn't the place to start (especially deep fried squid!), but start somewhere. Your kids are getting messages about food all the time, whether it's the food pyramid at school (unbelievably boring) or from the television (Cheese curls that will turn your whole mouth blue?). This is not a lesson to delegate to others. What we eat affects our physical and mental health and our future. It's too important to ignore or leave in the hands of people who don't love our kids like we do.

Ideas for healthy snacks:
Nuts – shelled or not (Removing the shell is half the fun!)
Dried fruit of any kind (apricots, cranberries, cherries, raisins)
Fruit (fresh or frozen)
Fruit salad (mix up everything you've got on hand)
Fruit kabobs (layer food on skewers)
Celery & carrots (and dip if you must)
"Ants on a Log" (celery sticks or bananas with peanut butter and raisins)
Pickle tray (assorted pickles, olives, and the very important-toothpicks)
Cheese and crackers
PB&J tortilla rollups (sliced up in small colorful sections)
Cheese tortilla rollups (sliced up)
Hard-boiled eggs in "egg cups" (you can pick up egg cups at garage sales)
Toast with honey and cinnamon
Pooh Sandwiches (whole grain graham crackers with peanut butter and honey)
Power mix (nuts, seeds, dried fruit, chocolate chips mixed together)
Homemade Soft Pretzels

Hard pretzels with mustard for dipping
Nachos (whole grain chips with cheese melted on top, add tomatoes or olives)
Oil Popped popcorn (use olive, canola, or for a real treat – coconut oil!)
Sunflower seeds (spitting like the ball players makes this a good outdoor snack)
Pumpkin seeds
Big kosher dills
Cheese sticks or cut cheese (great dipped in sweet mustard sauce)
Smoothies of every variety

Challenge:

Basic: Make healthy, attractive snack options.

Serious: Let your kids help plan the menu. Talk about the important elements of a healthy meal. Limit your kids/self to one snack per day or cut out the snacks altogether.

Extreme: Ask your kids what foods they've never eaten but would like to try. Make plans to cook the new food together. Resolve to change your own eating/buying habits so that you can make healthy options readily available on a daily basis. Ask your kids what they want to grow in the garden this year and make it happen.

8

Who's in Charge Around Here

What is it about children and couches? Is it just my children who cannot walk past a couch without upending a cushion, pitching a throw pillow, twirling an arm cover on one finger, or dragging the throw-blanket away for a superman cape? My biggest regret when it comes to decorating my house is buying a couch with unattached cushions.

A day does not go by when I don't have to track down and return some critical seat or back cushion to our couch. I put the couch back in order and no more than leave the room before the cat appears wearing an arm cover as a head piece or a child flies past me with a seat cushion strapped to his chest as a shield. I always know when my youngest has been messing with the stereo, not because of the sound but because of the huge stack of couch cushions positioned in front of the cabinet so that he can reach all the knobs. On the scale of life's difficulties I know that replacing the cushions and washing the pillow covers once again is relatively low. But what drives me nuts is that I could have prevented this.

Parenting is all about prevention. Kids grow up, this is inevitable. Our job as parents is to create an atmosphere that is safe and sane and gives them enough freedom without turning ourselves into shrews who constantly yell, "Why is the couch cushion on the swing set?" We need to be smart because kids' brains are gaining on us every day. Prevention. I'm telling you that is the key.

Buy couches with attached cushions and save the throw pillows until you have teenagers. Parenting preventatively is parenting intentionally. You can prevent battles you don't want to have.

Reduce the screen options. If you don't want your kids watching ten hours of TV a day, cut the cable (and break your own habit too). At the very least, limit the time. Computers can be programmed to shut down during chosen hours. This has been a lifesaver for me. I don't have to stand over my child hollering at him to turn it off, the computer does it for me. If that video game seems way too mature for kids, get it out of your house. Things get lost occasionally around my house – it happens.

Learn to say no. If you don't want your kids to have it, then don't give it to them. And for heaven's sake, don't fall for that "all the other kids are doing it" line. My kids still don't know how to play Nintendo and have no idea what a reality TV show is. And it's not making them social pariahs. Our house is filled with extra kids every weekend.

You want your kids to read more? Don't tell them to read, fill the bookshelves. Take them to the library. Talk about the books you read and ask them what they're reading. Hit the used book sale or Goodwill and tell them they can buy five books!

The same goes for eating healthy and organic. If you don't want your kids to eat things that aren't good for them – don't buy them. Of course kids aren't going to choose the healthy snack when there are Transformer Fruit Snacks on the next shelf. Fill your cabinets, fridge, and counter tops with healthy options like fresh fruit, nuts, cheese, whole grain snack food, and yogurt. I left a bowl of freshly picked apricots out on the counter recently and my kids ate every last one in two days. (Of course, I found pits all over the house too, but that's the price I'll pay.)

Just because many kids are allowed to watch inappropriate adult television shows, play hours of violent video games, and eat corn syrup saturated diets while society shrugs its collective shoulders, doesn't mean it's okay. Whatever you decide is right for your kids, be clear with them because making no decision is certainly making a decision. Kids know this and they capitalize on it.

Think through what you really want for your kids in terms of lifestyle, habits, eating, and priorities. Take a hard look at your home – make the changes you need to make. Kids aren't supposed to have all their impulse control mastered yet so we need to set them up to be successful. Sometimes teaching them about healthy choices means not having any unhealthy ones available.

I look at it this way – I've only got a few years of real influence on their lives. I have to make the most of my time, my example, and my decisions now. Sure they may make all kinds of unhealthy choices the moment they set out on their own, but at least I'll know the foundation I helped them build is strong and there is a good chance that some habits will be hard to break. Just remember - you don't get another shot at raising your kids.

Challenges

Basic: Reconsider your house rules. Make the necessary changes and explain to your family why you're doing it.

Serious: Clean out your pantry and fridge. Throw out or donate anything you don't want your family to eat. Take their suggestions, but then make your own decisions about what to refill it with.

Extreme: Think about how you want your children to spend their time and find ways to lead them to it. Drop the dish, cut the cable, and/or toss the satellite. Use the savings to take a vacation. Consider adding a Wi-Fi or screen-free day to your weekly schedule.

Intentional

EATING

9

Superfood!

We talk a lot about the bad ingredients we don't want in our food, but let's talk about a few good ingredients we need to eat *more* of in our diet. I think of these foods as *superfoods* and look for ways to incorporate them into all my recipes.

The first, and perhaps the superfood above all superfoods, is **coconut**. Coconut oil is nature's best source of lauric acid, an essential fatty acid that boosts the immune system and protects us against viruses, yeasts, parasites, and other pathogens. Lauric acid is used to make baby formula. It also occurs naturally in mother's milk. It's a fatty acid with antifungal and antimicrobial properties. It may even be a key to fighting heart disease. In her book *Nourishing Traditions*, Sally Fallon writes:

> Demographic indications are that countries whose populace consumes large amounts of coconut have very low incidences of coronary diseases. In one study of two groups of Polynesians, those consuming coconut oil as 89% of the fat intake had lower blood pressure than those whose coconut oil intake was only 7% of fat intake. In Sri Lanka, a major coconut

producing and consuming nation, the1978 rate of heart disease was 1 per 100,000 contrasted with a rate of 18 to 187in countries with no coconut oil consumption.

As heart disease surpasses cancer as the leading cause of death in this country, we might all be wise to find ways to add more coconut to our diet. The more I've read about coconut oil the more convinced I am that it can have a huge impact on our health, and not just the immune system.

When my son was first diagnosed with alopecia areata, I had never even heard of coconut oil. If I ever ate it, it was by accident. I never liked the texture of coconut, and didn't realize anything like coconut milk existed. Now I find all kinds of ways to sneak coconut into our diet. I add it mostly in the form of coconut oil, but I also use coconut milk and raw coconut as much as possible.

Coconut oil is fairly expensive, about as expensive as good olive oil. It's worth every cent. Look for coconut oil that is non-hydrogenated, otherwise you'll lose out on some of its benefits. Good quality coconut oil tastes like coconut. It is semi-solid in cooler weather and liquid oil in warmer weather.

You can use coconut oil in place of butter or oil in baked goods. I substitute coconut oil for half the butter in all my cookie recipes and my kids don't notice it other than to brag about how good my cookies taste. It can also be used to sauté if you keep the temperature at 350 degrees or less (350 is its smoke point). Coconut oil in waffles, pancakes and breads gives them a rich flavor that never fails to bring on the complements.

Very finely chopped raw coconut, or coconut flour, substitutes nicely for part of the flour in baked dishes. Add it to graham cracker crusts for a scrumptious treat (try it with banana cream or chocolate cream pie!). Coconut flour is an excellent gluten free alternative.

Coconut milk can be used in soups and cooking dishes. One of my favorite dishes is coconut rice. You can also use it in puddings and ice creams. It does tend to separate, so be sure to shake it before you open the can.

Need one more reason to put coconut oil in your shopping cart? It's great for your skin. When I come to the end of a jar in my cooking, I scrape out what's left and rub it on my arms and hands. I wouldn't waste an ounce of that precious stuff. I once had a health professional tell me that if I used coconut oil on my skin every day, I'd look ten years younger. I don't know if that's a comment on how powerful the stuff is or how old I look for my age!

Coconut Rice

2 cups long-grain brown rice
2 tablespoons butter
2 tablespoons extra virgin olive oil
3 cardamom pods (critical – don't leave this out!)
2 cups Chicken Stock
2 cups Coconut Milk
½ teaspoon sea salt

1. In a heavy pan, melt butter and olive oil. Open cardamom pods and add seeds to the pan. (Note: I open cardamom pods by rolling my rolling pin over them a few times).
2. Sauté rice in butter and oil, stirring constantly, until rice begins to turn milky. Pour in liquid, add salt and bring to a rolling boil. Boil, uncovered, for about 10 minutes until water has been reduced to the level of the rice. Reduce heat, cover tightly, and cook for about 45 minutes or until done (you can cook longer, the original recipe calls for cooking up to 3 hours!).

A Little Bit Healthy Chocolate Chip Cookies

½ cup butter
¾ cup coconut oil
1 cup sucanot (or 1 cup white sugar)
1 cup brown sugar (or 1 cup rapidura)
2 teaspoon vanilla
2 eggs
1 cup organic white flour
2 cups whole wheat pastry flour

1/3 cup almond meal (optional)
¼ cup ground flax
1 teaspoon baking soda
½ teaspoon salt (I use Celtic sea salt and increase it to almost 1 teaspoon)
2 cups grain sweetened chocolate chips (or use a semi-sweet good
chocolate chip, cheap chips cheapen the cookie in ways other than price)

Directions:

1. Preheat oven to 375.
2. Cream butter, oil, and sugars. Add vanilla, eggs, and flaxseed. Beat well.
(If it's cool out and I'm using coconut oil it will be kind of hard, so I beat it
much longer than if I do when it is warm to ensure that it is evenly spread
through the batter.)
3. Mix together flours, almond meal, baking soda, and salt with whisk.
Add to batter. Beat until mixed well. Add in chocolate chips.
4. Use mini ice cream scoop or melon baler to drop small tablespoons on
to baking stone or sprayed pan.
5. Bake for 8-10 minutes, depending on the size of the cookies and
whether you heated the pans. It also depends on your oven, so watch
your cookies carefully the first few times.

My number two favorite superfood is **Flaxseed Meal**. A few
years ago my husband's cholesterol was reaching levels that were
kind of scary. The doctor threatened to put Nick on drugs for
cholesterol and implored him to change his lifestyle. Now, let me tell
you about my husband's lifestyle – he's thin (he prefers the term
"lean"), splits wood, runs, and rides his bike on occasion, doesn't like
sweet food, and eats most of his meals here at our house where his
crazy wife won't buy processed foods and is always coming up with
another new "healthy" recipe.

Since I couldn't convince him to give up his coffee or beer, there
wasn't much we could do about his lifestyle. I began reading about
cholesterol and stumbled upon the news that flaxseed has been
proven to lower cholesterol in men (I don't know if it doesn't have the
same effect on women or if scientists haven't done studies with
women yet). I began adding flaxseed meal to everything I could –
pizza crust, bread, cookies, and just about anything baked. I couldn't

get away with putting it in anything where it's pasty texture would be noticed, but if it went in the oven, it had flaxseed in it.

Guess what happened? At his appointment, approximately six months after I began the flaxseed assault, his cholesterol was just fine. The numbers that were supposed to be low, were low, and the numbers that were supposed to be high, were high. That was enough proof to make me a believer in the benefits of flaxseed!

Flaxseed comes from the flaxplant and has been around for centuries. In fact, King Charlemagne, back in the 8th century, ordered all his subjects to eat it because he believed in its health benefits. Somehow, we lost the King's memo, but mark my words, you'll be seeing a lot more fields of flax in the near future. Fields of flax will be beautiful, too. The flower is a pretty blue color with tiny delicate petals on long stems.

Flaxseed contains three ingredients that make it such a phenom:

1) ***omega-3 essential fatty acids*** I know you've heard about these and their heart-healthy effects. Each tablespoon of ground flaxseed has about 1.8 grams!
2) ***Lignans*** These are antioxidants and flaxseed contains 75-800 times more lignans than other plant foods.
3) ***Fiber*** Both the soluble and insoluble kind.

The experts say the optimal dose is 1-2 tablespoons a day. I have to warn you that eating it straight could be tough. You can buy flaxseed oil, but it doesn't have all the benefits of the straight seed. It's best eaten in a ground form (flaxseed meal) because our bodies process the ground form more efficiently than they do the whole seeds. I add ¼ cup of flaxseed meal to many recipes, including breads, pizza dough, and cookies. You'll have to experiment and figure out how much is too much for your family. Flaxseed meal can easily be substituted for part of the fat in recipes. Store it in the freezer so it stays fresh, especially if you buy it ground.

Ever since I've learned about flaxseed, I've been seeing information about it everywhere. It's kind of like when you buy a new car you think is uniquely you and you start seeing the exact same car everywhere, even the same color. One tip I read suggested putting flaxseeds in a spice grinder (like you use for pepper or salt) and grind some on whatever you're cooking. The idea being that if it's handy, you'll be more likely to use it. At the feed store recently they were selling big bags of flaxseed to feed your chickens so their eggs will be higher in Omega 3's. Made me wonder if chicken flaxseed is the same grade as flaxseed for humans (it was a bit cheaper, but I decided not to test out the idea).

Need a few ideas for adding flaxseed meal to your diet beyond baking it in? How about putting it in pancakes, waffles, chili, meatloaf, meatballs, soup, oatmeal and casseroles? Want to try it whole? Here's a delicious recipe.

Spiced Nuts and Seeds

3 cups whole nuts (walnuts, brazil nuts, cashews, pecan, almonds)
¼ whole flaxseed
¼ cup quinoa
2 egg whites
2 tablespoon honey, agave nectar, or maple syrup
1 ½ teaspoon coarse salt
¼ teaspoon cayenne pepper
¼ teaspoon cumin
¼ teaspoon cinnamon
¼ teaspoon ginger
1. Heat oven to 325 degrees.
2. Mix together all ingredients except nuts.
3. Toss with nuts and spread on baking sheet.
4. Bake for about 30 minutes, stirring occasionally, until dry.
5. Scrape from pan and let cool.

My number three super food is **walnuts.** Besides being loaded with omega-3's, which we all know are good for your heart and your brain, they also have more antioxidants than other popular nuts. But for me, it's the taste. Walnuts are delicious. I eat them every day on my salad, and add them to my baking in whole (if no children will be dining with us) and ground versions. Walnuts are fun to crack open and their empty shells are perfect for craft projects, which can be an entry point for getting the super nuts into your kids.

Here's my favorite lunch salad I eat almost every day.

Lime-Garlic Salad with Walnuts

One huge bowl of fresh lettuce, baby kale, and/or spinach
¼ cup walnut halves or pieces
1 hard boiled egg (sliced)
1-2 tablespoons shredded raw milk cheddar cheese
Dressing:
¼ cup garlic grapeseed oil (or olive oil)
¼ cup lime balsamic vinegar
splash of cranberry shrub (or a tsp of agave nectar)
¼ teaspoon salt
½ teaspoon black pepper
any seasonings I'm in the mood for – Italian seasonings, fresh herbs, dried oregano, and/or minced garlic
1. Shake dressing ingredients together in a bottle.
2. Toss lettuce with two tablespoons dressing, top with walnuts, egg, and cheese.

The fourth superfood I'm going to highlight is **wholegrain wheat flour**. It may not belong in the superfood category, but it is decidedly better than plain white flour. Whole grain flour contains all three parts of the grain – the bran, the endosperm, and the germ. Refined white flour removes the bran and the germ, leaving only the endosperm. All the key nutrients, vitamins, minerals, healthy fats, protein, and fiber are in the bran and germ. So white flour becomes quite literally nutritionless.

When I teach classes on Intentional Life and healthy eating, people always ask how much whole wheat flour can be substituted for white flour. The simple answer is – all of it, but you might not want to do that at first. Until your tastes (and your kids' tastes) grow accustomed to it, you might want to start by substituting about 1/3, increasing to ½, and then even higher. You'll soon be able to recognize the empty taste of baked goods made with all white flour.

The same holds true for whole wheat pastas. Start by mixing them in. You'll need to cook your pasta more al dente when working with whole wheat pastas or they can become mushy. These days you can find pastas made with every kind of healthy flour under the sun – black bean, spinach, artichoke, beet, tomato, etc. There's absolutely no reason to ever eat a nutritionally-void, tasteless white pasta again!

The last food I would encourage you to work into your repertoire is actually an entire food group – **berries**. Sure they carry a bit of sugar with them, but the sugar is countered by their amazing antioxidant value and the fact that most people actually like berries. Blueberries are the number one superfood in this group. Eat them as much as possible. Every day isn't too much. Pick berries when they're in season and freeze them to eat all year round. Cranberries are also excellent. Cranberry sauce is simple to make and shouldn't be restricted to Thanksgiving. It cans and freezes easily. Raspberries are precious and expensive, but are also one of the easiest fruits to grow since they're basically a weed and will multiply quickly. Fresh raspberries don't last long, so if you don't gobble them up, freeze them to add to fruit salads and smoothies later.

Berries out of season can be dearly expensive, so make a point of buying (or growing) plenty of berries in season and freezing some for later use. To freeze berries, wash, spin dry, and spread out on a jelly roll pan. Freeze overnight. The next day, you can transfer them to labeled containers and store in the freezer for up to a year.

Cranberry Sauce

½ cup rapidura (or dark brown sugar)
½ cup fresh orange juice or more if you like (About 2 oranges)
¼ cup water
1 ½ tablespoon honey
1 (12 oz) package fresh cranberries
1 (3 inch) cinnamon stick

1. Combine all ingredients in a medium sauce pan over medium-high heat; bring to a boil.
2. Reduce heat, and simmer 12 minutes or until mixture is slightly thickened, stirring occasionally.
3. Discard cinnamon stick; cool completely.

Challenges

Basic: Try adding some healthy pastas to your regular white pasta.

Serious: Pick two of these foods and come up with a plan to incorporate them into your diet.

Extreme: Re-design your menus to add in all five superfoods.

10

Waste Nothing!

Those of us who didn't grow up during the Great Depression are only now beginning to appreciate what it means to use what you have, make do, substitute and wear things out. I am of the generation that thought nothing of buying a new stereo because it was *better* even though the one I had sounded just fine. My husband appreciates the finer points of the latest tweeter or woofer or what have you and will argue the need for newer and better until he's on his deathbed, so maybe I should choose a better example than stereos. Let's say clock radios or dish racks or couch cushions. Most of us are inclined to throw out or give away our old, but perfectly good stuff, when something nicer catches our eye. I see that trend changing some in light of the current economic situation and this is good for our planet, if not our factories.

If your cabinets and refrigerators look anything like mine they have all kinds of unidentified objects cowering in the very back - a jar of bean curd or anchovy paste purchased two years ago for some complicated recipe you never got around to making, the orange marmalade your kids won't eat because it tastes like Motrin, a gourmet dip mix you were suckered into buying for some fundraiser.

My husband pulled out a can of clam sauce recently and said he remembered buying it at the grocery where we lived two houses ago! We've actually moved some of this stuff. Thanks to modern preservatives though, it's still good! I used to be famous for starting a recipe and realizing halfway through that I didn't have a crucial ingredient. My ever-patient husband would run to the store for fresh ginger or confectioners' sugar in the wee hours of the night on too many occasions. He'd still do it if I asked, but now I either modify the recipe or save it in-process and make something else. On lazy days when I don't have a meal planned, we don't order take out. Instead, I search the back of the cupboards where rare and forgotten treasures still roam.

Vegetables are one thing I can't stand to see go to waste. It was this issue, plus the multitudes of cucumbers we were drowning in one summer that led me to create my favorite salad. I call it Chopped Salad. It's basically everything in your crisper drawer (even the rubbery celery), plus anything still growing in your garden, chopped up really small with a food-chopper or processor and mixed together – kind of like coleslaw but without the cabbage (unless you have the remnants of a cabbage head rolling around your vegetable drawer). To this concoction I add my favorite dressing, cashews, and croutons (made from leftover bread). Not only is this a great way to use what you have, it's low in calories and makes a huge crispy salad that you can eat for days.

I won't waste fruit either. One cold and rainy day my fridge went on the fritz and froze everything in my fruit drawer (or maybe some kid, I'm not naming names here, messed with the temperature control). I couldn't bear to let anything go to waste, especially expensive, organic fruit. There were 12 apples – the last of the local crop still available at the farm market, plus a bag of organic lemons that had been reduced for quick sale, and some grapes I was talked in to buying when I broke my own rule and took a kid to the grocery store. So the damage wasn't too bad. Still, I would never throw out good food so....

I thawed out the apples, peeled them and made fresh apple sauce for dinner. The kids were so excited to have warm fresh applesauce, they ate the whole pot.

Not much you can do with frozen lemons other than thaw them out and make lemonade, which is what my husband did. It was a rainy, miserable weekend so hot applesauce and cold lemonade were pleasant surprises for all of us. My kids even discovered that frozen grapes are fun to eat, so nothing went to waste after all.

Our adventures with the fruit drawer brought home an important part of living intentionally – waste nothing! As much as I love composting, I would never compost something that I can use now. When the organic free trade bananas get too brown, I peel them, break them in to sections and freeze them. Then anytime I want to make banana bread or banana milk shakes, I've got the perfect overripe bananas at the ready. I paid a small fortune for those bananas, heck if I'm gonna toss them out over a few brown spots.

We grow gorgeous Georgia Rattlesnake watermelons every summer. They're several feet long and weigh as much as a toddler. We can't possibly eat them all while they're fresh, so I cut the rind off and freeze the fruit. Watermelon freezes well and is perfect for smoothies all year long.

When we come down to the ends of our bread or there's just a couple slices left on the French bread loaf, I make croutons out of what's left. If I don't need croutons, then I make breadcrumbs.

You don't have to have grown up in the Depression to know that nothing needs to go to waste, although I do think of my mom whenever I'm tucking another plastic container of bananas in my freezer. She is never one to let anything go to waste and always leaves our house after Thanksgiving with the turkey carcass in the trunk. We let her have it because we know it will come back in the form of her famous homemade turkey noodle soup. Waste not, want not.

Challenges

Basic: Clean out your vegetable crisper and make a chopped salad.

Serious: Clean out your pantry, cabinets, and drawers. Make a list of what's in there and work the food into upcoming menus. If you know you won't use a fresh item, figure out how to save it. If you're certain you won't use a non-perishable item, donate it. Inventory what's in your freezer and make a list you can place on the outside so you don't have to open it and dig to consider your options.

Extreme: Don't buy anything from the grocery store for one week except fresh produce and milk. Use what you have to design your week's menu. Enlist your kids/spouse in this challenge. Then take them all out to eat on the money you save! Reorganize and label the remaining food so that nothing gets lost again.

Bonus Challenge: Imagine that some national disaster has occurred and you only have the food in your house to live on. See how many days you can survive without going to the store. I'm guessing that if we truly had to, most of us could survive for months, maybe longer.

11

Bake Your Own Bread

The smell of bread baking makes a house more appealing. I traced my highlighter over the words in the magazine. We were selling our first house and our real estate agent convinced us to price the old farmhouse optimistically high for the market. I was doing my part to make it happen. Each time a prospective buyer was scheduled to visit the house, I'd pop a loaf of dough in the oven to fill the house with the smell of fresh bread baking. I bought the tiny loaves six to a pack and kept them hidden in the back of the freezer. We ate a lot of bread that spring, and we sold the house for top dollar, too. There's something about fresh baked bread that soothes our souls.

Bread is the sustenance of life. Most of us eat it every day, so finding a healthy version should be a priority. Organic bread is available in most grocery stores, but it's pricey. Bread freezes fairly well, so you can buy it in bulk, but it takes up a lot of real estate in your freezer.

When it comes to healthy, delicious, inexpensive bread, the best advice I can give you is to buy a bread maker. You might not need to buy one because you may have one tucked away in your basement or attic, a relic from your wedding shower. If not, ask around, I bet someone you know has one.

If you strike out locating a free breadmaker, your next stop should be the Goodwill. I've never paid more than $6.97 for one at the Goodwill and several were brand new and had the owner's manual, but you can always download an owner's manual online. It's not necessary though, because all breadmakers are basically the same. The only difference is the size and shape of the loaf.

Baking bread with a breakmaker is ridiculously simple. It takes five minutes. The trick is dumping the ingredients into the pan in the correct order - wet ingredients, followed by dry ingredients, and then yeast. I'm not sure it's necessary, but I make a little indent in the flour to put the yeast in, sort of like the *nest* my kids make in their mashed potatoes for the melting butter. (The first recipe I used gave this direction, and I've kept the habit.)

Once everything's loaded, simply press the button. My house smells divine because I bake bread almost daily! I love coming home to that warm, yeasty delicious fragrance. I hope that even when they are grown and gone, my kids will associate the smell of bread baking with home.

Storing your odd-shaped breadmaker loaves can pose a challenge as a traditional bread bag or Ziploc won't cover it. I use a plastic adjustable bread keeper especially designed for the upright loaves produced in a breadmaker. It easily fits my 3 pound loaves and has an exhaust hole, so if the bread is still warm it won't sweat. You can also buy specialty bread bags that claim to keep bread fresh longer. I use these when I have more than one loaf to store, but I can't say they make homemade bread last longer. Without the preservatives loaded in store-bought bread, homemade bread only stays fresh 3-4 days, any longer and you'll want to put it in the fridge to keep it from growing moldy.

In the beginning, it's tempting to have a slice slathered with butter every time you pull a gorgeous freshly baked loaf from the breadmaker. I would wager that there is very little in life that is as satisfying; and that said, you should definitely indulge on occasion. I promise that once you're baking your bread on a near daily basis, you'll be able to resist. It's like everything else – once it's no longer only for a special occasion, you'll take it for granted.

When I make bread for sandwiches or toast, I pack it with healthy ingredients like flax meal, a powerhouse of omega 3's and fiber that also makes the bread moister. I add pepitas (pumpkin seeds) for their anti-oxidant value, but grind them up so the kids won't be alarmed when they find a green seed in the PB&J. With so many different healthy flours available that the options are endless.

For consistent loaves, it's best to weigh your flour, instead of measuring. When I figured this out it was a turning point in my bread making career. If you dip a measuring cup into your flour canister, you'll get a different amount every time. Flour can compact when handled, so to get a consistent measure you must weigh it instead of filling a cup. My scale is an Escali Digital scale and cost about $25.

Baking your own bread will save you big money. One loaf costs about a quarter of the cost of store-bought Bread. But more valuable than that, it will also be good for your spirit. Creating something simple, healthy, and delicious will nourish your body and soul.

Below are a few recipes to get you started. Once you play around with your machine, you'll figure out your own recipes. I use my machine for sandwich breads, rolls, pizza dough, even bagels. When I want a good dinner bread, I make that by hand. That recipe is below, also. It never fails me.

Whole Wheat Flax Seed Bread with Pepitas

(for bread machine, three pound loaf)

1 7/8 cup water
2 tablespoons oil or butter (I use butter-flavor grapeseed oil)
3 tablespoons honey
15.4 ounces whole wheat flour (freshly ground if possible)
7.4 ounces white bread flour
1/3 cup ground flax seed (make this a heaping ¼ cup)
1/4 cup ground pepitas (optional)
1 teaspoon salt
2 teaspoons yeast
1. Place in bread machine in order listed and use whole wheat setting.

Crusty Bread
(makes three loaves)

4 tablespoons oil
4 tablespoons sugar
2 tablespoons salt
5 cups warm water
4 ½ teaspoons yeast (2 packages)
Lots of any kind of flour (6-8 cups at least)

1. Put oil, sugar, and salt in a big bowl.
2. Pour about 5 cups warm water over the top so the sugar dissolves.
3. Add 2 packages yeast until it bubbles and then enough flour mixed in to make a kneadable bunch.
4. Knead, set aside for 20 minutes or so.
5. Punch down. Divide in to 2 or 3 loaves. (It make 3 BIG loaves.)
6. Put in cake baking pan with sides touching. Let sit another 20 minutes.
7. Bake at 375 for 45 minutes.

You can add other ingredients – different flours, beer, etc. It is classic – doughy and soft inside with a wonderful crust. I make one recipe and freeze two of the loaves.

Pizza Dough (in bread machine)

1 ½ cups water
3 tablespoons olive oil
3 cups whole wheat flour
1 ½ cups white flour
1 ½ teaspoon sugar (or sucanat)
1 teaspoon salt
3 teaspoons yeast
Optional: pizza spices

1. Add ingredients to machine in order listed. Use dough cycle.

Pizza Dough (by hand)

1 ½ cups warm water
3 teaspoons yeast
1 ½ teaspoon sugar (or sucanat)
1 teaspoon salt
3 T olive oil
3 cups whole wheat flour
1 ½ cups white flour
Optional: pizza spices

1. Place water in large bowl.
2. Add yeast and sugar, stirring to dissolve. Let stand a few minutes. Add salt and oil, stir well.
3. Add white flour and 1 cup wheat flour. Stir to combine.
4. Add remaining flour and work into dough.
5. Place dough in greased bowl, cover with towel and let stand in warm place for about 1 ½ hours, or until dough doubles. Punch down and let rest five minutes.

Challenges

Basic: Find a good brand of organic or naturally made bread and stock up. Be sure to read the label carefully. Choose a brand that uses whole grains and whose ingredients list is not ten lines long. Especially avoid brands that contain high fructose corn syrup or food dyes.

Serious: Make a loaf of fresh bread from scratch and surprise your family. The Basic Bread recipe listed in this chapter is super easy, it makes three loaves but takes A LOT of flour (just warning you). If you want an extra challenge, make pizza dough! Also consider purchasing a good food scale and weighing your flours so that your loaves are more consistent.

Extreme: Buy, borrow, or acquire a breadmaker. Try out several recipes. See how many good ingredients you can sneak into one loaf. If you're really adventurous, see if you can make hot dog rolls, bagels, or pretzel rolls. For the best tasting breads, locate a grain mill and buy your flour freshly ground to order– you'll be blown away by the difference in taste!

12

Start Your Day Intentionally

Starting your day intentionally means eating breakfast. I shouldn't have to say that, but apparently I do because breakfast is the most-skipped meal of the day. According to the Journal of the Academy of Nutrition and Dietetics, 10-30% of people skip breakfast every day. After evaluating 47 studies examining the association of eating breakfast with nutritional adequacy, body weight, and academic performance in children and adolescents, a group of doctors and scientists found that children who ate a nutritious breakfast were more likely to have a superior nutritional profile, be a healthy weight, and have better memory, test grades and school attendance.

Skipping breakfast forces your body into a 10-20 hour fast on a daily basis. I'm certain that places unnecessary stress on your body and brain whether you're a child or adult.

What does a healthy breakfast look like? A balanced breakfast should include whole grains, lean protein, dairy, plus fruits and/or vegetables. This is not rocket science, nor is it news to any of us. As my kids became teenagers, they began to skimp on breakfast in favor of more sleep. Instead of growling at them to get up, I began making breakfast for my teens much like I did when they were toddlers. It's not important to them that they eat a good breakfast, but it is important to me. Which makes it my problem, not theirs. Am I spoiling them? Maybe, but my hope is that I'm giving them a leg-up on their day and teaching them about the importance of breakfast.

Making our own healthy breakfast as opposed to buying a convenience food like breakfast bars or overpriced cereal is not only better for us, it saves money.

Have you ever wondered what the profit margin is on breakfast cereals? Think about it. How can a company charge $5 a box for something made with corn and rice and not feel guilty? It's not the product you're paying for; it's the marketing and our insatiable appetite for convenience. While I haven't figured out how to make frosted flakes from scratch, I have discovered how simple (and cheap!) it is to make instant oatmeal. I will never again pay nearly $5 for a box of 8 little packets of artificially sweetened oatmeal. The packaging excess alone shames me.

Instant Oatmeal

4 cups old fashioned rolled oats (not quick-cooking)
¾ teaspoon salt
1/3 cup brown sugar
1 teaspoon cinnamon

Process ingredients in food processor or blender and grind to the consistency of wheat germ. Fill your bowl, add enough boiling water to make it the consistency you like, and let it stand one minute. Add milk, nuts, and/or dried fruit. It does look a little more like cream of wheat than instant oatmeal, but my kids didn't complain. This recipe is so simple it seems criminal that we paid so much for instant oatmeal all those years. If only I'd known.

Another exorbitantly expensive cereal eaten on a regular basis in our house is granola. I can understand the hefty price tag on granola because nuts and dried fruit cost more than oats. Still, making my own saves money and eliminates packaging. Plus, I know what goes in to it (and what does not), so I feel better about feeding it to my family.

Homemade Granola

9 cups rolled oats
1 cup chopped almonds
1 cup chopped pecans
3 Tablespoons brown sugar or rapadura
1 teaspoon Celtic sea salt
1/2 cup maple syrup
1/3 cup honey
1/3 cup pineapple juice
1 teaspoon almond extract
½ cup dried cranberries
½ cup golden raisins

1. Preheat oven to 300.
2. Combine first 5 ingredients in large bowl.
3. Mix together syrup, honey, juice, and extract. Add to oats and stir well.
4. Spread mixture evenly on three jelly roll pans. I use stoneware pans, but if you're using something else, coat pan with cooking spray first.
4. Bake for 45 minutes, stirring every 15 minutes.
5. Stir in cranberries and raisins. Cool completely. Store in air-tight container.

My absolute favorite breakfast cereal to date is *Chocolate Coconut Oats* made with steel cut oats. It does require that you plan ahead, but it's well worth it.

Chocolate Coconut Oats

1 cup steel cut oats
2 cups whole milk
2 teaspoons coconut oil

½ teaspoon sea salt
2-4 teaspoons chocolate chips
½ cup nuts (almonds or walnuts), chopped (optional)

1. Mix the oats and milk and refrigerate overnight.
2. In the morning, warm oats in a pan on low heat, add coconut oil, sea salt, and chocolate chips and stir frequently until mixture warms and begins to thicken. Remove from heat, top with nuts. Makes 2 BIG servings. YUMMO.

My boys' favorite breakfast is Cream Eggs and Ham. We normally serve this as a dinner and then eat it leftover for breakfasts. It starts with homemade english muffins. You can buy english muffins at the store, but the homemade muffins are healthier, taste better, and are easy to make. It's worth the effort.

English Muffins

¼ cup warm water
1 tablespoon yeast
2 tablespoons sugar
2 cups flour
2 cups wheat flour
¼ cup flaxseed meal
2 teaspoons kosher salt
1 large egg
1 ¼ cups warm milk
2 tablespoons butter, melted
Cornmeal

1. In a standing mixer, beat together water, yeast, sugar, 1 cup of each flour, flaxseed meal, and salt.
2. Add egg, milk, and butter and continue beating until creamy.
3. Add remaining flours and knead until smooth and elastic. (Add more flour if needed to make a nice dough.)

4. Place dough in bowl coated with oil. Cover with a towel and let rise 2 hours (until doubled).

5. On a clean surface, sprinkled with corn meal, roll the dough out to a thickness of ½ inch. Don't stretch the dough. Use a biscuit cutter or the top of a drinking glass to cut out muffins. Reroll scraps and cut out more muffins. Try not to work the dough too much – the more you work it, the tougher the muffins become.

6. Heat a cast-iron skillet until very hot (I use a jenn-air griddle for this.). Place muffins in hot pan (don't crowd). Turn down the heat to medium so the muffins cook through without burning, about 10-15 minutes per side. They will look just like the ones you buy at the store – lightly browned in the center. Remove muffins to a cooling rack. Split with a fork before toasting.

Cream Ham and Eggs

1 dozen hardboiled eggs, peeled and chopped
2-3 cups of ham cut into bite-size pieces.
6 tablespoons butter
6 tablespoons flour
¾ teaspoon salt
½ teaspoon white pepper
3 cups milk

1. Melt butter in saucepan over low heat.
2. Blend in flour, salt, and white pepper with whisk.
3. Add milk all at once. Cook quickly, stirring constantly, until mixture thickens and bubbles. (You can add cheese or other flavorings at this point. I like to add lightly blanched asparagus.)
4. Mix eggs, ham, and sauce together and warm.
5. Serve over toasted english muffins.

Challenges

Basic: Make 5-minute oatmeal (from whole oats) or Chocolate Coconut Oats for breakfast.

Serious: Get out your food processor and create instant oatmeal. Experiment with flavorings, and package correct portions in individual containers so your kids can serve themselves! Make granola. Develop your own version. And once you do that, package some to give away as gifts.

Extreme: Make an intentionally healthy breakfast every morning for one week. Make english muffins in large batches and freeze for future use. Go hog-wild and find some recipes for the cereals your kids love most. There are plenty to be discovered on the internet!

13

Stop Drinking Soda

There's not a gentle way to say this, so I'll get right to the point, *cut out the soda.* I know this is hard for many people, but if you are striving for a more intentional and healthy life, this should be a priority. Loaded with sugar (or artificial sweetener), sodium, caffeine, artificial colors, and artificial flavorings, there is truly nothing in a can of soda that your body needs. I'm realistic enough to know you can't completely ban soda, unless you're a better mom than I, which is entirely likely. My kids drink soda at restaurants and friends' houses, but I don't keep soda in my house because I know the basic rule of feeding kids: *If you don't buy it, they can't consume it.*

If you need a few more reasons other than your health to cut out the soda, I can tell you that not buying it will save you serious money. You will be shocked at how much lower your grocery bill is when you stop buying soda. You'll also lose weight when you lose the soda. Many people drink soda like water and the calories add up. Even diet soda increases your weight. I had a pleasant surprise when I finally gave up my beloved Fresca. I'm not sure if it was eliminating the sodium clogging up each can or no longer being plagued by sugar cravings brought on from drinking diet soda, but when I dropped the diet soda, I dropped five pounds!

Giving up my soda habit was not easy. Diet soda was my water for years. Now I keep a pitcher of home-brewed tea in the refrigerator. I enjoy experimenting with new teas, especially green tea because of its many health benefits.

Mint tea is delicious and growing mint is so easy it's dangerous. Mint will consume an entire garden, so I recommend planting it in a container of some sort. Simple dried mint makes delicious tea. Drying mint is easy. Cut it and wash it well. Then hang the mint in a dry, dark space for a few weeks. A basement with a dehumidifier is a perfect spot. When it's dry and crumbly, it's ready for tea. Put the crushed mint in cute canisters and give it as gifts. Try different varieties like chocolate mint or orange mint.

A word about caffeine – it's a drug. If you don't believe me, try giving it up. But do give it up if you can. You'll sleep easier and probably discover you don't need as much sleep. You'll be healthier, happier, and the people around you won't be victim to your caffeine fueled mood swings. Don't start your kids on the bad habit either. You have the power to get them off caffeine now – use it.

Water, milk, tea, and the occasional apple cider or homemade lemonade are the options at my house. A pitcher of ice cold water in your refrigerator has more appeal than you would expect. If you want to get fancy (or you're on city water), add some lemon, lime, orange, or strawberry slices - even better.

Instead of thinking of how hard it will be to give up soda, start thinking of all the alternatives you can choose instead.

Challenges

Basic: Cut down your soda consumption.

Serious: Limit sodas to weekends or special occasions. Place a pitcher of water in the fridge as an attractive option. Plant a pot of mint or buy some to dry and make your own mint tea.

Extreme: Stop buying soda completely and stock your fridge with a pitcher of water, ice tea, or homemade lemonade. Use the money you save for a family outing/prize. Pay attention to how your body feels once it's soda-free.

14

The Simpler, The Better

I live in Amish country. Besides the buggies and one room school houses, the Amish are also famous for their food. Amish food is *plain*. Sometimes it's too plain for me. Personally, I feel any dish tastes better with more garlic, pepper, or heat. I do think the Amish are on to something, though, with their simple food. Added unnecessary ingredients, particularly salt, sugar, and fat is one of the hallmarks of processed food. Salt and sugar are an inexpensive way to bring out flavor in poor quality ingredients or mask the taste of fillers and additives. Added salts and sugars also increase the shelf life of a product. Extra fats are added for appearance, taste, or "mouth feel".

Many foods don't need those added ingredients. In fact, two of the best processed foods don't require a single added ingredient.

There's no better comfort food in the world than warm, homemade applesauce. Once you've made your own, I promise you'll never be able to stomach another bottle of store-bought applesauce again. The bonus is that making your own is easy. The other bonus is that making your own will impress your friends and family. They will be in awe. And they'll want a bowl. Wait! There's one more bonus –

it will save money because store-bought applesauce is ridiculously overpriced!

In late summer and early fall, apples are fresh, cheap, and plentiful. There are so many varieties available it can be overwhelming. I think the best applesauce comes from mixing varieties together, but making applesauce from fresh apples you just picked yourself is pretty stellar too. I try to get my kids out to a pick-your-own farm each year. There is nothing in the world like a fresh apple eaten moments after it is picked. It is sunshine in every bite. Don't take my word for it – go find out.

Most fruit markets sell apple *seconds*. When making applesauce, quantity is important and looks aren't. I like to go to the Seconds Room at my market and ask for a few bushels of mixed apples, any kind except Red Delicious. Red Delicious may be yummy for eating, but they make only mediocre sauce. A mix of varieties makes the taste richer and more complex.

Making applesauce is not a precise science, so don't get hung up on following a recipe. Personalize your own. Here's what I do:

Applesauce

1. Core, peel, and slice enough apples to fill a big pot. Periodically, splash a few squirts of lemon juice on the apples to keep them from turning brown.

2. When the pot is full of apples, add water to fill the bottom quarter of the pot and put it on the stove.

3. Working on a medium-high setting, bring the apples to a boil, mashing them with a spoon and stirring often. Once the apples are boiling, turn down the heat a little and continue to mash them with a spoon or a potato masher as they cook.

4. Continue cooking and mashing occasionally until the mixture looks like applesauce. It will depend on your pot, your stove, and your apples as to how long this takes. It can take 15-30 minutes, but there is a point where the apples become really easy to mash and the whole mixture suddenly looks like applesauce.

5. This is where I stop and move on to canning, freezing, or eating, but if you don't like chunky applesauce (which is one of the qualities I love about homemade applesauce), you can now put your concoction through a food processor and eliminate all those chunks that make your kids say, "Did you make this?" Although, once your kids have tried real homemade applesauce warm from the pan with a sprinkle of cinnamon they'll change their tune.

A great way to increase your kids' enthusiasm for homemade applesauce is to enlist their help in the process. If you own an apple peeler/corer/slicer contraption, get your kids in on the action. They love to eat the long, curly apple peels. Most peeler/corer/slicers only work on perfectly shaped apples, so if your seconds are particularly asymmetrical and/or overly ripe, don't get too frustrated when the handy contraption doesn't work. You may just have to revert to the old fashioned knife to do the job.

We can some of our applesauce and freeze the rest in repurposed large yogurt containers. Slightly thawed, frozen applesauce is a wonderful dessert treat. But the best way to eat it is still warm from the pan. I make applesauce in large batches in the fall, but I make a small batch anytime I have apples getting wrinkly in the bottom of the fruit drawer. Don't think you can only make applesauce when you have time for the big production it can become. Grab a little sauce pan and peel, core, and slice 3 or 4 apples. You do the same thing your do for a big batch, just modify your amounts. Fresh, warm applesauce makes a yummy side dish anytime. Toss in some fresh cranberries to add some zing.

Peanut Butter is another processed food that has been abused for too long. You can make your own great-tasting peanut butter with just one ingredient – peanuts.

Five reasons why you should make your own peanut butter:

1. If you have young kids – this is probably one of their main protein sources.
2. Homemade peanut butter is WAY healthier than store-bought.
3. It's incredibly easy to make.
4. It tastes AMAZING.

5. You can make it just the way you like it.
6. Bonus reason: It'll impress everyone who stops by for lunch.

Here's how to make your own scrumptious peanut butter :

Step one - buy peanuts.
Step two - put them in your food processor and process. (This can take several minutes.)

That's it. The only ingredient necessary to make peanut butter is peanuts. I use lightly roasted and salted peanuts so there's no need for added salt. I toss in honey roasted peanuts for added sweetness. You can add other nuts – cashew, pecan, whatever you like. But you don't need to add oil or sugar or even salt – three things that processed peanut butter has in spades; along with a bunch of other stuff I can't pronounce.

I buy peanuts in bulk and store them in the freezer so we never run out of peanut butter. I can whip it up fresh in minutes. Keep your yummy homemade peanut butter in the refrigerator. If you like crunchy peanut butter, simply process for less time. If you have less-picky children, you are blessed and you can also incorporate your jelly straight into your peanut butter making PB&J's easier.

Let me quickly address the fear that most people have about *natural* peanut butter. Traditional processed peanut butter is chock full of emulsifiers and other artificial ingredients to keep it from separating. Natural peanut butter doesn't contain these emulsifiers so it is sometimes separated – as in there is a gross pool of oil at the top and the bottom is chunky and dry. If you must purchase commercially-made peanut butter, choose an organic or natural brand. When you open it the first time, use a good strong mixing spoon or spatula to stir it thoroughly to incorporate the oil which may have separated. After you've stirred it, store it in the refrigerator. The peanut butter won't separate again unless you heat it up.

My homemade peanut butter never separates. Never. This is not because I add emulsifiers (I don't), it's because it doesn't contain extra oil and therefore doesn't require emulsifiers to help it maintain its consistent texture. There, now you can put that little phobia back on the shelf and move on to making your own natural peanut butter.

I know I harp on this, but I have to say it once again: Read labels. Look for foods with fewer ingredients. More is not always better. Food does not need to be complicated to taste good. Applesauce and peanut butter are proof of that.

Challenges

Basic: Find an organic peanut butter with ingredients you recognize. Make a small pan of applesauce today with the apples growing rubbery in your crisper drawer.

Serious: Make your own peanut butter. Find a source for apples and buy a half bushel. Make a big batch of applesauce and take some to a teacher, friend, or new neighbor. Enjoy some warm as a side dish with dinner and freeze the rest.

Extreme: Experiment with different kinds of peanut butters, adding other types of nuts or jelly or even chocolate chips or bananas. Find a pick-your-own apple farm and pick several bushels of apples. Make and can or freeze homemade applesauce. Bonus: Enlist your kids' help. Extreme Bonus: Plant your own apple trees.

15

Use Oils that are Good for You

The price of oil dictates many of our decisions, from the cars we purchase to the budget we (and our country) live on. Many of us have few options when it comes to fuel oil for our vehicles or houses, but let's talk about our options when it comes to the oils that fuel our bodies.

There was a time when the grocery store simply stocked big plastic bottles of golden cooking oil. It was cheap and we used it for everything. As I've grown up and learned about health, cooking, and appreciating the taste of warm bread dipped in fresh olive oil, things have gotten much more confusing, at least for me.

By now we've all had it beaten into our heads that trans fats are bad. But do you know why? Or for that matter, do you know what a trans fat is? Manufacturers create and add trans fats to foods because trans fats make it possible for oil to be solid at room temperature. This is a good thing when you're creating a cheese curl that can survive for centuries in any climate. Trans fats are created by heating the oil to extremely high temperatures and infusing it with hydrogen gas. This causes the chemical makeup of the oil to be changed, or hydrogenated.

This isn't a situation that would naturally occur, so processing partially hydrogenated anything isn't something our bodies are designed to do. In fact, partially hydrogenated fats increase your cholesterol more than unhydrogenated fats. They can actually block your body's utilization of essential fatty acids, and cause inflammation throughout the body. Research has found connections between the consumption of trans fats and heart disease, cancer, autism, diabetes, autoimmune diseases, and allergies. Is it any wonder these problems increased at the same time many of our foods became filled with trans fats? Thankfully, trans fats are now listed on food labels for us to see.

So trans fats and hydrogenated-anything isn't good, but what about other oils? How the oil was extracted from its original source is important. When horses were still important to our daily existence, oils were extracted by a stone press. Basically you squeezed the heck out of the seed or nut, and the result was oil. That's not how most oils are produced these days.

Manufacturers have discovered that by adding refiners like hexane (a petroleum by-product used to make plastics, glue, and solvents) they can extract even more of the oil, very quickly. More oil from less raw materials creates a bigger profit. Never mind that workers in shoe factories utilizing hexane in their processes developed nervous system and respiratory system failures. Never mind that teenagers looking for a quick high sniffed hexane and ended up paralyzed. Much of the hexane evaporates once it does its job, and the rest is removed by boiling the oil, causing most of the remaining hexane to leave in the form of steam. The US government allows a tiny percentage of hexane in oils and doesn't require companies to note it as an ingredient.

And how to get that gorgeous clear, clean color? Refine the oil more by degumming, bleaching, and then deodorizing it. Now it's beautiful, but is it safe? Hard to say, since laboratory mice don't process oil the way we do, studies have been few and far between.

Here's my take on oils. Look for oils that say on the label that they are *cold-pressed, expeller-pressed*, or *unrefined*. Although the US does not yet regulate cold and expeller pressing, they're still better for you than mass marketed oils. Europe has strict standards for expeller pressed oils. These oils are more expensive, but we generally use small amounts of oil, so I think the splurge is not only justified, but necessary.

Look for dark or green glass bottles when buying oils. Oils can be damaged by light if they are unrefined. Buy your oils in small amounts; they only taste fresh for a few months after opening. Vegetable oils will last longer, but olive and nut oils should be used within 3-6 months.

If you use canola oil, choose organic because nearly all canola oil comes from genetically modified ingredients. Organic canola oil, grapeseed oil, or butter are the best oils for cooking at high temperatures. You lose the flavor and much of the nutrient value when you heat olive oil above 400 degrees.

I use mostly olive, coconut, and grapeseed oils in my cooking. Occasionally I'll use sesame or peanut for Asian dishes. These oils and a little butter get me through just about any recipe.

Making healthy food choices for you and your family, requires reading labels. Like so much involved in living a healthy life, we need to slow down and act consciously. It's dangerous to assume that just because the broader culture accepts a food, activity, or attitude as acceptable, that means it's safe or sane for any of us. Bottom line, with oils, as with anything, *know what you're eating*.

Challenges

Basic: Stick to olive oil, butter, and organic canola oil in your cooking.

Serious: Read labels and buy expeller pressed oils whenever possible. Rid your cupboards of corn oil, vegetable oil, and any oils that are past their prime.

Extreme: Cook with coconut oil, olive oil, and butter as your primary oils. Try substituting coconut oil in your baking, and olive oil in your cooking. Experiment with other healthy oils like grapeseed and almond oils.

16

Process Your Own Food

Processed food (said with the appropriate wince in your voice) has become a term that encompasses all that is bad about our food system. It's quite a catchall label. I'm as guilty as the next person of condemning it. And I do condemn processed food if it's loaded with chemicals, additives, sugars, and excess salts that are not good for the body. But nearly all food could be considered *processed* if it isn't eaten in its raw state.

I think the answer is to process your own food from healthy ingredients. When you read the label on the side of a box of Cheezits or a bottle of pancake syrup, you can be easily intimidated. *I can't possibly make that.* No, you can't, and you wouldn't want to. But you can make your own healthy version of both.

Kids (and spouses) generally cringe at the idea of eating healthy because they believe it means giving up all their junk food and desserts. While there's no physical reason to eat junk food or desserts; there are lots of emotional reasons. It's possible to make foods like Pop Tarts, brownies, pretzels, even potato chips with healthier ingredients than the ones you find on the shelves of the average grocery store. I'm not saying these foods will be good for you, but at least they won't be dangerous.

I find it a fun challenge to figure out how to make popular processed foods. Many times my versions are yummier and sometimes I can even slip in a few redeeming ingredients. The internet is rife with copycat recipes. It's a simple matter to find these recipes and use better ingredients.

A few things to note about your processed food versus store-bought processed food:

✓ Your processed food will not keep as long as the processed food you buy at the store. I don't think it's a good thing that a Twinkie will last several years. In my opinion, no one should eat a food that can last a few years (except maybe a pickle, pickles are meant to keep).

✓ Your processed food may not look *exactly* like the processed food you buy. Expectations are a powerful thing and many of my masterpieces are snubbed based on appearance alone. Don't despair, if you do it right the taste will override their objections (that and your flat-out refusal to buy the store bought junk!).

✓ Your processed food may not cost the same to make as the store's. In terms of dollars, sometimes it will cost remarkably less! And sometimes it will cost more. In terms of time, it will most likely cost more, unless you factor in travel time and time wasted stalking the aisles of the store. I can make peanut butter in less than the time it takes you to drive to the store!

✓ Your processed food may be healthier than the same store bought food, but healthier is relative. Sugar isn't healthy in any form. A calorie is a calorie is a calorie. A food loaded with white flour, butter, and sugar can be perfectly organic, but that doesn't make it good for you.

Making your own processed food is a simple matter of, as Don Henley wrote in his famous song – *how bad do you want it?* Sometimes it's worth the effort. Sometimes it's a better idea to give up the habit. And sometimes you have to compromise rather than die on that hill. If the rest of your diet is improving, an occasional chemically laden treat won't make that much of a difference. The problem arises when it becomes a habit or you succumb to the desire to eat the entire bag.

All of that said, I'll share a few of my favorite processed food recipes.

Toaster Pastries (Pop Tarts)

First make a basic pie crust (or cheat and buy a crust in a tube or in the freezer section of the grocery store. It won't taste nearly as delicious, but maybe that's not the point with a pop-tart).

Crust
1 cup whole wheat flour
1 cup, plus 2 Tablespoons flour
16 tablespoons butter, cut in pieces
1 teaspoon salt
2 teaspoon sugar
6 tablespoons Ice water
Filling
Jam of your choice
Coating
1 egg
1 tablespoon water
Powdered sugar (optional)

1. Place flour, salt, and sugar in food processor and pulse to mix. Add butter and process until crumbly.
2. In a large bowl, use your hands or a pastry cutter to blend flour mixture and ice water. Handle as little as possible because the more you work it, the less flaky your crust will be. Wrap in plastic wrap and place in refrigerator for at least 30 minutes.
3. After crust is chilled, working in batches, roll half of it into large sheets and cut out rectangles the size of a toaster pastry. Use flour to keep the dough from sticking to the surface or roller (or your fingers).

4. Place pastries on nonstick or well-greased baking pan. Paint the pastries with egg mixture (one egg plus one tablespoon water mixed together). Place one tablespoon of filling in a thin line down the center of the pastry. Don't be too generous with your tablespoon of filling, especially if you're planning on toasting these puppies, otherwise they'll be lumpy. In this particular case, lumpy might be good.

5. Roll out the rest of the dough and cut into rectangles for the tops. Paint with egg mixture. Seal the edges of the pastry using a fork and then poke the top two or three times.

6. Bake at 375 for 15 minutes.

7. After they have cooled, sprinkle with powdered sugar. Total yum.

Note: You can make a savory version with spinach and cheese or tomato, feta, and black olives!

Cheese Crackers (Cheezits)

3 tablespoons cold butter, cut into small pieces
1 cup flour
½ cup whole wheat four
1 teaspoon dry mustard powder
1 teaspoon salt
1 ½ cups shredded cheddar cheese (or any cheese you have around – I used Swiss and asiago for the ones I took to book club and there were no leftovers)
2 teaspoons white balsamic vinegar (or plain white vinegar if that's all you've got)
1 ice cube
¾ cup water

1. Combine butter, flour, dry mustard, and salt in mixer. Mix on low speed until crumbly (about 30 seconds).

2. Add cheese and mix on low speed briefly.

3. Combine ¾ cup water, vinegar, and ice cube and let sit for a moment to get cold.

4. Add 6 tablespoons of the vinegar mixture to the dough and mix on medium speed for 20 seconds. Continue to add liquid, 1 tablespoon at a time until the dough clings in a ball to the beater. Then mix for an additional 30 seconds.

5. Wrap dough in waxed paper, and refrigerate for at least 2 hours, and up to 3 days.

6. Remove the dough from the fridge 15 minutes before you are ready to roll it out. Preheat the oven to 300 and grease two baking sheets. (If you have baking stones, preheat them – even better.)

7. Place dough on floured surface and use rolling pin to flatten dough to less than ¼ inch thickness. Cut dough in squares or circles or whatever shape floats your boat.

8. With spatula, transfer crackers to greased baking sheets. Keep a little distance between each so all the edges are crisp.

9. Bake for 20-25 minutes, or until the crackers are slightly golden, rotating the trays halfway through baking.

10. Turn off the oven, but leave the trays in the oven as it cools for at least 1 hour. *(I don't always have the patience for this step, but it does make your crackers much crispier.)*

Double Chocolate Brownies

(this recipe is from my kids' godmother Kate Busa – NOT a light recipe!)

¾ cup flour (white or whole wheat or combination)
¼ teaspoon baking soda
¼ teaspoon salt
1/3 cup butter (or coconut oil)
¾ cup sugar
2 tablespoons water
1 12 oz package chocolate chips
1 teaspoon vanilla
2 eggs
½ cup chopped nuts

1. Preheat to 325 and grease 9" square pan.

2. Combine dry ingredients in small bowl.

3. In sauce pan, mix butter, sugar and water – bring just to a boil then remove from heat. Add ½ the chocolate chips and the vanilla – stir until smooth.

4. Add eggs one at a time. Beat well after each.

5. Mix in dry ingredients.

6. Add remaining chips and nuts.

7. Bake 30-35 minutes.

There are no better brownies! Be sure to take them out when they still look a little gushy- that way they won't dry out and they'll be extra yummy and gooey! Served warm with ice cream - they are crazy-good!

Potato Chips (or Sweet Potato Chips)

2 medium potatoes, scrubbed and sliced to 1/8 inch (use mandolin slicer, don't cut off your fingers!)
2 tablespoons organic canola oil or grapeseed oil
½ teaspoon coarse salt
Optional seasonings: Old Bay, vinegar, rosemary

1. Preheat oven to 400 degrees.

2. Toss potatoes with oil and divide between two rimmed baking sheets. You can also cook chips on a cooling rack placed on top of baking sheets to cook chips more evenly, but if you haven't got one, no biggie.

3. Sprinkle with salt and seasonings.

4. Bake for 10 minutes.

5. Flip chips (unless you're baking them on cooling rack) and bake an additional 5-10 minutes until golden and crisp.

Chicken Nuggets

1 pound chicken (boneless breasts and/or thighs), cut into 1-2 inch pieces
¼ cup whole oats
½ teaspoon dried parsley
1 teaspoon garlic powder

½ teaspoon onion powder

¼ teaspoon black pepper

1 teaspoon kosher salt

1 cup panko bread crumbs

¼ cup parmesan cheese, shredded or grated

1. Preheat oven to 375 degrees.

2. Place first 7 ingredients in food processor and process until chicken is finely chopped.

3. Mix bread crumbs and cheese in a shallow bowl.

4. Roll 1-2 tablespoons chicken mixture into nugget shapes. Press into bread crumbs to coat. Place nuggets on a cooling rack set over a baking sheet. (Or place nuggets on a baking sheet and freeze for several hours before packing them in freezer bags for later use.)

5. Spray nuggets with cooking spray (I like to use coconut oil spray).

6. Bake for 15 minutes.

Challenges

Basic: Take a long, hard look at your processed food habit. Choose a few to do without.

Serious: Try making some of your favorite processed foods from scratch and/or enlist your kids to do this.

Extreme: Give up processed foods for a month. Either do without or make your own version.

17

Get Canning!

When I mention to people that I "can," they are amazed. That is, unless they also can and then they know it's really no big deal. Canning is not difficult and requires only a few special tools.

You'll need a **canning pot.** These large enameled pots have a wire separator inside that keeps the jars from touching the bottom of the pot or crashing into each other. My pot holds seven jars. I do traditional hot bath canning as opposed to *pressure canning*. Pressure canning requires a different pot, high temperatures and a stove other than the one I have which is glass top. In fact, the only stove recommended for pressure canning is a straight-ahead electric coil type stove. I'm happy with hot bath canning so I stick with that. If you want to can meat or certain non-acidic vegetables (green beans, beets, carrots, corn, peas, and potatoes to name a few) you'll need a pressure canner (and a different writer). I freeze meats and non-acidic vegetables.

Canning pots are not expensive. A brand new one at the most expensive hardware store in my town only costs about $20. You can also find them frequently at Goodwill and yard sales as many of the people who *can* are moving to retirement communities.

Besides a pot, you'll need a **jar lifter** and **funnel**. A jar lifter is just what it says. It's used to lift hot jars in and out of the canner full of boiling water. A jar funnel is used to fill the jars. It is wider on the bottom than your standard funnel to allow you to neatly fill your jars. It makes ladling hot jams and sauces into jars much easier. Mine is metal and very old. Many of the new ones I've seen are plastic. If you can find a metal one I would opt for that as heat and plastic are never a good combination. Neither a lifter nor funnel are expensive and can be found at old time hardware stores and kitchen stores where they sell canning supplies.

And of course you'll need **jars.** When you buy a new case of jars they will come 12 to a case and include the lids and bands. After that you can recycle the jars and bands, but need to buy new lids. The lids are sold separately anywhere you can buy jars. I stock up at the end of the season when all the canning supplies go on sale. I always buy more jars, too, because I need more for the next year – some break and some are given away. Jars can be found at yard sales but are rarely much cheaper than new ones. The people selling jars know they hold their value. If you do buy used ones, be sure to check carefully for chips along the rim. Any chipped edges will make it impossible to get a good vacuum seal.

Jars come in half pint, pint, and quart sizes. They make smaller jars, but that seems silly to me. The tops can be regular-mouth and wide-mouth. I use regular mouth jars for most everything except pickles which are easier to take out of wide mouth jars. It is completely personal preference, so do what you want – the recipes are the same for either type of mouth.

Okay, have everything you need? Let's can!

1. **First, heat your canner.** Don't wait until the recipe is finished to start heating the water because this step takes TIME. I place seven jars in the canner and drop the lids around them. You can sterilize your jars and lids by hand or in the dishwasher, but if they are clean to start with, heating them with the canner does the trick and saves you time and effort. Fill the jars and the pot with water (you'll want to fill the jars first so they don't float around in the canner). You need enough water to cover the jars. Turn the burner on high and go prepare your goodies.

2. **Cook up whatever you are planning to can.** We can spaghetti sauce (do not use oil in your sauce – not safe for canning), diced tomatoes, pizza sauce, salsa, barbeque sauce, pickles, tomato-basil soup, fruit sauces, fruit syrups, and jams. Each year I try to add another recipe. Canning has made a comeback in recent years and you can find plenty of recipes online, but my favorite recipes can be found in the *Ball Complete Book of Home Preserving*.

3. When you are ready to fill the jars, remove them carefully from the canner using your jar lifter. Use tongs to fish out the lids. Next, **ladle your yummy concoction into jars** using your canning funnel. You'll want to fill until about ¼" – ½" from the top. The recipe will tell you. Then take a knife (we have a super skinny spatula that does the trick) and work it around the edges of the jar to force out any air bubbles. (Most recipes tell you to do this, but I forget this step frequently and haven't had a jar go bad, so if you forget and your jars are all finished, don't toss them out.) Wipe the rims with a clean wet cloth. This is important because if there is food left on the rim, it may prevent you from getting a good seal. And if there is food left on the outside where the bands meet the jar, the band may rust to your jar and make it difficult to open your jar six months from now. Place the lids on and screw on the bands.

4. Using your jar lifter, **place the jars carefully in the canner** so that they aren't touching. Try to angle the jar into the water as opposed to dropping it straight down. I find this produces less boiling water splash. (Ouch!) The water should cover the jars by at least a ½ inch. It may be necessary to remove some water if you're using quart jars so that the water doesn't overflow the canner.

5. **Bring the canner water back to a boil and process** for 10-40 minutes depending on the recipe and your level of paranoia to be sure all bacteria are good and dead.

6. When the timer sounds, **turn off the stove and take the lid off of the canner**. Give it a minute to let out all the steam. (Don't open the lid with your face over the canner. I know of what I speak and have to remember this the hard way every year.) Set a dry dish towel on your counter next to the canner and take the jars out and place

them on the towel. The towel will catch the water that comes out with the jars and also prevent any of them from slipping off the counter (heaven forbid).

7. Now here's the best part! **Your jars will make a tinny "pop" sound as each jar creates its vacuum**. This usually happens in the first few minutes after you remove the jars from the canner, but can sometimes take longer. On long canning sessions when the last jar of spaghetti sauce or salsa is finally sitting on the counter, I love to crack open a beer, sit back and listen to the pops. Satisfaction. Even if it's midnight, I'll hang around until I hear the last pop. If you take up canning, you'll come to love this sound too.

And that's it. Simple. Really, it is. I tried to break it down to the barest directions for you. Things can go wrong on occasion, but if you follow the recipe and the processing times, it's rare. Knock on wood, I've never had a jar go bad. I once opened peaches that got lost on a move and were over five years old. They tasted just fine. If the lid of your jar can be pressed up and down easily, then the vacuum didn't happen. You'll want to put that jar in the fridge and eat it first.

I highly recommend the book *Ball Complete Book of Home Preserving*. It has answers to any questions you might have about what can and can't be canned.

Sometimes I prepare a recipe one day and can it the next. All this requires is that I bring the recipe back to a boil again for a few minutes before canning it. When I'm doing a big project like spaghetti sauce or applesauce where I'm canning 30 jars or more, this makes it easier. I'll cook up the goods in several pots on the stove and then place the lid on while it's still boiling and turn it off. This keeps it sterile until I'm ready to can the next day. There are only so many burners on my stove, so this method is more efficient for me.

If you've never canned before, start with something simple like tomatoes or applesauce. Take your time and follow the directions. I promise you'll find great satisfaction in canning and it just might become a habit. My husband and I do much of our canning late in the evening when it's not too hot to heat up the kitchen with all the boiling pots. We enjoy the time together, listening to music and creating food that will nurture our family all year long. Canning is more fun with company, so enlist some help.

While canning is very, very simple, it is important that you pay attention. What follows is the story of one of my canning disasters, plus a recipe for blueberry syrup. I share it with you for entertainment purposes and also as a warning that multi-tasking and assuming you know what you are doing are two dangerous sins in the art of canning (and raising children). This story was originally published in *Hobby Farm Home*. (Great magazine if you're serious about growing or raising some of your food.)

Golden Rules of Canning

We learn some of life's most important lessons in kindergarten. Robert Fulgham wrote a lovely book on that premise. One of those critical lessons is to always use the potty before setting off on any adventure. I dragged my canner out for the first time this season and learned the hard way that one really should use the potty BEFORE one starts canning.

That's become my first rule of canning – use the potty first. My second rule is PAY ATTENTION. Canning is not difficult. I regularly try to convince people who are afraid of jars and lids and boiling water and fresh produce that it's quite simple. It's so simple in fact that I tend to do too much multi-tasking while I'm canning. That might be okay when you're canning jars number 265 and 266, but when you are canning jars 1-7, you need to focus on what you're doing.

I tell you my story, not so much to amuse you or make you feel sorry for me, but to help you see that even those of us who have canned hundreds of jars, can still mess it up. And that's okay. The thing is not to let it discourage you.

My tale begins on a bright warm morning when I dragged my three children to the local blueberry patch. This was their third trip there and let's just say they were less than enthusiastic. One refused to get out of the car when we arrived and rather than making a scene that might alert the authorities to potential forced child labor violations, I let her stay in the car with her attitude and her book. The boys and I hiked out to the fields. The smallest child found a full bush and parked himself under it proceeding to eat his fill and spending the rest of the time calling, "Are we *ever* going to leave?"

I was down to one assistant picker, but the two of us managed to fill our buckets and enjoy a peaceful conversation about how you know when a blueberry is the ripest (it's shiny purple) and whether or not Harry Potter and Voldemort might be related (we were currently reading Book 3 of the series). This isn't the part where you feel sorry for me; I'm just trying to make it clear that these blueberries were harvested with great effort and sacrifice.

The next morning I decided to make blueberry syrup. While it's not difficult to make, it does take a bit of time to crush and cook the blueberries. We taste tested the first batch on pancakes and unanimously decided the syrup was awesome. So I decided to make more to can.

I pulled out seven pint jars from the basement and found seven lids and rings, put them all in the canner, and got it boiling to sterilize the jars and lids. The problems began as I waited and waited for the huge vat of blueberry sauce to reach a boil. The directions said to boil for five minutes. The process of prepping the berries and sterilizing the jars had taken the better part of an hour. In that time I'd also finished two cups of tea.

The syrup was going well, but I had to pee. I waited and waited for the syrup to reach a boil so I could get it in the jars. For a very long time it seemed *about to boil*. I didn't want to leave it unattended, but I couldn't wait any longer so I dashed off to use the downstairs powder room. There wasn't any toilet paper and as many of you probably know, only mothers are capable of finding the extra toilet paper and replacing the roll. So now I had to hurry to the closet upstairs for more toilet paper.

By the time I made it back to the kitchen, the syrup had boiled up and over the top of the pan, all over my stove, down the cabinets, into the vents and along the counter top. I said a few choice words and spent the next hour cleaning up the stove and kitchen.

Undeterred, I put the pot back on to boil and watched it very carefully. The next time it boiled I was ready. My husband brews beer and he loves to quote his beer making guide which says "a watched pot never boils, but when this pot boils you better be watching." Those words haunted me all day.

I was still able to fill five jars and save a small amount for breakfast on Saturday. I secured the lids and screwed them down with the rings. I placed each jar in the canner and set the timer for 10 minutes according to the recipe directions.

While I waited, I emptied the dishwasher, mixed up a batch of dough for hamburger rolls and negotiated a truce between warring parties over the computer. When the timer went off I lifted the lid on my canner expecting to see five jars of blueberry syrup, but there were only four.

I vaguely remembered that I had an extra lid ring leftover after I started processing my jars, but figured I'd miscounted when I set them out originally. Turns out there were five jars in my canner, but in the dark blue water I couldn't find the empty fifth jar that I'd apparently put in the canner without screwing on the ring that secures the lid until the vacuum forms.

More blueberry mess to clean up, but in the end I did have four jars of delicious blueberry syrup. I tried to focus on that and promised myself that next time I'd remember the golden rules of canning: 1) Pee before canning and 2) Pay Attention.

Blueberry Syrup

8 cups blueberries
6 cups water, divided
1 tablespoon grated lemon zest (it makes a difference- use a fresh lemon)
3 cups sugar
2 tablespoons lemon juice (again, fresh lemon if possible)

1. In a large stainless steel saucepan, combine blueberries, 2 cups of water and lemon zest. Bring to a boil over medium heat and boil gently for 5 minutes.
2. At this point, many recipes call for you to strain the skins out of your syrup. Not me, we don't mind the skins in our syrup. It does make for lumpy syrup but we like it that way. I just try to mash the blueberries really well while they're cooking using a potato masher. And I figure, like so many other fruits and vegetables, there's good nutrition and fiber in those skins.
3. In a large stainless steel saucepan, combine sugar and remaining 4 cups water. Bring to a boil over medium-high heat, stirring to dissolve sugar, and

cook until temperature reaches 230 degrees. Add blueberries. *HERE'S WHERE YOU NEED TO PAY ATTENTION*. Increase heat to high, bring to a boil and boil for five minutes. Remove from heat and stir in lemon juice.

4. Ladle hot syrup into jars, leaving ¼ inch headspace. Wipe rim. Center lid on jar. Screw down band on jar lids (important).

5. Place jars in canner. They should be completely covered with water. Bring to a boil and process 10 minutes. Remove canner lid. Wait 5 minutes, then remove jars, cool and store.

Challenges

Basic: Find a friend/relative/neighbor who cans and ask if you can help.

Serious: Borrow a canner from friend/relative/neighbor, buy a box of canning jars and can something – I recommend applesauce. It's easiest. (There are directions for making applesauce right in this book!).

Extreme: Procure your very own canning supplies and get to it! I promise you'll be an expert in no time and won't look back. (And then you can buy the t-shirt I just put on my Christmas list that says, *I CAN, what's YOUR superpower?*)

18

Drink More Water (Plus Bonus Soapbox Sermon on Plastic!)

Drink more water. I know you've heard that before. I think I'm part camel because I'm able to go nearly all day without a drink. But I'm trying to do better.

Here are just a few of the things water does for you (if you drink enough): increases energy level, reduces joint/back pain, prevents headaches, aids in digestion and prevents constipation, ensures proper circulation, increases metabolism, regulates appetite, and keeps us alive (we can live a month without food, but only a week without water).

Recently I read *Stiff* by Mary Roach. In her book, Roach investigates what happens to our bodies once we die. The book considers all the possibilities from donating your body to science to becoming human compost. It sounds gruesome, but the book was a really fun read and taught me two valuable lessons.

The first is that we all need to think through what will happen to our bodies after we die. We should not leave this to the people who love us. It's not fair to burden them with the details of what happens to our remains. Find out the options and pick one. Today. Write it down somewhere and tell the people you love where that somewhere is. It's the only way you can help them through your death, which will hopefully be a long time from now, but could ultimately be tomorrow. Do this.

The second lesson I learned from the book is that water has a powerful effect on our skin. In one chapter, Roach visits a morgue and watches a body being prepared for a funeral. As the technician pumps the body full of fluid, Roach sees facial lines disappear and the dead person looks not only more alive, but decades younger – instantly. I immediately got up and poured myself a glass of water. Drinking water helps our systems function better, keeping us hydrated and healthy, but it could also be the single most important part of your skin care regime. As a bit of a skin care junkie myself, this hit home for me. If you're not drinking water for your health, drink it for your complexion.

How much water do we need? Every body is different – some need more, some need less and this can depend on how much you exercise, sweat, and eat. It can also depend on your size, age, and health. The Institute of Medicine (a non-profit, non-governmental agency that is part of the National Academy of Sciences) recommends 1.9 liters for women and 2.2 liters for men. This is slightly more than the infamous 8 eight-ounce glasses of water spouted by most fitness gurus. Keep in mind that some of your water may come through the food you eat. You can get as much as 20% of the water you need this way, especially if you eat a lot of fruits and vegetables.

If you exercise a lot, you need more water. If you are pregnant, you need even more. The weather and the temperature also affect how much you need to drink. Obviously when it's hot and dry, you need more. One thing that is not a reliable indicator of how much water you need to drink is your own thirst. By the time you register thirst you are already dehydrated.

Our kids need to drink more water, too. Most of us are dehydrated. We need more water. One of my children gets migraines and the first thing the neurologist asked us was – *is he drinking enough water?* Dehydration is a big trigger for migraines, or any headache for that matter. Drinking plenty of water every day is a critical lesson we need to impart to our children. Water should be available to our kids all day long and I'll do what it takes to make that happen. Here are a few of my water ways:

- ✓ Never walk by a drinking fountain – always stop and drink. I'm sure this is a nuisance for teachers, but it's a good habit to instill.

- ✓ Even short trips in the car call for an accompanying water bottle. Sure, this leads to lost water bottles and a car rattling with empties on the floor, but it's worth it.

- ✓ The only beverage that can be carried outside of our kitchen is water. That means if a child wants a drink while watching TV, playing outside, working on the computer, or playing in his room with friends, water is the only option. Water is the one thing you can have at our house anytime, anywhere.

- ✓ Get rid of the juice. Fresh fruit has more nutrients and fiber with fewer calories per serving.

- ✓ A pitcher of ice water is inviting when it's all ready to go. Keep one in the fridge or set one on the table at snack time. Make it available and appealing.

- ✓ Instead of asking your kids if they'd like some water, fix them a glass and give it to them. Say something like, "I thought you might be thirsty." They get busy like us and forget to drink enough.

- ✓ Make it easy for kids to get their own water whenever they want. Store kids' drinking glasses in a low cabinet they can easily reach so they can get themselves a glass of water whenever they're thirsty.

- ✓ For the first time ever we have a fridge with water and ice on the outside. It's definitely worth the splurge in terms of encouraging kids to drink more water.

✓ Good water bottles are something worth buying. Find trendy fun bottles with the carbineer clip and give them to your kids as gifts. Buy a cool one for yourself and set the example.

✓ Serve water with every meal at home.

✓ Always ask for water when you are out at a restaurant. If you don't like the taste of tap water, ask for a slice of lime or lemon. Order water for your kids too.

✓ Don't buy bottled water. I know you didn't ask for it, but here's my two cents on bottled water. Just hold on a moment while I climb on my soapbox…

Bottled water is a ridiculous waste of money. Water is free. Can you imagine if someone told you back when you were a kid that someday people would pay $2.50 for a small plastic bottle of water? It would be like saying you have to pay to breathe the air. You'd have thought they were nuts, yet we spend over 100 billion dollars a year on bottled water. How much could be done with that money? The Water Project estimates that the cost of just one case of bottled water could supply a person in Kenya with clean, safe drinking water for the next five years!

Never mind the cost – how about the benefit? There are no regulations specifying that bottled water has to be anything beyond decent tap water. I've heard all about the special springs where this water comes from, but I'm certain that for many of these companies, that special spring is a hose in the factory where the water is bottled. Someone's making lots of money because we've never learned the lesson of the Emperor's new clothes.

This is an easy one, folks. Instead of spending your money on bottled water, buy some really nice stainless steel water bottles and refill them. You'll be helping the environment and your pocketbook. If you're concerned about taste, spend $30 bucks and get a water filter pitcher or attachment for your sink.

I'll step off my soapbox now, but seriously, we all should drink more water in whatever container we can. It's one of the best things you can do for your health - and for your complexion.

Challenges

Basic: Stop buying bottled water.

Serious: Purchase a few nice water bottles for you and your family. Label them. Use them. Keep a clean water bottle in your car so you can fill it if you get thirsty when you are out.

Extreme: Keep water in a pitcher in your fridge, maybe even add a few lemon slices to it to make it more enticing. Drink a full glass of water when you get up, before every meal, and before you go to bed. Teach your children to do the same.

19

Are You Eating Too Much Protein?

When she was young, my daughter ate very little meat, unless you count hot dogs. And even hot dogs were mostly just a spoon with which to eat ketchup. One spring when she was eleven, impressed by her Catholic friends who were giving up something for Lent, she announced that she was giving up meat for the month of April. ("Not for Lent, Mom, for April!") I bit my tongue and did not say what I was really thinking which was, *How convenient – giving up something you already don't want to eat! And why exactly does April demand this kind of sacrifice?* I didn't launch into a lecture on the meaning of Lenten sacrifice. I just said, "Hmm," which caused her to glare at my doubt and march out of the kitchen.

As the month progressed, she sat smugly at dinner passing the steak, chicken, or pork and reminding us, "Remember, I don't eat meat." We stressed to her that she still needed to take in enough protein and worried that her sullen mood was caused not by her impending hormones, but by her lack of protein.

Somewhere along the line I had become as brainwashed as the rest of America into believing that meat = protein. The meat industry has worked hard to hammer home that belief. As Mark Bittman points out in his book, *Food Matters,* "Per calorie, cooked spinach has more than twice as much protein as a cheeseburger." Meat is not the only, or necessarily the best, form of protein. He goes on to explain (what quickly becomes apparent when you read the stats on protein), Americans eat way more meat than they need. "If the American high protein diet were the ideal, you might expect us to live longer than countries where meat consumption is more moderate. We're the second-to-last in longevity among industrialized nations."

But was my daughter getting *enough* protein? She was 11 years old at the time of her meat-free month and according to the government's recommended daily allowance she needed somewhere in the neighborhood of 34 grams of protein a day. She could get that from any of the following non-meat sources:

1 oz cheese = 7 grams protein
1 cup milk = 8 grams protein
1 egg = 6 grams protein
2T peanut butter = 8 grams of protein

Throw in some whole grain breads and cereals (2-4 grams) and a few veggies (1-3 grams) and there's every reason to believe that my daughter was doing just fine on her protein intake despite her meat protest.

And what about the rest of us? Women ages 19-70 need about 46 grams of protein. The typical 8 oz steak serving has 50 grams of protein and the yogurt I eat each morning for breakfast has about 18 grams. Throw in the copious amount of vegetable matter I consume and my fondness for cheese, and I'd say I'm getting more than my fair share most days.

And what happens when you eat too much protein? According to Gail Butterfield, PhD, RD, protein expert, and nutrition lecturer at Stanford University, too much protein can lead to a buildup of ketones in your system which puts your kidneys in overdrive in their effort to flush them out. This stress on your kidneys can lead to dehydration, bad breath, and weakness. I would guess it could also lead to weight gain. Excess protein can't be stored, so we either break it down and burn it as energy, or we store it as fat. I like to run, but even my long runs couldn't possibly require the amount of protein I'm taking in. Other researchers believe that eating too much protein can lead to calcium loss and to the immune malfunction that causes food allergies.

So what's a person or a parent to do? Pay attention. Reduce the portion sizes of the meat you eat which will save you money and calories. Plan more meat free meals. Try to break the strangle hold that meat has on our understanding of a healthy meal. We don't need to eat it every meal, let alone every day. Just reducing your family's meat intake slightly will have a substantial impact on your health and your budget. Teach your children that protein can be found in many other sources beyond meat.

Here are a few meatless dinners to consider:

- ✓ Pasta *(endless options here)*
- ✓ Mexican recipes *(substituting beans for meat)*
- ✓ Vegetable egg rolls and veggie fried rice
- ✓ Pizza *(nix the pepperoni)*
- ✓ Eggs *(so much you can do with an egg!)*
- ✓ Salad bar *(Nuts, dried fruit, hard-boiled eggs, and cheese can add protein)*
- ✓ Meatless Chili *(crock pot time)*
- ✓ Seafood *(who doesn't need an excuse to eat more seafood?)*

My daughter did go back to eating meat that May. Which meant she went back to eating hot dogs and nibbling around the edges of a small piece of chicken on occasion. For her, giving up meat wasn't a huge sacrifice. I'm glad she did it though; it gave me a chance to educate myself about our need for protein. We don't need to eat meat at every meal, but it will take some re-wiring to change our habits.

Challenges

Basic: Plan one meat free meal this week.

Serious: Tally up how much protein each member of your family eats in a normal day and how much each needs. Discuss it with them and brainstorm ways to reduce the amount of protein you eat. Plan to have at least one meat-free meal each week.

Extreme: Make meat-free/lower protein meals at least three times each week. Eat smaller portions of meat when it is on the menu. Consider having a vegetarian day, week, or month. Pay attention to how your body feels when you eat less protein.

20

Cut Down on Sugar in Your Diet

We all know you shouldn't take candy from strangers. But what about parents-of-kids-you-know who offer you candy? And what if you're old enough to know your mother will likely be annoyed that you're eating candy at 9:30 at night? (Especially when that same mother is about to arrive and has already promised to stop for ice cream on the way home to celebrate a recent academic achievement!) Maybe this sounds like something that only happens in fairy tales or Law & Order re-runs, but this actually happened to one of my children! Sure, maybe I'm overreacting, but here's how it went down:

I pulled up only a few minutes late to pick up my child from the evening's sporting practice. As I looked in the building, I could see my child crouched in front of a candy machine, reaching to retrieve something. I thought, *Gross, he's grabbing for leftover candy in that filthy machine!* I spotted my child's friend leaving the practice with his father and waved to them. I hurried to fetch my disgusting child who was now shoving candy in his mouth as fast as possible and trying to look innocent.

When I confronted him, he told me that no, he wasn't gathering leftover candy, he purchased the candy. *With what?* I asked, knowing full-well that this child was flat broke. He told me that his friend's dad, who had just left, handed him a dollar and told him to go buy some candy. An avalanche of emotions rushed through me at that point. Anger, because who was this guy to think he can order my kid to eat candy? Embarrassment, because I knew the father's motivation came from my child's claim (more or less truthfully) that his mother never buys him candy. Frustration, because I was sick of being the odd one out in nearly all parenting situations. Sadness, because apparently my devoted spawn felt deprived. And then back to Anger, because I had promised this little Einstein that we would stop for ice cream at Handel's (where they make all the ice cream fresh every day from real cream!) on the way home that night.

This episode traveled with me for a few days. As much as I wanted to hunt that man down and explain to him why my child's diet doesn't consist of daily sugar loads, I resisted. I'm sure he thought he was earning brownie points with my kid (although for the life of me, I don't understand why parents want to impress kids, their own or anyone else's). I'm sure he never gives the dangers of sugar a second thought, but I do.

Sugar is not good for any of us. As recent research is bringing to light, sugar, not fat, may be the real cause of our collective health issues. According to Dr. Robert Lustig, a UCSF professor of pediatrics and very eloquent and passionate anti-sugar advocate, Americans are consuming about 141 pounds of sugar per person per year and we weigh 25 pounds more than we did 25 years ago. His lecture, *Sugar: The Bitter Truth,* presents a fascinating and very convincing argument; sugar is a poison that is slowly killing us all. We are eating more sugar now than we ever have. A 12 ounce soda has 8 teaspoons of sugar in it. (Lustig points out that the "normal" soda from a machine these days is actually 20 ounces.) How many sodas does the average person drink in a day? I only pick on soda because it's frequently cited as the number one source of sugar in the American diet.

The USDA website labels sugar "empty calories" and makes recommendations about how many "empty calories" are acceptable in a typical diet.

AGE	Calories	AGE	Calories
Children 2-3	135	Children 4-8	120
Girls 9-13	120	Boys 9-13	160
Girls 14-18	160	Boys 14-18	265
Females 19-30	260	Males 19-30	330
Females 31-50	160	Males 31-50	265
Females 50+	120	Males 51+	260

The average soda (and I'm going to assume it's only a 12 oz can, silly me) has 145-160 calories. All of which, would be empty. So there's your day's worth of empty calories if you're the average kid. Hope you don't plan to eat any other junk food or processed food today because you've already reached your limit. And if you're hankering for a candy bar, you better divide it up between several days or you'll blow 2-3 days' worth of your empty calorie limit in one day.

Bottom line: Many people are consuming way too much sugar. Besides soda and candy, sugar is one of the primary ingredients in pretty much every processed food you buy. If you don't believe me, head for the grocery store and check for any of the following names for sugar on the ingredients list of your favorite cracker, prepared meal, frozen burrito, seasoning, dressing, or what-have-you: *anhydrous dextrose, brown sugar, confectioner's powdered sugar, corn syrup, corn syrup solids, dextrose, fructose, high-fructose corn syrup (HFCS), honey, invert sugar, lactose, malt syrup, maltose, maple syrup, molasses, nectars (e.g., peach nectar, pear nectar), pancake syrup, raw sugar, sucrose, white granulated sugar, sucanat, rapadura.* Just because it doesn't say sugar, doesn't mean it isn't sugar.

Dr. Lustig's belief (shared by other doctors and researchers) is that sugar is the main culprit in causing not only obesity and dental diseases, but diabetes, heart disease, and a host of other ailments, effectively poisoning us. Sugar has been linked to immune disorder issues, chromium deficiency, cancer, arthritis, and even learning disabilities. While sugar gives you a temporary "high," your body quickly crashes from the surge of false energy and you're left grumpy and tired. So what do you do? You crave more sugar.

As a confirmed sugaraholic myself, I would never tell you to cut out sugar completely because you can't. We get natural sugar from fruits, vegetables and grains, but the refined sugar we can do without. I might know this, but offer me a slice of key lime cheesecake and I'll take back everything I said. Sugar is a powerful thing.

Still, cutting out as much as possible might be the best thing you could do for your health and your child's. Here are a few ideas for reducing the amount of sugar in your diet.

Read labels. If sugar (in any form, see list above) is one of the first four ingredients, put the package down.

Cook from scratch as much as possible. Make your own smoothies with fresh fruit. Bake your own cookies, pizza dough, bread, applesauce, etc. Most prepared foods have extra sugar and salt to mask the taste of the extra preservatives and additives.

Consider using stevia, a natural sweetener derived from a plant, 300x sweeter than sugar with no calories.

Eat lots of fresh fruit and limit dried fruit which has considerably more sugar by proportion.

Cut out soda completely. You don't need it and it is only damaging your health. Drink water or tea instead. It's simply a matter of changing habits.

Control the sugar added to what you eat. Buy your tea unsweetened. Buy plain yogurt and sweeten with fruit. Make plain instant oatmeal and sweeten it with dried fruit (those tiny, seriously expensive oatmeal packets are more sugar than oats!)

Buy only 100% juice if you must drink fruit juice, with no added sugar.

Be careful of "fat free" foods. Many times the manufacturer compensates for the lower fat with higher sugar (and salt).

Start dialing back your sugar gradually. If you normally add two packets of sugar to your coffee, go for 1 ½, same with your kids oatmeal, cereal, etc.

Curb cravings with fruit. When the urge for sugar seems to overwhelm you, reach for fruit. It's still sugar, but with some extra fiber and a few less calories. I keep dried cherries on hand for these moments. Distract your kids' cravings by offering fruit after a meal or as a snack.

Try using sucanat in place of white sugar, and rapadura instead of brown sugar. The calorie count is about the same, but at least with less-processed sugars you get some of the same health benefits of molasses, plus traces of potassium, calcium, magnesium, iron, and vitamin A. These sugars are more expensive and you use them 1 for 1, so if you're budget doesn't have room for it, stick with straight sugar – just less of it.

Giving up sugar is not something I can claim I've done. When I'm able to reduce my refined sugar consumption, I see an improvement in my moods and energy level, plus it reduces the amount of sleep I need. But I'll be the first to wrestle that chocolate out of your hand if you tell me I have to give up all my sugar forever. This I do know: If I can reduce the amount of refined sugar in my children's diet, I'll be helping them to not only be healthier and avoid cavities, I'll be helping them to think more clearly and handle their emotions more consistently. That pay-off makes the battle worth fighting.

I still don't know why that dad gave my child money for candy, but the next time I see his kid, I might just tempt him with some fresh, homemade, organic applesauce laced with cinnamon! So there!

Challenges

Basic: Cut out, or at least cut down, your soda consumption. Explain to your children how much sugar is in one soda. Make it a special-occasion only drink.

Serious: Make more food from scratch and experiment with lightening the amount of sugar used. Consider using sucanat or rapadura.

Extreme: Cut out all sugary drinks. Make more of your food. Strive to stay under the USDA recommendation for empty sugar calories. Use stevia in place of sugar. It's tricky and somewhat of an acquired taste, but it doesn't mess with your blood sugar and doesn't have any calories, so it may be worth the effort.

Ultra Extreme: Give up sugar for a week or a month. Pay attention to how it makes you feel. It takes about two weeks for the cravings to go away. Don't give up!

21

Buy Better Eggs

Egg cartons have a lot of terms on them. It can be confusing for the average consumer, let alone a college-educated- overly-cautious-chicken-hobbyist mom. Why do some cost more than others and how do you know which ones are worth the big bucks? Looking over the labels at our grocery store, I realized two things – 1) my eggs are valuable and 2) my hens have it good. So what do all those terms mean? Here's a few definitions that might clear it up (or confuse you more).

Certified Organic: These birds live inside barns but not in cages and are given outdoor access (but there's no definition of *access*). They're fed an organic diet which is vegetarian and free of antibiotics and pesticides. *De-beaking* and *forced molting through starvation* are permitted. The US Department of Agriculture's National Organic Program verifies all this. (You may or may not want to know that *de-beaking* means cutting off the sharp end of a hen's beak so that she can't hurt her neighbors. This is necessary in close quarters because while hens may flock together, they don't necessarily like each other, and when they're forced to share close quarters, they tend to fight just like kids in the back seat of the car.)

Forced molting through starvation means depriving a hen of food so that she will molt, or drop all her feathers and grow new ones. All hens molt once each year and they don't lay eggs when they're molting. I'm assuming that forcing them to molt all at the same time makes management of large numbers of birds easier. Although it sounds like less-savory characters could potentially game this system, *certified organic* is probably a good thing, unless you're a hen.

Free-Range: There are no standards for *free range* egg production. Generally, *free-range* egg laying hens are uncaged inside barns or warehouses and have some outdoor access – which might be a concrete slab or a beautiful pasture, who's to say since no one is, literally, watching the hen house. There are no rules about what the hens are fed, how much outdoor access they have, or how closely they're packed inside their housing. They can, hopefully, engage in their natural behaviors such as nesting and foraging and these more relaxed conditions mean fewer eggs. De-beaking and forced molting are permitted, but there is no third party auditing.

I used to think my girls (and boys) were only considered *free-range* part of the year (the non-vegetable garden season when I turn them loose), but because they have access to their outdoor pen every day, they qualify as free-range all year, even when they aren't pooping on my porch and digging up my mulch. Seems to me, free-range could mean a lot of things and you shouldn't take the carton's word for it. It would be helpful to talk to the farmer. At my natural grocery store pictures of the hens are pinned up along the coolers with the eggs, so you can see from whence they came. The hens are outside in the grass and look very happy.

Certified Humane: These birds are uncaged, but may be kept indoors all the time. Still, they must be allowed to carry out their natural behaviors such as nesting, perching, and dust bathing. There are limits to the number of hens in each space and rules about how many perches and nesting boxes must be provided. Forced molting is not allowed, but de-beaking is. *Certified Humane* is a program of the Humane Farm Animal Care program.

De-beaking doesn't seem very humane to me. Maybe it's humane to the birds around you, but if you're the one having her beak cut off, that just doesn't sound very pleasant. There are very few animals, and pretty much no farm animals I can think of who are happy living inside all the time. But at least they are able to nest and perch and take their dust baths. For those of you who are curious, chickens have this crazy need to roll in dirt. They dig a hole and then lay down and roll around. Then they stand up and shake to get the dust out. The first time one of my hens did this I thought she was dying or at the least, grievously injured. I called my chicken-expert neighbor in alarm and she assured me this was a natural thing chickens do. Now I just mutter curses at them when I trip over freshly dug dust bathtubs in my barn.

Cage-Free: As the name implies, these birds don't live in cages, but they generally don't have access to the outdoors. There is no third-party auditing, so this term invokes visions of the huge chicken houses with tens of thousands of birds crammed inside that were pictured in the movie *Food, Inc.* De-beaking and forced molting are permitted, but the hens can engage in natural behaviors if space allows. It's good to be cage-free, but again without the blue sky up above you, what's the point?

United Egg Producers Certified: Almost all US Egg companies comply with this voluntary program which permits routine cruel and inhumane factory farming. Hens are afforded 67 square inches of cage per bird, less than the area of a sheet of paper. Forced molting is prohibited, but de-beaking is allowed. Compliance (to what?) is verified by third party auditors. This is a program of the United Egg Producers and might be a certification to avoid. It's like a superstore such as Wal-Mart stamping a Mass Market Producers certification on their own products. The official certification makes you think it's a good thing, but when the people doing the certifying are also making the profit it's meaningless.

Vegetarian-Fed: These girls are fed a more natural feed than the traditional factory farm birds, but like *grass-fed,* this term is not regulated, so unless you know the farmer, this label is basically meaningless. And honestly, how can a hen ever be completely vegetarian fed? The feed I buy does not contain animal byproducts and I don't feed my hens bacon, but they do eat bugs and when they discovered a nest of mice recently they ate all the babies. I'm sure that even a caged chicken reaches out and snags a fly or a gnat or a mosquito from time to time, so really, how can any chicken be a vegetarian?

Natural: There is no legal definition of *natural* as it relates to food products. According to the US Department of Agriculture any food that contains "no artificial ingredients or added color and are no more than minimally processed" may be considered *natural*. But what is *minimally processed*? I'm sure you're smart enough not to be fooled by that *natural* label by now.

Fertile: These are eggs which (if they hadn't been refrigerated already) could develop into chicks. They are no more nutritious than other eggs, but typically cost more. These are generally cage-free eggs because the hens would have to be in the company of a rooster or two for their eggs to be fertile. I think our eggs all taste great but I certainly couldn't tell you which ones are fertile and which ones aren't. There's no visible difference, so don't worry that you're going to crack open a fertile egg and find a half-formed baby chick.

Omega-3 Enriched: These eggs have a higher content of omega-3 fatty acids than the average egg thanks to the flaxseed added to their feed. These eggs are probably worth paying more for. I buy flaxseed, which is expensive, and mix it in with my chicken feed. I'm always looking for more ways to get Omega-3's in my family.

Hormone-free: This label might as well say, "rip off," because the use of hormones in the poultry industry has been banned since the 1960's, so all eggs are hormone-free by law. If a carton has this label, they are assuming you are a sucker worth suckering.

No living thing should have to live the way most chickens do on traditional poultry farms. You can read about it in *Omnivores Dilemma* or watch it in *Food, Inc.* I know first-hand how stupid chickens are, but I also know they have personalities and display emotions like fear and anger. They clearly display joy when I arrive with a box of stale cereal or a bowl of uneaten popcorn. I'm not a vegetarian, and I plan to raise some chickens for meat once my kids move out and I find a willing butcher. Still, I believe all living things are entitled to dignity and decency even if their ultimate purpose is to end up on my dinner table.

Gathering all this information has made it clear to me that my hens lay golden eggs! The eggs that I collect each night are *free range, cage free, hormone-free, organic* (albeit not certified), *humane* (again, not certified), *free-roaming, vegetarian-fed, natural, fertile,* and even *Omega-3 Enriched*! Just imagine how much they'd go for in a grocery store!

Just in case you can't get enough, here's some more fascinating facts about eggs –

The really big eggs sometimes have double yokes. Eggs come in all kinds of colors other than white and brown. Our Americana chickens lay green and blue eggs. Our Bard Rock chickens lay light brown eggs just like you see in the grocery store, and our Rhode Island Reds lay beautiful deep brown eggs that are sometimes speckled. The shades of the eggs vary day to day probably due to diet, temperature, or maybe their mood that day.

I've kept fresh eggs in the refrigerator for 3-4 months and they're fine. If an egg goes bad you will know it before you crack it. All eggs have pores so a rotten egg will stink up your entire fridge. Other chicken farmers have taught me that a fresh egg just plucked from the nest will keep on my counter for three weeks. I know you're thinking – it's not the rotten egg I'm worried about, it's the one with salmonella. I couldn't find any documented cases of salmonella poisoning coming from a person eating a homegrown egg.

When an egg is laid it has a protective coating on it, called the "bloom". The protective coating keeps bacteria from getting inside the egg while it sits in the hen house or on the counter. All eggs have it unless they have been scrubbed clean to look pretty at the grocery store. Some store bought eggs that have been cleaned are then given a sheer spray of mineral oil to protect them. That's why they sometimes appear shiny.

You, too, can have golden eggs. Plenty of people keep chickens in the suburbs and even the city. All you need is a large dog run and a "house" of some kind. Chickens are cheap, easy to keep and pay for themselves. Just in case you were wondering, and you might be since people ask me this all the time, you don't need a noisy rooster to have eggs. You only need roosters if you want to hatch more chickens. Another lovely by-product is chicken poop - true fertilizer gold for your gardens.

Additionally, chickens make great pets. Kids love them. My daughter trained one of ours to walk on a leash (with a small dog harness). With enough attention, they can become docile and friendly.

Challenges:

Basic: Read the labels at your grocery store and decide what you're willing to pay more for. Purchase a dozen eggs from a farmers market or neighbor who keeps chickens and have a blind taste test.

Serious: Buy eggs from a farmers market or neighbor who keeps chickens. Ask the farmer/neighbor about the chickens' living conditions.

Extreme: Start keeping chickens yourself. Check with your neighborhood association or township/borough for regulations.

22

Buy Your Beef (or Pork) By The Cow (or Pig)

Friends raised their eyebrows when I told them we were buying a cow. They'd come to expect extremes from me in terms of food, but putting a bovine in our suburban pasture seemed a little crazy, even for me. When I explained we were only buying half a cow, they shook their heads in disbelief. Buying meat by the animal is much cheaper than buying it in Styrofoam cartons. And don't worry – it doesn't arrive on four legs.

The first task is to find a farmer you trust who sells cows whole, half, or quarter. Ask around at your local butcher shop, farmer's market, or check online. Two great websites to get you started are localharvest.org and eatwild.com. You want animals who have been primarily grass-fed and raised without the use of growth hormones or unnecessary antibiotics. You'll also want to be certain that the farm uses a butcher who dry-ages the meat.

Grass-fed animals offer huge health benefits over factory farmed animals. Grass-fed meats have significantly less saturated fat and are higher in omega-3 fatty acid. Omega 3's are good for your heart and essential for your brain's health, helping to ward off depression, attention deficit disorder, schizophrenia, and Alzheimer's. Grass-fed meat also has more vitamin E, beta-carotene, and vitamin C than grain-fed beef. Maybe the most powerful argument for the health benefits of grass-fed meat and dairy products is that they are high in CLA (Conjugated Linoleic Acid). CLA is a powerful anti-carcinogen which has been shown to reduce the risk of cardiovascular disease and fight inflammation. The Journal of Dairy Science states that grass-fed animals can produce 300-500% more CLA than grain-fed animals. (When checking my facts on CLA, I came across this gem: *Kangaroo meat has the highest concentration of CLA.* Just thought you'd want to know in case it ever comes up on Jeopardy.)

Half a cow feeds my family of five for nearly a year. We eat beef about 1-2 times a week. The price sometimes goes down if you buy an entire cow, so you might try to find a friend to split the cow. There are a few terms you'll want to understand when buying a cow. The *live weight* is what the cow weighs when it arrives for slaughter. The *hanging weight* is the cow's weight after it has been slaughtered and the non-usable parts removed. It's the carcass' weight before it's been aged and the butcher gets to work. The hanging weight is the weight that matters most – it's how the price is calculated. The *retail weight* is the weight of the beef you actually cart home. Generally, it's 60-70% of the hanging weight, but it can sometimes be more if you've got an experienced butcher.

When you order your cow, be sure to ask if the price includes the butchering and packaging (most do). You'll be asked to specify details like how much steak you want versus how much hamburger, how many pounds per roast, and how thick the steaks should be cut. It makes me feel like royalty when I direct my steaks to be cut 1½" thick and order the percentage of fat I'd like in my burger. Oh, and package my burger in one pound packs with a few three pound packs thrown in for parties. Nobody grants my wishes like the butcher.

It generally takes about two to four weeks from when you order your cow until you're firing up the grill. The meat arrives flash-frozen and vacuum packed in plastic packages. We had an exceptionally big cow one year and some of the hamburger was in our freezer for over a year but still tasted great.

All that savings and convenience is well and good, but the taste is the best reason to buy your cow local, fresh and untainted by growth hormones, antibiotics, and excessive fat created by corn-feeding. The key is the dry-aging which makes the meat deliciously tender. We ordered a grass-fed cow once and had it cut by a conventional butcher. The meat was tough and gamey. Once we discovered the wonders wrought by dry-aging, we never looked back. Dry-aging is the process of hanging the meat for several weeks before cutting it. This allows the enzymes to work on the meat as a natural tenderizer. Basically, you're letting your meat mold, but a good butcher knows how long to let it hang and how to cut the fuzz off without losing too much meat. I always request that our cow be dry-aged as long as is legal.

Prior to our switch to grass-fed, dry-aged beef, my kids refused most steaks. If they did eat steak, they would chew it like gum and leave it in unsightly lumps on the edges of their placemats. But that was before they tasted "*our cow*". That was before we could afford to feed them filet mignon on a Tuesday because we paid the same price per pound for the filet mignon as we did for the hamburger we grilled over the weekend. The beef they're eating is better than beef they would get in most restaurants. It melts in your mouth and is so tender it never needs a steak knife. I could go on but suffice it to say – buy your own grass-fed dry-aged beef and you will never go back to eating plain old steak. The year we began buying our beef by the cow is the year all my children decided they liked steak (even the vegetarian one).

After experiencing grass-fed beef, we took it a step further and went whole hog by purchasing our very own grass-fed pig. The process worked much the same, but we had to turn to the Amish to find a hog that was not cured with nitrates. I try to stay away from added nitrates since they are known carcinogens.

I know your first concern is –where do you put all that meat? It doesn't take as much room as you would think. The hog fit neatly in two big coolers when we picked it up. We have a standing freezer; the cow and pig take up about two thirds of it. We don't order them at the same time though, so it never comes to that.

My adorable nerdy husband plans to make up a spreadsheet showing the cost of buying by the cow and pig compared to buying the same cuts from the grocery store just to make a point, but I don't need the numbers to tell me. The food is fresher, healthier, tastes better, and supports my local farmers. It's just an added bonus that it costs less too!

Challenges

Basic: Buy grass-fed, dry-aged steak and taste the difference.

Serious: Gather some friends together and go in on a cow and/or a hog. When it's delivered, have a party to celebrate and divide up the meat.

Extreme: Buy your own split-side of a cow (if you buy only a quarter, you'll be asked to choose between the back or the front – go for back.).

23

Fast Food Fight

I realize writing this may be pointless, but I'm going to write it anyway. Maybe I'm a hypocrite because I'll confess right up front that during family road trips we almost always wind up eating at a fast food joint. And yet, I must carry on with this rant.

Please, please, please don't eat fast food. I understand that when you have children in the car who are pulling your fingernails out one-by-one with their incessant whining while they wither away to nothing with bloated bellies and sunken eyes in the back seat, you feel as if you have no choice but to pull into the fastest food joint possible. But let's be honest here, folks. Sometimes we choose fast food because it's easy. It makes the kids happy. And heck, it tastes good.

You know what else it does? It makes our country fat and unhealthy. It makes our kids develop tastes for foods that are over-salted, drenched in unhealthy fats, and coated with sugar. It teaches them that eating fast food is an acceptable choice for their meal, rather than a last-ditch, there's-no-where-else-to-eat, it-might-make-us-sick, but we-have-no-choice option. My three kids will never eat at McDonalds without at least feeling bad about it. When they open up that Combo Meal, they know that what they are really eating is not so much food, as animal by-products molded into a recognizable shape, lard-coated pesticide-enriched, white potatoes, and chemically created drug-filled sugar water.

It's every mother's duty to give their kids some baggage. And this is one of the carry-ons I'm loading on mine. I think it's a good one. To be sure, you can occasionally find something nutritionally redeeming at a fast food restaurant. But my guess is your kids aren't choosing the carrot sticks or fruit cup. And if they go for that baked potato, it's sure to be smothered in artificially-colored cheese food product.

Grilled chicken seems harmless until you ask about the chicken's heritage and discover it was raised amongst millions of other chickens crammed in a dark, closed-in house with horrible ventilation and hopped up on antibiotics to keep it from dying from the bacterial infections that are common in such set-ups. Don't be fooled by those lovely pictures of chickens sitting on a fence. Those chickens can't even walk, let alone hop up on a fence because they've been bred to have grotesquely large breasts that prevent them from even moving. Egg to deep fryer in about 12 weeks' time. If they live any longer, they'll die from congestive heart failure because their bodies can't support their breasts. (No lie – I know someone personally who didn't get his chickens butchered in time and this is how they died!).

Almost everyone I know thinks factory farming is horrible. And yet many of them eat at fast food restaurants on a near weekly basis. Is this just the cumulative effect of little white lies? Or did we not understand the unit on cause and effect in middle school science class?

If my ranting and raving isn't enough to make you steer past those golden arches and smiling freckled-faces, consider this fact from The National Center of Health Statistics -*The average weight of a ten-year-old boy in 1963 was 74 pounds; by 2002 the average weight was nearly 85 pounds. The average weight of a ten-year-old girl in 1963 was 77 pounds; by 2002 the average weight of a ten-year-old girl was 88 pounds.*

Or how about this gem - A *person would need to walk 9 miles (14.5km) to burn off the 923 calories found in Burger King's Double Whopper with cheese.*

So what's an overloaded, stressed-out mom to do?

If you're in town, go home to eat. A peanut butter sandwich or a frozen pizza are healthier choices. They're just as quick and cost less.

If you're traveling – pack food. Stuff a cooler with fruit that travels well, like cherries, apples, bananas, and blueberries. Toss in several bags of baby carrots. Wheat crackers, raisins, craisins, apricots, nuts, and cheese sticks are easy on-the-go food, too.

When all else fails, remind yourself and your kids that HUNGER IS NOT AN EMERGENCY. There are very few people starving to death in the US. Your kids can go several hours (at least) between meals. Hunger will pass and many times it's actually habit and/or boredom that drives us to demand food.

If you must stop, look for a place that serves fresh food quickly, instead of processed food. Chipotle Grill is one of my favorite stops and it's quicker than the average fast food. Stopping in a Mom & Pop type place can also be quick, if you tell the server you're in a hurry and ask what can be prepared quickly.

Find a restaurant with a good salad bar. Many supermarkets have salad bars. You can even get a pound of shrimp steamed quickly and enjoy a decadent treat instead of a mashed up hamburger wrapped in foil.

If you know you're going to have to stop and you can't bring yourself to pack food, remember you have other options beyond fast food. The internet gives you the power to find restaurants on your route that serve healthy fare.

Here's my bottom line. Fast food won't kill you, if you eat it once in a while. (It will kill you if you eat it daily – see the movie *Supersize Me* if you don't believe me!) However, what's more important is teaching our children that this is not a healthy way to eat. When we swing through the drive-thru on a regular basis, we are training our kids for a lifetime of unhealthy eating. Every mom I know loves her kids too much to want that for them. I know fast food is easy. I know our children love it (they love candy and potato chips, too). This is one of those things we must do for our children (like driving the speed limit and being nice to rude people). We need to teach them fast food should not be a regular part of their diet.

Besides the health issues raised by consuming fast food, I'd like to raise another point. When we eat "fast" we are not respecting the place food has in our life. It is our sustenance. When we choke down something in a wrapper while our children duck in and out of the Playland between bites of ground up chicken-parts coated in bread and fat, we aren't paying attention to the food we eat. When we sit down and face one another and eat good food together, it is a form of communion. We need to teach our children to taste their food, to appreciate where it came from, and who prepared it. We need to teach them the power they have in choosing what to put in their bodies and about the power food has to make our bodies healthy or unhealthy. Whatever decisions they make will be apparent at some point in their lives on the bathroom scale or the doctor's table. Teach them to make healthy, empowering choices for their bodies and their lives.

We only get one shot at raising our children. This is our one and only chance to teach our children about eating healthy and being healthy for a lifetime. It's more than a meal and much more than fast food.

Challenges

Easy: Limit fast-food meals to once or twice a month. Explain to your family the reasons for this.

Serious: Limit fast food meals to only-under-desperate-circumstances. Plan ahead and pack meals instead.

Extreme: Don't eat at fast food restaurants for one month. Use the money you save to buy a family treat – I recommend lobster! Watch *Supersize Me*. Make a pledge to stop eating at fast-food restaurants.

24

To Pack or Not to Pack, That is the Question

To pack or not to pack – isn't that the big question? A University of Michigan study demonstrated that children who eat school lunches on a regular basis are 29% more likely to be obese than kids who pack their lunch. I'm sure I don't need to quote any statistics about adults who eat their lunches out on a daily basis. We all know what happens to a typical adult on a daily diet of Burger King. Buying lunch every day isn't good for our waistlines or our wallets.

I allow my kids to buy school lunch only occasionally (they have the meanest mom in the world). I gave in to their repeated demands because it seemed that if I dug my heels in, they would only want to buy lunch more. They were asking for stuff like fish sticks and sloppy joes which they've traditionally hated. I agreed to allow them to purchase lunch one day a week. Amazingly, that doesn't always happen. The only exception is *Breakfast-for-Lunch* day. They can't resist pancakes and more importantly – syrup. I cringe at the thought of them fueling up on processed pancake mix, high fructose corn syrup mixed with artificial flavors and colors, and trans fat-laden home fries. But this is the sacrifice I make to keep the peace and to keep them from resenting our food choices.

School lunches, at least in my experience, are by nature loaded with processed food and artificial ingredients. How else can you feed so many children so cheaply? All I can say is - *Shame on our government*. I completely understand the budget restrictions and hard choices, but I don't accept them. Our children deserve better. Rather than climbing up on my soapbox, I'll just leave it at that.

When it comes to packing a lunch that your kids will eat, I've got a secret – *make them pack it themselves*. Even the youngest can do this if you give plenty of direction and plenty of options. The directions for packing lunches at our house are as follows:

Lunch should contain five things: fruit/veggie, carb, protein, water, and dessert. You can make your lunch as large or small as you like, but it should have at least these five things. Eating a healthy lunch will give you the energy and patience to survive the rest of your day.

Choose at least ONE OR MORE FRUIT OR VEGGIES: banana, apples, blueberries, peaches, oranges, sliced watermelon, strawberries, carrots, celery, or cucumbers. (Of course these choices vary according to season and my shopping whims.)

Choose at least ONE OR MORE PROTEIN: peanut butter & jelly sandwich, hardboiled egg, garbanzo beans, kidney beans, nuts, bagel with cream cheese, or cheese slices.

Choose only ONE carb: pretzels, crackers, popcorn, bagel chips.

Choose only ONE dessert: cookies, leftover dinner dessert, leftover candy from the last event (Halloween, birthday party, Valentine's Day, road trip, Mom's weak moment), homemade pudding, or zucchini bread.

Choose ONE OPTIONAL DAIRY: yogurt, cheese stick/slice.

Fill your water bottle. Add a clean cloth napkin and utensils you'll need.

When we first instituted the pack-your-own-lunch process, I paid the kids one mom buck (see chapter on my Mom Buck System) because they were taking over a job I normally had to do. As long as they packed their lunch without my involvement (this means I didn't have to nag them to do it), they earned a Mom buck. I encouraged them to pack the night before, but to-date no one has.

I hope by laying out the requirements for a healthy lunch, I'm imprinting that structure in their minds so someday when the choice is theirs, they'll put together a lunch that is balanced, healthy, and yummy. I do realize that this doesn't get me off the hook completely. It's still my responsibility to keep the house stocked with options they'll like, which may mean more trips to the market. The payoff has been more lunches eaten. There's nothing that frustrates me more than unpacking three uneaten lunches I carefully packed just that morning.

What do you pack that healthy lunch in? First rule - no plastic bags or aluminum foil to clog up the planet. Baggies are the bane of my existence. Have you ever considered anything so wasteful? You can't get around them on many occasions, but you can avoid them when packing lunches. Buy small re-usable plastic containers. Be sure to use plastic safely, though. Never wash plastic in the dishwasher. Wash it by hand, with warm water (never scalding hot) and soap. Also, don't pack anything hot in plastic. My kids have learned to eat their food and put the plastic containers back in their lunchboxes. There are some accidents occasionally (lost lids or crushed containers), but no one and no system is perfect. This works for us.

Challenges

Basic: Start packing lunches – it's infinitely healthier.

Serious: Use reusable plastic or glass instead of baggies or aluminum foil.

Extreme: Teach your kids to pack their own lunches.

25

Here Comes the Sun (and Vitamin D)

I got my Vitamin D today the old fashioned way – I went outside. I spent about an hour working on my latest project – a Quarter Horse gelding named True who is 4 years old and "unbroken." It's been a lot of years since I've "broken" a horse. Broken is a horrible term, I've always hated it. Hopefully, I won't be *breaking* True, I'll be *making* him, but we shall see. Anyway, 30 minutes spent teaching him the finer points of paying attention to me and respecting my personal space accomplishes two things. One, True is a tiny bit closer to allowing me to put a saddle on his back and two, I got my Vitamin D for the day.

Vitamin D has been all over the news lately. *New* scientific breakthroughs have revealed that there is much more at stake with our daily intake of Vitamin D. Are we getting enough? What happens if you're deficient? How do you get enough? What happens if you get too much?

Americans (probably most first-world nations) are spending more and more time inside. We are no longer a nation of farmers. Most people's work doesn't allow them a whole lot of time outside their cubicle or classroom or factory. And when we are home we tend to spend a good part of our free time in front of screens of one variation or another. Our yards are smaller and in some cases, not safe. When we do go outside, we are covered with technically advanced clothing that blocks UVB rays and slathered in sunscreen which prohibits our body from absorbing the sunshine necessary to make Vitamin D. Consequently, we aren't getting our Vitamin D on a daily basis. And this includes kids. Huge numbers of people are Vitamin D deficient.

Let me back up. What do we know about Vitamin D? You probably remember that milk is fortified with Vitamin D, and Vitamin D is necessary to build strong bones. A deficiency in Vitamin D can cause rickets in children and osteoporosis in adults. Vitamin D isn't technically a vitamin because it's produced in the human body. It's not found in any natural source except fish and egg yolks, and even then it requires the body to convert it to vitamin D. But the body can also use sunshine to create vitamin D. It then stores the extra Vitamin D in the fat cells to use for, literally, a rainy day.

How much do we need? The first government recommended allowances were 200IU of Vitamin D daily. In 1997, it was upped to 400 for kids and 600 for adults. New research is indicating that we need even more, perhaps 800 or 1000. According to the Harvard School of Public Health Vitamin D is more essential than at first thought. Scientists believe that Vitamin D is critical to the brain, prostate, breast, colon, heart, lung, muscles and our immune cells.

The auto-immune community has touted the benefits of Vitamin D for years. Many people who suffer from alopecia areata (the autoimmune condition my youngest son has) buy "happy lights" to get more UVB light. Vitamin D is powerful, helping normal cells grow, but also helping abnormal ones (cancer cells come to mind) die. It has been proven to destroy infectious agents, such as TB. Evidence is mounting that higher levels of Vitamin D can lower the risk of Type 1 diabetes, multiple sclerosis, depression, muscle weakness, and cancer.

Does this news make you want to grab your beach towel? It should. Being a person of incredibly fair skin, I am well aware of the dangers of too much sun. I have the freckles to prove it. I'm fairly sure that Vitamin D is not one of my deficiencies. Actually, all you need to get your vitamin D is 5-10 minutes of direct sunlight between the hours of 10am and 3pm. Maybe your plan could be to put the sunscreen on after you've set up your chair and had your snack.

You can get Vitamin D from supplements and fortified products like milk and orange juice. Some doctors, who worry about skin cancers, recommend you do that, but be aware that there is such a thing as too much of a good thing. While you can't overdose on Vitamin D from the sun, you can overdose from supplements. Experts at Harvard say up to 2000IU a day is safe.

Vitamin D aside, I know that sunshine is a real pick-me-up for me and for my kids. Sometimes it's tempting to stay inside, especially when it's hot, but 10 minutes won't kill anyone, and it just might save your life.

Challenges

Basic: Purchase Vitamin D for you and your kids to take, particularly in the winter.

Serious: Sit in the sun everyday – drink your coffee outside, meditate, take a walk, do something outside for at least ten minutes every day. Get your kids outside too – challenge them to run laps around the house, ask them to walk the dog, or invite them for a game of Frisbee. Teach them the importance of sunshine for their health.

Extreme: Get yourself and your kids outside every day for thirty minutes. This might be the perfect time to begin a daily walk or run. On cloudy or winter days, give your kids a supplement and take 1000IU (at least) of Vitamin D yourself. I take mine in a liquid. It's one tiny drop in my tea each morning. It doesn't affect the taste at all (proof being that I slip it into my hubby's coffee when I can and he's never noticed.)

Intentional

HOME

26

Create an Intentional Kitchen

Once upon a time, I organized our kitchen. I threw out things we never used and sorted the useful items into the prime drawers. I gathered all the spices, donated the duplicates, and lined up the jars with the labels facing outwards. I matched up all the plastic containers and tossed anything without a matching lid. I cleared the counters of erroneous items that had come to reside there by default. I even took every piece of children's art off the fridge. The entire kitchen looked ready for show. Because it was. The house was for sale. Why is it we never really clean out clutter or make our spaces truly tidy until we're either expecting the Queen or putting the house up for sale? Don't we deserve to live in such pristine places, too?

Creating a high-functioning, organized kitchen is not a job done in one morning. This is a job that takes determination, a large trash can, and several extra boxes for donations and indecision. An organized kitchen is an intentional kitchen because everything in it has a purpose and is easy to find. It makes creating healthy food from scratch an inviting project instead of a chore. Let me share my 10-step Intentional Kitchen plan with you!

1. **Subject everything to the *Four question Test***. I found this test years ago in a great book called, *Organic Housekeeping* by Ellen Sandbeck. As you sort out drawers and cabinets, consider every item and ask yourself -

Do I really need this? This can be a hard question, but if you've only ever used the item once or you've never used it at all, then you probably don't need it. And if you only ever use it on Thanksgiving or Christmas or when your mother-in-law visits, then it certainly doesn't need a place of prominence in your kitchen.

What would happen if I threw it away? I would recommend giving it away, not throwing it away, but it's still a question to consider. Would I miss it? Could I get another one easily? Is there someone who could make better use of it than me? Would it rock my world if this item disappeared tomorrow?

Do I need so many? This is the question that gets me. I don't need six rubber spatulas. Sure, at times when my daughter is baking two or three sugar-laden projects at once, she needs them because otherwise she'd be forced to wash a few, but *I don't need six*. I only need three. Consider how many of any tool, dish, utensil, glass or pot you need. It's quite definitely time to cull our coffee cup herd.

Will I care for this person any less if I give this away? This is a powerful question. We hold on to many objects simply because someone important in our lives gave them to us. They thought we needed it, but do we actually need/want/use it? And if we give it away does that mean we love this person any less? I vote no. Be gone. (This is probably a critical question to ask yourself when you sort out your closet or knick-knack collection, also.)

2. **Save the prime real estate for the most used items.** We have a little drawer between the fridge and the sink across from the stove which is undoubtedly the equivalent of Boardwalk on the monopoly board. It's prime real estate in our kitchen. I cleaned it out recently. And what did I find hiding in there? A few beer cozies, the wrench shaped bottle opener that Nick got at a trade show twenty years ago, six tiny corn spikes the kids used to hold their corn on the cob when they were preschoolers, and the instruction manual for my standing mixer that I wished I'd had the previous Christmas when I was trying to sort out what model it was for

replacement parts. There were also some wineglass markers and more than a few old corks floating around the drawer, plus some random metal screws whose origin was unknown to us. I shook my head when I spied the crab crackers which we failed to locate the last time we had steamed crabs and had to use the back of our knives.

I dumped the drawer immediately and only returned the bottle opener because it was the one item that saw regular use in our house. Now this primely located drawer holds ladles and spatulas within reach of the stove where they are normally used.

Think about what is in the drawers and cabinets that are easiest to access. Place the tools you use most in these places.

3. **Remove or relocate infrequently used items.** If you only use an item like a muffin pan, melon baller, or a double boiler on occasion, it doesn't need to be handy in your kitchen. Relocate it to an out of reach cabinet, a closet, or the basement. This frees up space so your cabinets and drawers are not jammed.

4. **Make use of drawer dividers.** When we designed our kitchen, I added lots of spacious drawers. The problem with spacious drawers is that everything in them becomes a jumble. You don't have to go out and buy drawer dividers. (But if you do, I recommend the wire mesh kind so they don't fill up with dust and those little bits of gunk that have no clear origin and give your visiting relatives the impression that you never clean your drawer dividers because you probably don't.) You can use empty boxes with the lids cut off or Tupperware containers.

5. **Prioritize your pantry.** If your pantry looks like mine used to, there are boxes and bottles stacked and tumbled clear to the very back. When I finally sorted it out, I found an expired can of organic coconut milk and a leaky tube of anchovy paste in the very back. For shame. Clean out the pantry and organize the contents. Just like the drawers and cabinets, put the foods you eat frequently near the front.

5a. Turn all the labels so they face outward. I did this when the house was for sale on the advice of a house-prepping guide, and wow- what a difference. It instantly makes your pantry look organized, but it has the added bonus of helping you keep track of what you have in there, also.

6. **Group the items you use together – together.** I created a baking center in one area of my kitchen and put everything I use to bake – spices, extracts, baking powder/soda, molasses, and other ingredients in the same cabinet with the tools I use to bake – sifter, chopper, nut grinder, food processor, hand mixer, etc. The measuring cups and spoons, and the tools like whisks, rubber spatulas, eggs separator, and citrus press are in the drawer below. When I bake, I can stand in one place and reach nearly everything I need.

7. **Look for underutilized storage space.** The space between the counter and the cabinets can hold a skinny shelf. We put a shelf there to store all my fancy vinegars and another to hold bottles of spices. They are off the counter, but easily accessible. How about under the sink? The bulk head? You could put a tasteful basket on top of your fridge and hide all manner of things.

8. **Clear the counters.** If your counters are clutter-free, it's much more inviting to cook. Move anything you don't use daily off the counters. We moved our coffee maker off the counter, because it's only used on the weekends and that opened up all kinds of space. Sugar and flour canisters can be put in cabinets to free up space. The only things sitting on my counter, are the standing mixer (because it's too heavy), the paper towel holder (because we haven't found a creative place for it yet), and a pretty pottery jug full of wooden utensils. Now, when I'm ready to cook – I've got room to work.

9. **Clear the front of your fridge.** I know this one is hard. I have a habit of letting mine fill up periodically, but when I clean off the fridge it makes the entire kitchen seem cleaner and less cluttered.

10. The Last tip comes from my brother-in-law, the chef – **"Clean as you go, sign of a pro."** We were cooking together years ago and he recited this mantra a few times with a chuckle. It stuck in my head, although I saw no evidence of him putting it in practice. In fact, whenever he cooked, we ate delightfully, but nearly every dish I owned was utilized and then left dirty on the counter. I suppose if you can cook like James, that's okay, but I can't, so I clean as I go so that someday I'll be a pro. It does make the difference if you take just an extra minute to wipe out a pot or rinse off your knives. If you clean up the drop of tomato sauce that

splattered on your backsplash a few moments after it happens, it's easy. If you wait until next week when you're cleaning for company – it's a bear and might even have left a stain on your wall. If you take the time to put away the wine opener or corn meal or the buttermilk immediately after you've used it, the clutter is kept to a minimum. If you clean as you go, no one becomes overwhelmed by the task of cleaning it up later. Say it with me– "Clean as you go, sign of a pro!"

Challenges

Basic: Clean out your cabinets and straighten your shelves.

Serious: Move everything you don't use *daily* off your counters. Move anything not used on a regular basis out of your kitchen to alternative storage. Do your best to clean as you go whenever you cook.

Extreme: Pull everything out and subject it to the four-question test. Clean your drawers and cabinets before putting your tools and dishes in the places that make the most sense in terms of their use. Consider adding additional storage space and/or drawer dividers.

27

Non Toxic Cleaning

Cleaning is not my favorite activity. My house is serviceably clean; it's not going to make anyone sick, but it isn't ready for a photo shoot by a long shot. I tend to clean on an as-needed basis. The toilet-bowl looks nasty? Time to clean. The dog's shedding? Time to vacuum. Someone spilled lemonade? Guess it's time to mop. Overnight visitors, holidays, and parties will also send me to my cleaning closet, but I resist it as long as possible. With three kids, a busy hubby, and a dog who all track in the remnants of six acres of gardens, horses, chickens, woods, and grass – I'm outnumbered and overwhelmed by the chore of cleaning.

I used to go for every new cleaning product that promised to make cleaning easier and faster. I tried everything and usually loved it for about a week. Then it got pushed to the back of the closet with the other bottles, sticks, cloths, and powders. These days my cleaning closet has only a few things in it. I'm saving a ton of money and cleaning the way my grandmother did.

I was motivated to purge my cleaning closet for the same reasons I was motivated to clean up our diet – health. In my battle to reclaim my youngest son's health, I started with household cleaning products figuring that the air we breathe affects every molecule of our being. We disposed of all toxic cleaning solutions, detergents, shampoos, and soaps.

Reading up on alternatives, I discovered that many of the things our grandparents cleaned with are all natural, safe, and work as well, sometimes better, than their modern equivalents. Plain white vinegar can do anything! You name it, vinegar can do it.

I use vinegar as my primary cleaning agent. I have spray bottles of vinegar stashed all over the house. I use it for kitchen counters, kitchen table, bathroom counters, sinks, and fixtures. It make stainless steel shine. It works wonders on mildew stains and tile. We have a bathroom ceiling in the older section of our house that constantly grows mildew spots. When we first lived in this house I chased after those spots with every kind of bleach available, only to end up with a headache from the fumes, foggy contacts, and tired arms. Nothing would remove them. Then I discovered vinegar and voila! I just spray, give it ten minutes, and then wipe away. A miracle! (I'm easily impressed.)

I use vinegar to remove any kind of stink from shoes, equipment, trash cans, coolers, and the inside of the free freezer we received that had been shut off with meat still stored in it. It cleans tile and wood floor, and diluted with water does an awesome job on windows.

My younger kids used to love to clean windows but I worried about the fumes they inhaled, and the Windex battles that sometimes ensued. Vinegar can't hurt them. No more worries about the toxicity of Windex, but sadly they've outgrown their love of window cleaning. To clean windows and mirrors, use a 3-1 ration of vinegar and water.

Sometimes when I share this advice with others, I'm told it leaves streaks. The streaks are not from the vinegar, they're from buildup created by commercial window cleaners. To get rid of the residue, add a squirt of liquid castile soap to your vinegar and water spray. After you rid your windows of the buildup you can go back to plain vinegar and water for regular cleaning. By the way, the residue left by commercial cleaners may contain 2-Butoxyethanol, a suspected hormone disrupter that causes skin and lung irritations. Just one more reason to get rid of the commercial cleaning agents.

Vinegar is a great fabric cleaner too. It removes food, crayon, and God-knows-what-else stains from my couch cushions. When I mop up one of my elderly dog's accidents on the carpet, I immediately douse the same spot with vinegar and scrub. The smell is virtually eliminated and vinegar doesn't discolor the carpet.

Vinegar also works well as the rinse-aid in the dishwasher. You have to fill it more frequently than regular toxic rinse aid, but at such a low price, it's no issue. Vinegar costs only about $2 a gallon. Talk about a deal.

A frequent worry I hear when teaching workshops on organic cleaning concerns the smell. People worry that their houses and clothes will smell like vinegar. They won't. The smell dissipates quickly and if you come to my house the only smell you're bound to encounter is bread baking. But if you can't tolerate the smell while you're using vinegar, you can mix it with a few drops of natural oil such as lavender or lemon.

When I first began cleaning organically, I used two things - vinegar and baking soda. Both cleaners are effective, but they should be utilized separately. While they have different purposes, I occasionally got carried away in my cleaning efforts and combined their forces. I soon learned that's not such a good idea. Combining vinegar and baking soda renders them both ineffective. Vinegar is acid and baking soda is alkaline, so the ingredients neutralize each other. Seems I didn't retain any valuable information from my high school chemistry class.

To clean with baking soda, dissolve 1 teaspoon of baking soda in hot water in a clean spray bottle and add a squirt of castile soap. This spray works well as an all-purpose cleanser for baseboards, tabletops, and other hard surfaces and it will last several months. Baking soda is also great for cleaning electric ovens. To freshen carpets, sprinkle baking soda on carpet, let sit 15 minutes and then vacuum.

If you're paranoid about germs and don't want to take my word for it that vinegar will kill them, you can also use hydrogen peroxide – it'll kill anything. Just add a spray nozzle to the brown hydrogen peroxide bottle and use it on toilets, counters, even fruits and vegetables. Hydrogen peroxide has no taste and no real smell, so you won't even notice it. Hydrogen peroxide is good for bathroom mold, too. Leave it on for an hour to let it eat away at the mold and do its job and then wipe it off. Hydrogen peroxide must be kept in a light-proof bottle otherwise all of its magical powers will disappear.

There's absolutely no reason to purchase commercial cleaners. Why would you willingly bring a toxic product into your home? There's a reason the warning labels on so many cleaning products tell you to dispose of it safely and keep out of reach of children. It's a risk you don't need to take. The internet is rife with eco-friendly cleaning ideas, but I've discovered over the years that good old fashioned soap and water almost always works as well as any of the fancy concoctions – eco-friendly or otherwise. I'm relieved to no longer worry about the toxic fumes and residue left by commercial cleaning products and when friends visit with toddlers, I never worry because pretty much everything in my cleaning closet and under my sinks is edible.

Challenges

Basic: Go through your cleaning closet and safely dispose of anything you don't use. As you use up your toxic products replace them with more eco-friendly commercial versions.

Serious: Mix up a bottle of baking soda all-purpose cleaner (mark bottle clearly). Buy vinegar and dilute it with water in spray bottles as a glass cleaner (bonus points if you let your kids wash the windows).

Extreme: Fill spray bottles with vinegar and keep one in the kitchen and every bathroom. Read up on organic cleaning and learn to make your own cleaning products. The book *Organic Housekeeping* by Ellen Sandbeck is a great place to start.

28

A Place for Everything

We had almost completed the 500 piece puzzle of the planets, when it became obvious that there was a piece missing. Before we could become too discouraged, my youngest son yelled, "I'll check the Missing Piece Drawer!" and ran from the room. The Missing Piece Drawer, you ask? As a mother, this is my best invention yet. Unlike my allowance plans, chore charts, and measuring cup-free recipes, this one actually works!

The Missing Piece Drawer was born when I finally got serious about cleaning my house. No matter how fast I moved, the kids and their mess moved faster. I found myself constantly picking up pieces that were left out – board game markers, dice, puzzle pieces, checkers, Legos, and all kinds of essential parts to toys and games that would truly not be the same without all of their pieces.

Tired of trooping back and forth to the playroom, digging through the toy bin, or dragging out the Trouble, just to realize that the piece in my hand is actually a marker for Sorry, I began putting the lost pieces in my pockets as I cleaned. Vacuuming unearthed the largest finds, especially under the couch. Many times the pockets of my jeans would be bulging with these lost pieces and I would forget they were there. I would find myself waiting in line at Parent-Pick up fingering the objects in my pockets trying to guess which game they went to. Once home, life would distract me and the pieces would remain there and go unnoticed until I heard them clanging about in the dryer on laundry day. Sometimes instead of replacing these pieces in their respective places, I would stash them on the nearest receptacle - dressers, shelves, and in closets until I would have time to put them back where they belonged, which rarely happened.

Finally it dawned on me that I did not have to put these items back where they belonged at all. What would be the point? That piece, or one just like it, would be waiting for me the next time I moved the couch to vacuum. In a moment of genius, I cleared out a deep drawer in our old mission table and declared it "The Missing Piece Drawer." There was room in the drawer for thousands of lost pieces. No longer would the onus be on me to return the lost pieces to their homes, now if the kids were playing a game, doing a puzzle, or building a Lego masterpiece, and they couldn't find a piece – they could look in the Missing Piece Drawer. Brilliant!

When it's time to have the yard sale, I always check the Missing Piece Drawer to be sure all of the proper pieces to any game or toy leave our home together. Other items that find their way to the Missing Piece Drawer are the directions to the 1000 piece Lego Building set, single playing cards, doll house furniture, parts for the numerous science kits and art kits that dot our house, and spare change (which gives some members of my family incentive to look through the Missing Piece Drawer on occasion and often times leads to some lost items being reclaimed and even put away in their proper place!).

Everyone needs a Missing Piece Drawer because life is much too busy to return every monopoly chance card to the box. And no matter how long I stare at it, I still can't be sure which Garfield puzzle is missing the orange piece I found in the couch cushions. The Missing Piece Drawer saves me time and energy and helps corral the flotsam in our busy home. On more than one occasion it has saved the day. "I found it!" yelled my six year old, racing back in to the room, hand held high clutching the missing piece – triumph!

In addition to plenty of toys and games, children require lots of paper. Maybe they didn't tell you that at the hospital, but no-doubt you walked out with an armload of paperwork and that was just the beginning. Preschool, church school, scouts, you name it; every organized child-oriented group produces mountains of papers. Some are artistic masterpieces, some are fundraisers, some are records, some must be signed, and some make no sense at all. As children grow older, there are homework papers, project papers, stories yet to be published, notes to friends, inspired music lyrics (daughter), Dungeons & Dragons character sheets (son), and wish lists for a birthday that is months away (youngest).

Where to put all these papers? The sheer number of papers that come home from school each day are enough to overwhelm my personal secretary (if I had one). How does a well-intentioned mother know which papers can be recycled and which are critical to the well-being of the universe? It's best to get a handle on the plethora of paper that comes with parenting. My system has evolved over the years, but I'll share what has worked for us.

Each of my children gets a *Personal Paper Bin*. It's a crate with his/her name on it. Whenever I stumble upon papers that are not clearly meant for the recycling bin (like the overdue library book letter or the nasty note written to Mommy in a fit of anger), I put it in the designated bin. When my daughter panics because she can't find that paper sent home two weeks ago about the project due tomorrow, she can dig in her crate and usually find it. Same goes for my son when he needs the piece of paper that had a dragon detailed on it during a critical moment in a D&D game. And when it's finally my youngest child's birthday, I can dig through his papers and find THE LIST he is always referring to. When anyone's crate gets too full, they are responsible for sorting out the unnecessary papers for recycling. It's our tradition to sort out the paper bins each year on the day after school lets out.

On sorting day, rather than grab the tall hat (that's for you Harry Potter fans), I put out the recycle bin, the keepsake bin, and the trash can. Each child sorts the contents of their crate. Things that hold no value go either in the recycle bin or the trash can. Items worth treasuring for all time (or at least until they move out), go in their keepsake bin (an under the bed box with their name on it stored in the basement). Things they aren't finished with yet go back in their crate.

All the important papers, like invitations, flyers and tickets for important upcoming events, I keep clipped together on the fridge and stacked in order by date. I find if I look at them every day, we're more likely to remember to be in the right place at the right time with the right ticket.

I have a friend who has a file system I envy. She uses a beautiful wicker file basket with hanging files. Each member of the family has a file folder with his or her name on it in which is kept important papers, homework, permission slips, etc. I like the idea of that system, but it never happened here. Permission slips still ramble around the counter in the hopes of being remembered and everything else goes in the appropriate crate.

I know the day is coming when everything will be electronic, or so they say. But until then, you need a system to organize the paper that layers your house or risk being suffocated by it.

Challenges

Basic: Give each child an assigned crate/basket/bin/box for papers. Designate a box or drawer for missing pieces.

Serious: Create a Keepsake box for each child. It can be an under-the-bed box like ours, a plastic bin or even just a cardboard box. Once or twice a year, help your kids clean out the missing piece drawer. Put the pieces back where they belong, throw out (or save for your art teacher) all the pieces that have no place to be returned to, and toss the trash.

Extreme: Develop your own system for important papers – a filing basket or in-box system, individual paper/project bins, and keepsake boxes. When your kids outgrow the need for a Missing Piece Drawer, make a collage using the missing pieces or fill a glass container with them to make a decorative lamp.

29

Their Laundry or Your Life

When I was working at a job outside of my home, I did laundry willy-nilly, throwing in a load whenever there was a spare moment and waiting until the mound was taller than me before folding anything. This resulted in a near constant stream of laundry and some very wrinkly looks. (I don't iron.) It hung over me all the time – *I need to do the laundry, I need to do the laundry*. It was never *done*. And once we were up to three kids the laundry threatened to overtake my life.

When I began working from home full-time, it became necessary to get the laundry under control. I started by putting a timeline on the laundry. In on Monday, out by Thursday (Saturday if it's been a really tough week). All the children, ages 13, 11, and 8 at the time, quickly learned if they wanted clean clothes for the coming week, their laundry hamper better be in the laundry room first thing Monday morning. For a while, my oldest son solved the problem by leaving the hamper in the laundry room and undressing there each night, but the self-consciousness of puberty soon ended that.

Holding the kids responsible for gathering and delivering their dirty laundry to the laundress took a little convincing in the beginning. There were weeks when my daughter was forced to wear every article of clothing in every drawer and on every hanger because she stubbornly refused to gather her dirty laundry. I take some responsibility for that erroneous belief. After all, for the better part of her life I dug the dirty clothes out from under the toys, books, craft projects, and stuffed animals that litter her room.

My youngest has the habit of pulling something out of a drawer, deciding it won't do for that particular day and then depositing the unchosen clothing on the floor, later to be placed in the hamper, never to actually be worn.

Which brings me to an important point that can save you time and money - You don't need to wash everything each time you wear it (or toss it on your floor unworn). When I sort clothing coming from the offending child's room, I take the things that have not been on his body (this is easy since anything he's worn could easily be used as a stunt double in a detergent commercial) and fold it for his clean pile.

As far as my own clothes, I don't wash them every time I wear them either. Unless I've been running, gardening, or working with animals, they are most likely pretty clean. At least clean enough to save the detergent, water, and energy that it would take to wash them. My husband installed two sets of hooks on the wall near our closet. Now when I undress, I hang my worn, but clean clothing on the hooks to be worn again. I give my clothes a quick look-over and if I don't find any food remnants, children's finger prints, ink stains, or puppy tracks, I hang them back up.

I don't know where we learned that we need to wash clothes so frequently. I know I didn't have this same compulsion when I was in college and the laundry was four floors down and required quarters. We tend to be a nation of clean freaks which isn't good for us and certainly isn't good for our environment. Clothes break down with washing no matter how gentle the cycle or detergent. Where do you think all that lint comes from? Clothes last longer if you wash them less.

Here are a few things to keep in your laundry room that might save you time and/or brain cells:

✓ **Lost sock basket.** Don't try to track down the missing partner for every lonely sock. Put the leftover socks in the sock basket. I assign my daughter the task of periodically going through the sock basket and pairing up socks. And don't forget leftover socks make great cleaning mitts.

- ✓ **Container for clothing that needs to be repaired**. I have an old Winnie-the-Pooh hamper from the baby nursery tucked in the corner of my laundry room. When Grammy visits, its contents await her sewing skills (Alas, I have none).
- ✓ **Box for giveaway clothing near your laundry area**. Anything that is stained beyond recognition, too small, or the wrong season, goes in this box. When it's full, I divide the clothes up between Goodwill, next sibling, next season, rag bag, or compost. By waiting until I have an entire box (or two) to sort, I save time. It also means less unworn clothing ends up piled on the dryer or clogging up drawers.
- ✓ **Small container for the laundry fairy**. I don't take the time to check pockets since my kids got old enough not to leave crayons or playdoh in them. I have a large oatmeal canister on a shelf above the washer where I deposit all the treasures that turn up in the washer or dryer. Each summer we take down the oatmeal canister and divide the spare change between the kids for our annual trip to Hershey Park. I saw a clever idea posted on Facebook recently. The mom took all the things she'd collected over the years from the washer and dryer and filled a glass lamp with them and gave it to her daughter to take to college.
- ✓ **Shelves.** Hang shelving above your washing machine and dryer if possible. You always need more laundry space and usually this is dead space that could be utilized to hold your detergent, vinegar, measuring cups, and all the miscellaneous items that collect on top of the dryer.
- ✓ **Something educational or at least interesting to look at**. I fold clothes in my laundry room and consequently spend a lot of time there. The walls are gray, so that's depressing enough. On one wall are the marks where we measure the kids heights periodically, which is nice to consider, but on the other wall I've hung a huge map of the world. While I fold laundry, I study it and try to learn the names of more countries and places. This is a personal effort on my part because I'm bad at geography (I never win at Trivial Pursuit). Having something to look at makes laundry just a teeny, tiny bit more interesting.
- ✓ **Extra laundry baskets.** They're cheap and can simplify the putting everything away part of laundry. I dread carting

everything to the different rooms and sorting it in to drawers. One day I realized I didn't need to do this for my older children. They're capable of putting away their own clothes. So I bought two extra baskets and put their baskets full of clean clothes on their beds (they'd never notice the baskets if I put them on the floor amongst the mess). I'm sure you can guess what my oldest son did - he just dressed out of the basket all week. So I made a new rule – no basket, no laundry. If you don't empty and return your basket, your clothes will remain unwashed. Clean clothes are quite a motivator.

✓ **Small container for lost buttons or other important items.** When I find things like Boy Scout pins or school IDs in the laundry, I don't put them in the Laundry Fairy basket because I know someone will miss them sooner than later. When that happens I know where to look.

✓ **Pair of scissors.** These are for cutting tags off of new clothes and loose threads on old clothes.

Challenges

Basic: Clean and organize your laundry room/area.

Serious: Establish a laundry schedule and figure out which aspects of laundry your kids will be responsible for.

Extreme: Redecorate your laundry room/area. Consider installing a clothesline. Teach your children to do the laundry!

30

Homemade Laundry

I had been using expensive environmentally-friendly laundry detergents for several years and was continually disappointed by their inferiority in cleaning and whitening as compared to conventional detergents. That, and their high price tag, led me to conduct my own scientific experiment in a quest for a better, or at least cheaper, green detergent option. (I guess I shouldn't call my tests *scientific* seeing as I'm not a scientist and they were really pretty loosy-goosy experiments of my own devising.) I made my own homemade laundry detergent and then tested it on my kids' laundry. I tried several formulas and compared them to the brand name *green* detergents.

In my search for the perfect laundry detergent, I discovered literally hundreds of recipes on the internet. I was going for simple and least messy, so I quickly narrowed it down to powder formulas. The liquid recipes involved adding gallons of water to each mixture and then stirring the slop before using. That's too much work for me as I am fundamentally a lazy laundry lady. I was looking for something I could just dump in and be done with it. After much trial and error, I finally hit upon a recipe that worked at least as well as any store-bought green detergent. I was happy to discover that making laundry detergent was simple and saved money. No longer did I have to choose between spending a fortune for green laundry detergent or feeling guilty because I was too cheap to pay the price.

The recipe I use has three ingredients: Fels Naptha bar soap, Washing Soda, and Borax. Washing Soda (or Soda Ash) is sodium bicarbonate, which means very little to me. It's most common use is in the manufacturing of glass. What did peak my interest is that it is effective in removing oil, grease, and alcohol stains. It can also remove wax. Washing Soda is pretty basic stuff and the most popular brand is made by Arm & Hammer. I found it in our local family owned grocery store right next to the Borax. It costs less than $3 a box. And that box makes about 12 batches of detergent.

Fels Naptha Soap required a bit more research. I found it in the same grocery store and it was just 99 cents a bar. If you aren't familiar with Fels Naptha (I wasn't), it's a bar soap that has been around for a century or more. It's what your grandmother used for laundry back in the day of washboards.

A quick internet search uncovered controversy surrounding the safety of Fels Naptha. Fels Naptha used to contain lye. Whether it still does or not seems to be debatable. I decided to believe that there isn't lye in the Fels Naptha. As you probably know you can find support for just about any idea you want on the internet. After reading multiple posts and getting completely confused as to the safety of using Fels Naptha, here's what I decided - It's probably safe. I sided with the 71 year old woman who wrote that she's been using it all her life and has never had a skin irritation from it. The primary complaint from the nah-sayers seemed to be that it can irritate skin, shouldn't be ingested, and the government has never done any kind of testing on it (same could be said of plenty of junk foods on the market). All of that said, it's your call whether you want to use it or not.

Several sources said that you can use other soaps in place of Fels Naptha and achieve the same results. So I tried this. I spent $4 on a bar of Dr. Bronner's organic castile soap and mixed up another batch of laundry detergent. It seemed to work fine on towels, but definitely didn't measure up on children's clothes covered with grass stains and the unidentifiable stains covering the front of my daughter's barn jacket. I've been using Fels Naptha for nearly eight years now with no adverse reactions.

Homemade Laundry Detergent

1 cup finely grated bar of Fels Naptha soap (or any other soap that does not have moisturizers, dyes or perfumes in it)
½ cup Borax
½ cup Washing Soda
Directions: Use 2 tablespoons per load. (I know that seems like a tiny amount of detergent, but truly, it's all you need.)

The original recipe I found on the internet said to grate the soap in your food processor. I couldn't risk it with my prized and critical-to-my-life food processor. At first I used an inexpensive hand grater, but with five people and a muddy hillside, that took too much effort to produce adequate quantities of grated soap. So I bought the cheapest food processor I could find. It makes quick work of the bar of soap and if my good food processor ever goes, I'll have a really clean back-up. One bar of soap makes 3 cups of soap shreds. Each batch of detergent is enough for 16 loads of laundry. I was happy with the results in hot, warm, and cold water.

Considering Fels Naptha costs $1 a bar and borax and washing soda are less than $3 a box. The total cost of a load of laundry is significantly less than with commercial soap.

White vinegar works well as a fabric softener (1/2 cup per load) and for really tough stains, I use earth-friendly dishwashing soap as a pre-treater. I rub some on the stain and let it sit for a few minutes, or hours (sometimes days if I get distracted and forget) before adding it to the washer.

Lack of whitening is always the biggest complaint about homemade detergent. My detergent does fine on everything except my hubby's undershirts. Some turn gray. Hydrogen peroxide works well as a bleach and there are commercially made earth-friendly bleaches out there. I've reached the conclusion that by the time the shirts become ugly-gray, they're ready for the rag bag anyway. Old undershirts are excellent torn in strips and used to tie up sagging tomato plants. You can also compost them.

Maybe even my simple version of laundry soap seems like a lot more work than picking up a bottle of detergent at the store, but consider the other costs. It's easy to mix up more detergent if I run low which saves on trips to the store and there is very little packaging used for each batch of detergent. But more than that it's one more way for me to take care of my family in a way that is good for the planet, good for them, and good for my pocketbook. It makes for intentional laundry.

One final thought I can't keep to myself – my oldest son had asthma for many years. He was on a preventative inhaler and steroids daily. After we switched to all natural laundry soap and vinegar for fabric softener, his asthma improved so much he no longer needed either medicine.

Challenges

Basic: Experiment with how little detergent you can use per load. Most manufacturers recommend more soap than you need. (I'm sure you understand their motivations.)

Serious: Use earth-friendly laundry detergents and switch to vinegar for fabric softener.

Extreme: Make your own laundry detergent recipe and commit to using earth-friendly products like vinegar for fabric softener, dish soap for pretreating, and hydrogen peroxide as bleach. Go hog-wild and put up a clothesline.

31

Become a Thrift Store Shopper

When I walked in the door with two bulging bags of *new* clothes, my husband raised his eyebrows. We had a budget freeze going on in our house at that time. I did my best Vanna White, showing off the three new sweaters for me, a name brand shirt for my oldest, Levi's jeans for my daughter, and two shirts emblazoned with sports heroes for my youngest son. Before he could say a word, I ran back to the car for a huge stack of children's books. As he looked on in frank disbelief, I produced the sales slip from my shopping spree - $24.00.

Don't believe me? You should. I was shopping at our local Goodwill. Goodwill has become my go-to clothing store for two reasons.

One reason is the financial constriction placed on a family with three active children and the rising cost of life. In his prime, my youngest son averaged three uses of a garment before he ruined it with unspeakable stains, ripped it in ways that far surpass my sewing prowess, or simply outgrew it. The options were to stop feeding him or find a cheaper way to clothe him.

The other reason I head to Goodwill is my personal conviction that our world has too much stuff. Our landfills, basements, closets, and lives are jammed as we buy more new clothes, gadgets, and toys. These purchases necessitate that we buy plastic storage bins and storage racks, or take yet another load to the curb. When our houses fill up, some of us rent storage facilities for all of our stuff. If it is true that one person's trash is another person's treasure, trading our stuff for someone else's might be a way to solve this dilemma. Why not use what we already have?

I'm amazed at the quality of the clothing I can find on a good night at Goodwill. I say a "good night" because the inventory varies day to day. It's important to be a regular if you want to score the good stuff. The Goodwill sorts clothing by color. This comes in handy when your daughter announces that she will no longer wear clothing that is pink or purple, and wants only black. Many times I find items still sporting their tags. I'm no fashion diva so designer labels mean little to me, but I can tell a good quality piece of clothing. While a teenager might bristle at the idea of wearing *used* clothing, once I bring something home and wash it, no one can tell if I paid full price at some fancy boutique, or if I plucked it off the bulging racks at Goodwill.

I am certain there are more than enough clothes already on this planet to clothe everyone for the whole year without wearing anything twice. It seems obvious when you take a look at the overstuffed racks at any department store. Maybe if more people shopped at thrift stores like Goodwill, clothing manufacturers wouldn't need to make as many new garments. Buying used clothing is recycling and makes a small statement about the condition of too many closets and landfills.

It's not just clothes you find for mere pennies at Goodwill. I've purchased breadmakers, a mini George Foreman grill (my youngest uses it to make his own grilled cheese sandwich!), a Pampered Chef Apple peeler/corer/slicer, and my much coveted Tupperware cake-carrier. I almost always leave the store with an armload of kids' books and too many new novels for me. At 47 cents a book – how can a person resist? Canning jars, DVDs, puzzles, and toys also worm their way into our house, making me pause only momentarily as I fill yet another bag to donate back.

I hope you are also blessed with a Goodwill near you, because the best part about shopping at Goodwill is that the money comes back to you. There are approximately 2200 Goodwill stores in the U.S. and together they generate 1.9 billion dollars. 84% of that money goes directly back to the community in the form of job training, career counseling, and employment for people with disabilities, welfare recipients, and others doing their best to enter the workforce. Goodwill believes that "work creates economic energy that builds strong families and strong communities." So your hard earned money is going somewhere useful in your community. And isn't that the best reason to shop Goodwill?

Challenges

Basic: Find out where your local Goodwill or thrift store is located and visit.

Serious: Pack up a few boxes to donate and become a regular shopper.

Extreme: Give your kids $5 or $10 and see what they can find at the thrift store. Have a fashion contest with your Girl Scout troop or youth group with a budget limit. Look for a Goodwill or thrift store you haven't visited and make a road trip.

32

Be Re-purposeful

I knew I was saving those bricks for something. Seven years ago, when we tore out our old brick patio, I painstakingly hauled all the bricks up the hill and stacked them carefully and artfully behind the barn. My husband shook his head. His plan had been to toss them in the back of the truck, haul them to the woods, and dump them where they could rot for all eternity, if bricks rot. But I insisted they were useful and that maybe I would use them someday to lay a brick aisle in the barn. He humored me but didn't help haul the bricks to the barn. I did that myself, using a wheelbarrow.

Since then the bricks have found a few uses. They've held down plastic tarps covering machinery or hay. They've been experimented upon by two small boys wondering just how hard you have to throw the bricks at the barn wall to actually break one. And the chickens have made good use of them as a place to roost in the sun or get out of the wet or snow covered grass. I mostly forgot about them along with my fantasy of laying a brick aisle in my constantly flooding barn.

Recently I found a purpose for them. I'm always on the lookout for new places to tuck in another garden. Last spring my daughter planted Jolly Jester marigolds all around one sunny corner of the barn. Those marigolds thrived. So much so that they spread themselves a good six feet out away from the barn in a perfect semi-circle. When I finally cut down their dying stalks, the ground that was uncovered was barren – no grass left. What else can you do with such ground but plant a new garden?

The only complication was that the nice neat semi-circle is on a hill, like pretty much every piece of ground on our property. When I informed my husband of my plan he told me I'd need a wall to contain the garden or it would just wash away down the hill. I didn't point out to him that the marigolds never washed away. In fact, they were pretty difficult to remove from their spot.

The next morning, I stood before the barren ground, ready to begin my new salsa garden. I had visions of tomatillos, cilantro, and a gazillion new types of peppers. But as I stared at the space, I had to concede that my husband might be right (don't tell!). It was a pretty hilly spot. So I fed the horses and pondered what to do. Still thinking, I began the nasty chore of cleaning out the chicken pen. It's really the only downside of chickens, but the manure collected from this nasty chore makes wonderful fertilizer. As I laid my broom against the huge stack of bricks next to the chicken coop, I had my eureka moment! The bricks! They've needed a purpose beyond stoking my guilt and supporting soggy chickens for 7 years! So I began hauling them once again.

I laid out a beautifully shaped garden using the bricks. I was not deterred by the absence of mortar or a mason. I once dry-stacked a beautiful stone wall that still contains our strawberries, lilacs, and mint, so I was pretty confident in my ability to build a sturdy wall into the hillside. Our neighbor's 150 year old farm house is built completely on a dry stack stone foundation.

There's nothing wrong with holding on to useful things. Some people call it hoarding, but those people are simply not very creative. Sure, it's a pain to store all this useful stuff, but in the end it's worth the pain. It saves you money. It doesn't load up the landfill. It saves you time because you don't have to go to the store. And it makes your neighbors and friends wonder if you're nuts, which makes them keep their distance (and think of you when their daughter's brownie troop needs 15 cream cheese containers!).

Saving stuff is akin to a holy act in my book. You should always hesitate before you throw things out – are you absolutely certain there is no use left for this object? I used to play a little head game with myself as I walked toward the trash can. I would imagine I was a homeless person or a member of a tribe on a remote island – is there something useful I could do with this object? Crazy, maybe, but our society throws things out too easily. We do this because we don't want to deal with our own trash. We pay our trash bill each month and the friendly guys in the bright yellow vests cart it away. But it goes somewhere, because just like the information on your computer – nothing disappears. Repurposing, re-using, and saving useful things are not only money-saving acts, but an exercise in creativity, ingenuity, and resourcefulness. These are great traits for any of us. And perhaps one key to preserving our planet for those who come after us.

Being a repurposeful person only requires that you see beyond the present. When my older son spied the shoe sorter my daughter was removing from her closet (the shoes were never actually sorted, most days they were piled on top of the little shelf). He laid claim to it. He's repurposed it as a cabinet to hold all his game pieces for the complicated games he and his best friend invent.

My youngest son cleaned out his room and re-discovered his marshmallow shooter which isn't really repurposing, unless you consider that its old purpose was to lie under his bed and collect dust.

My daughter, lacking a decent jewelry box (cheap parents!) decided to turn her lamp shade into a jewelry box. She poked holes through the shade to hang earrings and secured a thumbtack (with an eraser on the other side) to hang her necklaces. Makes the lampshade very useful and actually, better looking.

All of these projects arose because of a need and instead of running to the store, we looked around for a solution to our problem. That's all it takes to be re-purposeful. We ran to the store for plenty of years and now we're drowning in the stuff we've acquired. So before you dash off to the store, or the trashcan, take a moment to consider your options. You have more than you realize.

Challenges

Basic: Make it a habit to think twice before throwing away useful things.

Serious: Comb through your home and look for unused items that can be repurposed. Include the outside and the garage in your search.

Extreme: Find some big boxes or bins and mark them "repurpose" and begin filling them with items you might otherwise throw out. Pick a project you've been wanting to get to and figure out how you can take it on without spending a cent. (Hint: see the next chapter for where to get free stuff.)

33

Make it an Earth Life, Not Just an Earth Day

Earth Day frustrates me. It's ridiculous that on one day each year we talk about the importance of reducing, reusing, recycling, and caring for our earth, and then the next day we go back to business as usual. Why is it we feel driven to keep our homes immaculate and in perfect running order (some more than others I know), but we don't feel the same way about our planet? Isn't our planet truly our home?

It's our responsibility, *each one of us,* not just the hippie lady who picks up trash along the side of the road. We wouldn't walk by a bag of trash lying on our living room floor, so why is it so easy to look the other way at the trash lying on the sidewalk? We wouldn't throw away money, so why is it so easy to throw away products that could be recycled? I'm as guilty as anybody. I'll throw out the empty jar of mayonnaise rather than try to clean it out for the recycling.

We recycle when it's made easy for us and when it's not we look both ways and then pitch the item in the trash. It's just one bottle, can, newspaper, envelope, whatever. But that's just it. We don't think one person's actions can make a difference and maybe that's true. But one person's actions times a million makes a huge difference.

My local newspaper's obligatory Earth Day article on the front page recited some interesting facts: Recycling just one aluminum can creates enough savings to power a TV for three hours. I don't know how they got to that number, but think about it. It's kind of like trading your carbon rights. You recycle that can, and you get to watch TV for three hours and not feel guilty. (Personally I think three hours in front of a TV should make you feel guilty or at least bored out of your mind.)

Another statistic said that each person, on average, creates 4.4 pounds of trash each day. That's nuts! But I'd guess it's fairly accurate. As I crushed another cereal box for the recycling bin and dropped the apple peels in the compost, I realized that trash has changed a lot since I was a kid. Back then (and I won't say when "back then" was) we threw everything away. We certainly threw away more than 4.4 pounds of trash per person. I remember we had three big trash cans in our garage filled to the brim. The garbage men walked up our driveway, lifted the garage door, and carted the cans out to the street. Then they put the trash cans back in the garage and closed the door again. I can't imagine the men in yellow vests that patrol our streets every Thursday morning at dawn, smashing recycling bins and leaving garbage cans rolling the street in their wake, would ever walk up our long hilly driveway to retrieve our trash.

My kids have grown up with compost and recycling. They don't know any different. They know all about saving the planet and global warming. They are concerned about the rainforest. Teaching your kids to live a life that is good for them and for this world isn't as hard as it used to be. Being green is in. Beyond that, it's simply *what they know*. They can't imagine throwing away a can or dumping the dregs of their cereal in the trash.

Each March there is a great opportunity to create a memory for your children and do something good for the planet. On a designated day, from 8:30-9:30 pm, people all over the world turn off all their lights. In 2010, 50 million people participated in Earth Hour and created the largest voluntary power-down in history.

Find out when this year's Earth Hour is and learn about it at *Earthhour.org*. Earth Hour is a worldwide event. You can check out posts, videos, and tweets from all over the world. You can even watch the lights going out via satellite around the globe.

Preparations for Earth Hour at our house include gathering candles and games and yummy snacks. At 8:25, we send the kids all over the house to turn off everything. Even though Earth Hour organizers only direct participants to turn off lights, we go for broke in our household. We have a gadget that tells us how much power we're using in our house at any given moment and we try to make it say "0." We light a fire if it's cold and burn candles and then for one hour we have fun without using any electricity.

Earth Hour is an opportunity to teach your children about conservation and have a great family memory to show for it. It's important to find ways to pass on our commitment to intentionally care for our planet. Plus, it's exciting to be part of a global challenge!

While recycling is a great way to care for the earth, it doesn't always mean sorting your trash. It can also mean giving things away, or acquiring "recycled" items instead of buying new. *Freecycle* and *CraigsList* allow you to give away or claim all manner of stuff for free!

I listed a big box of broken crayons on Freecycle and had eight takers within hours! The plastic fish-shaped candy molds were gone the next day! When I listed our VCR/DVD player that only works as a DVD player, we had too many takers to count. We've given away old TVs, kids plastic table and chairs (colored by paint, permanent marker and fifteen years of heavy use), a huge bin of parts for hot wheels tracks from two boys' worth of Christmas gifts, and a bucket of paint opened and rejected ("That's not the color I was picturing!"). None of these items would have been appropriate for Goodwill, but they weren't ready for the curb either.

Freecycle is moderated for inappropriate people and all posts have to be approved by the moderator before they appear in the feed. I've rarely met the people I've bequeathed my junk too. Normally we arrange via e-mail for the transfer of treasures, and I leave them on the porch.

The evening I picked up my free breadmaker found on Freecycle, my husband and I followed the directions down a country lane to a darkened house tucked beneath old oak trees. No streetlights, no porch lights, not a single light left on. I found the breadmaker in an unmarked brown paper bag in front of the garage. When we pulled in my husband was sure this was actually a drug deal. That was one of the best breadmakers I've gotten, and the original owner e-mailed me a few days later to be sure I got it and thank me for putting it to good use.

It's much easier to haul unwanted but potentially useful items to the curb, but giving them away not only keeps them out of a landfill and meets someone else's needs, it feels really good. I kept a box of half-finished craft projects in the basement for over twenty years. I couldn't bring myself to throw the contents away; but who wants a barely-started cross stitch set, a giant coloring poster partially colored in, or the pieces to a stuffed Noah's Ark set that were never sewn together? You'd be amazed. The woman who came for those things, plus an entire box of shells I'd collected over my childhood beach vacations, was grinning ear to ear with excitement at taking on all of these projects. Her basement had recently flooded and ruined her craft supplies. "I'm a crafter; it's what I do," she told me as we hauled the boxes to her car. "I could never afford to replace all the things I lost. Thank you so much!"

Craig's List is another place to find and give away stuff. There is a whole section for free stuff. I gave away two annoying roosters within three hours of when they got on my last nerve. We also gave away an old lawn mower that was too small for our place and was leaking oil. A lawn-mower racing enthusiast was thrilled to come cart it away! Who knew?

America Recycles Day is November 15. Consider celebrating the day by getting rid of the items that are just taking up space in your life and pass them along to someone who will treasure them (or at least use them). This is a great project for your kids. Maybe they can list items to give away and then list an item they'd like to have. I'm sure someone has the Rockem' Sockem' robots in their basement or a paint-by-number set that's barely been used collecting dust in a closet. It's worth a shot!

Teach your children how great it feels to give new life to old things. Talk to them about the importance of recycling. There is enough stuff for all of us already on this earth. Any time you have the opportunity to recycle or upcycle or precycle or whatever you want to call it, you're making a play to preserve our planet. And that's the most important reason to celebrate recycling on any day!

Challenges

Basic: Observe Earth Day or Earth Hour or America Recycles Day this year. Attend an event or watch a documentary about conservation. (*No Impact Man* or *Craig's List Joe* are excellent choices).

Serious: Join a Freecycle board and start monitoring the activity. Check out your local Craig's List, too. Help your kids come up with a list of things your family can do to help the planet. Look up earthhour.org and share the pictures with your family.

Extreme: Commit to cleaning up a stream or street on a regular basis. Become vigilant about recycling – designate recycling containers, start a compost pile, or give away a few items on Freecycle or Craig's List. Spread the word about Earth Hour by hosting an Earth Hour party.

34

Strive for an Empty Mailbox

How many catalogs do you recycle each day? My mailbox used to be laden with unwanted catalogs. It was rare that I ever bought anything from any of them, but they wasted plenty of my time. I hate to recall the hours I spent leafing through their glossy pages fantasizing about buying things I would never buy like $200 blue jeans or thigh-high boots or a hand-tooled Australian Stock saddle. Sometimes I circled items I really liked, even choosing colors and sizes. The catalogs floated around on the counter for a few days and eventually ended up in the recycling.

Then I discovered the answer to the catalog time/paper-suck. It's a website called *Catalogchoice.org*. The site allows me to opt out of catalogs I don't want to receive. Catalog Choice has extracted commitments from companies to honor my choices. Not every catalog I would like to do away with is listed on Catalog Choice, but most are. In fact, there are catalogs I've never even dreamed of. And therein lies the danger.

As I comb the list for catalogs to cancel, I can't help but notice all the intriguing titles for hundreds of catalogs I've never heard of. Catalog Choice assists you in canceling catalogs, but they will also be happy to hook you up with some new ones. It's a temptation to find out what they sell in the Bliss catalog or what constitutes a Boundless Journey. Just what does a person buy from Bounty Hunter? If you're not careful, canceling catalogs with Catalog Choice could be counterproductive. Who can resist requesting a catalog called Long Elephant Legs? What do they sell? Is it a catalog for tall people? Oh the mystery!

Some companies don't make it easy for you to cancel, you may have to visit their website or send an e-mail, but Catalog Choice tells you exactly how to remove your name from just about any company's list. When you choose to stop the catalog, they ask you to click on a reason. Your options include: *prefer not to answer* (this way you won't hurt their feelings), *prefer shopping online* (I worried that this would be a greenlight for said company to swamp my e-mail), *no interest in these products* (slam!), *I want to help the environment* (I hide behind this one mostly), and *other* (but no space to write 'because I think your products are overpriced and unnecessary').

When you opt out, some companies offer options to receive their catalog only once per year or season. My husband likes studying his Crutchfield catalog dreaming of all the electronics he could have if he didn't have children, but he doesn't need to do that two or three times a month. Catalog Choice even has a system for complaining if a catalog continues to be delivered to you.

It's a brilliant website, and I'm sure someone is making a buck from it. I don't know how our activities are tracked online, but I bet there's a kickback or two when someone discovers Bounty Hunter catalog while trying to cancel their Brookstone catalog.

Another way to ease the crowding in your mailbox is *Opt-Out Prescreen,* the official Consumer Credit Reporting Industry website that accepts and processes requests from consumers to Opt-out or Opt-in of receiving offers of credit and insurance.

It's fairly simple to get your name off the books. You can choose to do so online and it's good for five years, but you can also print out the forms, sign them, mail them back and your name will be removed PERMANENTLY. Pretty cool, huh? I had no idea that one agency could control the mass of mailings that have littered my life.

Before we opted out, we received offers for credit cards, mortgages, and insurance daily. It's hard for me to fathom the number of companies making these offers. It's even harder to imagine the amount of money they must rake in if they can afford to send such frequent glossy over-sized propositions.

I assume these come-ons must work or companies wouldn't keep mailing. It's discouraging when you think of the sacrifice of paper, energy, and resources. Normally I tear the offers in two and throw one half in the recycling and one half in the trash. And then I worry that some creative thief will figure out my system and start pairing up my trash and recycling and steal my credit/identity/money. I know people who mail the free reply envelopes back empty, but that seems wasteful in an entirely different way.

I do feel some worry for the USPS if everyone opts out; I know they need the business. I'm still waiting for the day when we get zero mail. We're getting closer. The only mail we get now are bills, magazines, real letters, and college admissions literature. The bills are disappearing, not because we've come in to some serious money, but because I'm paying them online. I've begun canceling the magazines that nobody actually reads, the real letters are few and far between, and I'm hoping the college mail ends when the kids move out. Mail-free days are coming. I just know it.

Challenges:

Basic: Establish an account with Catalog Choice and start canceling catalogs.

Serious: Tell family and friends about Catalog Choice and Opt Out Prescreen. Sign up online for Opt Out Prescreen.

Extreme: Request the paperwork and mail it to Opt Out Prescreen to have your name permanently removed (remember you have to do this for you and your spouse or anyone else receiving mail at your address). Seek out other ways to achieve the goal of a completely empty mailbox!

35

Yard Sale Happiness

There seem to be more yard sales every year. Maybe it's the economy, maybe we're all motivated to recycle, or maybe we just have too much stuff. For me, it was about the stuff; three children generate a lot of stuff. Our basement was crammed, so we filled the back of the pickup truck and joined friends in their driveway for their neighborhood yard sale. Since we don't live in a traditional neighborhood, we have to adopt others. (We do the same thing at Halloween. We've been trick or treating in the same neighborhood for so many years now that I'm sure the residents think we live there.)

This particular yard sale had very reasonable hours, 9am-3pm. We began setting up at 7am, which I quickly learned is not early enough when your yard sale begins at 9am. By 7:15 there were early birds picking through my boxes along with me. The kids set up a stand and began selling breakfast of painfully sweet lemonade and homemade chocolate chip cookies. They did a brisk business all morning until their interest petered out around 9:30. Lucky for us, other neighborhood kids were quick to take their spots, and no one made it up the driveway un-accosted by adorable kids yelling "Don'tcha want some lemonade?"

I love to go to yard sales. Love to find treasure in someone else's trash. But it's been a long time since I was the seller at a yard sale. I forgot how much I hate the haggling. For heaven's sake, here I am laying out all my junk and asking just a few pennies for it and you're going to come along and ask me if I'll sell it for even less than a few pennies? As one of my fellow yard salers pointed out – *that's the point*. Still, I'm uncomfortable with the haggling; I'm terrible at it, too. Even if the guy said, "Hey, you give me a dime and I'll take that old frying pan off your hands," I'd say, "Sure." I made every deal. Which I guess was fine since my entire motivation for participating in the yard sale was to get rid of my stuff. But by 8:30am I was already thinking "Why didn't I just box all this stuff up and take it to Goodwill?"

At lunchtime the kids had made more money on cookies and lemonade than I had on all my junk. Next time I think it would be a better strategy to put the cute kids behind the saw horse table full of dishware and I'll sit on the plastic chairs out front with the lemonade. Still it was fun to hang out with our friends and we did meet some nice people and send them off happy in the knowledge that they had totally scammed me.

As I watched the latest satisfied customer leave with a barely used Calphalon pot for a buck, it dawned on me that maybe the best thing to do would be to give it all away. That way I wouldn't have to stress about being taken advantage of, the customers would be happy, and just maybe all the stuff would go and I wouldn't have to box it up and take it home. By 1:30, I had convinced the other yard sale proprietors in the driveway that my plan made sense, so we posted a sign at the end of the driveway that said, "*Everything's Free! Really!*"

Customers walked up the driveway hesitantly, not sure if the sign was a joke. When we told them it wasn't, they carefully selected a few items and scurried away asking, "You're sure?" I smiled and thanked them for coming to our sale. This was my kind of yard sale.

I loved it when a very young couple with three little kids came up the driveway and I was able to make their oldest daughter grin like it was Christmas morning as she wheeled away my daughter's old pink bike that sat for two years in our driveway collecting rust. That smile was worth much more than the $5 price tag that still clung to the handlebars. The rest of the afternoon went on in this fashion. I loved the smiles we created on grateful faces and wished we'd switched to the new pricing system much earlier. I went home with $60, an empty truck, and the knowledge that I had made lots of people very happy that day.

I don't think I'll ever sit on that side of the table for a yard sale again, but just in case you do, here's my advice:

Have your kids set up a lemonade stand with homemade baked goods alongside your yard sale. It keeps them busy and draws the right kind of customers. People who stop for lemonade stands generally have kids or grandkids and they're more likely to buy your stuff, which is probably mostly kid stuff. Plus, it teaches your kids some responsibility, garners them a few marketing skills, and gives them an opportunity to do a little math in the summer.

Price everything before you actually get to the yard sale. I didn't price things before I got there and it was very stressful to price things while the professional yardsalers looked on and dug through my boxes. Put a sticker on everything. I bought a pack of stickers with preprinted yard sale prices on them and that made this easier.

Set up your stuff at least two hours early or put up a big sign that says "NO EARLYBIRDS!" (Although I'm not sure a sign will really scare off the true professionals.)

Join other families having yard sales at the same time. You can share in the expense and work of signs and advertisements. The signs and advertisements are key to getting lots of traffic. And it's really nice to have company while you suffer through the humiliation of selling stuff you're embarrassed you ever bought in the first place.

Consider having a rain date. We had perfect weather, but it would have been a miserable day if it had been rainy.

Bag up kid's small toys in plastic bags. It's too hard to price every small toy, bags are easier to handle. We put toy Power Rangers in a bag with a Power Ranger video, Barbies in bags with extra clothes, and all the Cars movie toys together.

Have lots of extra plastic bags for your customers to use and newspapers to wrap dishes and breakables.

Consider having a "free" box. If you have junk that you doubt anyone would want, but you can't bear to throw away, fill a *free* box. You'd be amazed what people will take when it's free. Now it will clutter their life and not yours!

Work out a pricing plan with anyone who's sharing your yard sale space. Pick a time to go to half price. If everyone's willing, pick a time to make everything free. I promise this will be your favorite time of the sale.

Remember that the bottom line is- you don't want to take anything home. It will just sit in your basement cluttering up your home and your life and your conscience. Make the deal!

Take leftovers directly to the Goodwill or thrift shop. Don't take them home first or you'll be tempted to hang on to things you were planning to get rid of just that morning.

Challenges

Basic: When a friend or neighbor has a yard sale, ask if you can bring a few things or a table full of things (plus the table) and join in.

Serious: Rent a space at a bigger yard sale.

Extreme: Organize and host a yard sale and set times when everything will be half price and when it will be free. OR host a "free" yard sale. (You could let your kids operate a not-free lemonade stand at the same time.)

36

Don It or Donate It

Americans have too many clothes. Okay, maybe that's not fair. I have too many clothes, and my children have too many clothes.

One spring morning, as I hung clothing on the line to dry, I considered our collective wealth of clothing. I studied each article as I shook it out and determined how many clothespins it would take to keep it from flying off into the wind that whips up the hill from the hollow. Jeans require four, shirts two and underwear requires anywhere from one to four clothes pins depending on who it belongs to. My daughter would be none too happy if her panties went sailing into the grass to be discovered by her little brother's friends. (Three clothespins minimum even though the panties are barely bigger than a tissue.)

According to the United States Department of Labor, the average American spends $1600-$1700 on clothing each year. That seems astronomical to me. I can't help but think of how many impoverished countries we could clothe with only the stuff in our closets we *don't* wear. I'd like to spend less than I do on clothing, but the first step is to wear what I have.

Even if a few items on the line took to flight, we still had too many clothes. Our drawers were stuffed to overflowing and our closets crammed. No one could possibly wear all of it. *Or could they?* I stood on my porch watching our clothes wave in the wind and devised a challenge for myself. I'd share the challenge on my blog so I'd have no choice but to go through with it.

Don It or Donate It Challenge

Commit. Pick a month long period. I chose a spring month.

Prepare. Clean out your closets and drawers and under-the-bed boxes and boxes in the crawl space and the stuff on hangers stored in your children's closets. Find the fat clothes (or skinny clothes), too, and decide what you believe you will actually wear. Get rid of the things that don't fit your body or your personality. Gather empty boxes and bins to help you keep straight what has been worn and what hasn't (and to fill up with the clothes you will toss at the end of the challenge).

Wear It. Over the course of your designated month, you must wear everything in your closets/drawers. You may designate a "safe area" for your slinky black dress or your just-in-case-we-get-invited-to-a-wedding wear. Everything else is fair game.

Toss It. After the month is over, pull all the unworn clothing out and box it up for Goodwill. Or if you're too chicken to do that, put all of it in a holding box in your basement with the date written on the box. If you don't go desperately looking for anything in that box by next year, give it away **without** opening it.

FAQ

How do I keep track of what I've worn and what I haven't worn?
You'll need to devise your own system for this. My closet has a neat divider, so I simply move everything to one side at the start and as I wear something I move it to the other side. For the clothing in my drawers, I emptied one or two drawers and after I'd worn and washed an article I put it in the safe drawer. This had the added bonus of forcing me to clean out all the flotsam that had accumulated in the bottom of my sock and undie drawers (what to do with all those baby teeth??).

What about out of season stuff?

That's simple. When you are in the preparation phase, box up the out of season stuff. That'll give you more room and safeguard things that you still love but it's too hot/cold to wear. You'll need to do this experiment one more time in the opposite season to truly clear things out. This is a great New Year's project!

What if I really, really love something but I never wear it?

This is your call, but if you really, really love something you should be wearing it every week. Your other option is to put it in your holding box.

I posed this challenge to my kids, too. But, to date, no one's taken me up on it. If any of them were to become game, I'd help them devise their own system for sorting. And I'd promise a reward at the end. The logical reward is new clothes, but then that just perpetuates the problem. So I'll have to think of something else.

I don't know about you, but in the mornings when I'm faced with a bulging closet of clothes, I'm overwhelmed by the options and almost always go for the same few outfits. *Don It or Donate It* forces me to cull the herd. No longer can I say to myself, "but I might wear that...." I'll have to prove it on my next round.

How about you? Are you brave enough to face down your closet?

Challenges

Basic: Go through your closet/drawers and fill a box to donate.

Serious: Make it a policy to keep the same number of clothes – when you buy a new article of clothing, give away an article of clothing you seldom/never wear.

Extreme: Take the *Don It or Donate It Challenge*!

37

Be a Good Neighbor

One spring, I came home to find boxes and buckets filled with hundreds of hostas in my driveway. These were a gift from my neighbor Nan who lives at the bend in the creek that snakes along our road. She is blessed with plentiful morning sun and soil made overly fertile from the many natural springs that feed our creek. Hostas grow like crazy at her house and so that spring her husband cleared out hundreds of hostas to keep them from overtaking their entire yard. I ran into Nan in the grocery store earlier that spring and somehow our conversation turned to hostas (I have that effect on people). I told her they were one of my favorite plants. When I thanked Nan for the hostas, she told me they had the same problem with daylilies and sure enough, multiple loads of lilies appeared later that same spring.

We decided to plant the hostas on the steep banks that flank the base of our driveway. When my husband and I pulled the truck laden with hostas, shovels, and our great intentions up beside the banks, we quickly lost steam. It was 95 degrees (which broke a record here that spring). The bank seemed much bigger when the job became a reality. The weeds and grass that needed to be removed to make room for the hostas were very committed to staying where they were. We wrestled with the elements for about 15 minutes when our neighbor Chris happened along in his truck. He laughed when he saw the mountain of hostas and I explained our plans. He shook his head knowingly at my husband and said he'd be right back with his front end loader. It took Chris only a few minutes to scrape away the offending weeds and expose our muddy bank. I spent the next few hours planting the hostas and reflecting on what great neighbors we have.

Another spring my daughter wanted her very own flower garden, which is to say she wanted to plant her very own garden and then let me water and weed it. I was thrilled to cultivate her interest in gardening, but not so thrilled to spend lots of money on the plants of her dreams. Lucky for her, my neighbor Mary who has a garden that looks like it stepped off the pages of a magazine, gave us some seeds she had saved from the 'spider flower' plants that Addie loves. Between those seeds, the marigold and zinnia seeds we saved from the previous year, and the seed packets that were given out free at the Fall Fest garden demo, we had seeds to spare. We spent a beautiful morning planting the seeds, and Addie made markers so we would know what was what. We talked about all the people we could give our seeds to after we harvested them later in the year. We even envisioned starting our own seed swapping club.

Living intentionally means being a good neighbor. We don't live in a traditional neighborhood, so when I say neighbors I'm talking about people who live a mile down the road. It can take a while to cultivate a neighborhood in these parts. To that end, we hosted a neighborhood potluck the first year we lived here. I made up a flyer and my kids and I took them to all the houses in a one mile radius. We met lots of neighbors.

Building a community should be a priority for an intentional life. There is great security in knowing there are people nearby who will help you in a crisis or even just bring their tractor over to help you plant your hostas (or give you the hostas in the first place). Sharing gardens, babysitting, and manual labor are just a few of the benefits of cultivating good neighbors.

When I grew up, we knew all our neighbors. These days it seems we are often insulated in our own lives, busy with home, work, and family. We don't know the people who live only a few doors down.

But we need each other, and if we take the time to get to know each other, we might discover there is much that connects us besides geography.

Challenges

Basic: Invite a neighbor you've met over for a cook out.

Serious: Organize a neighborhood pot luck, cook out, or progressive dinner. Make real invitations and personally deliver them.

Extreme: Organize a Neighborhood meeting and talk about the ways you can help each other. Create a neighborhood directory of e-mails and phone numbers. Consider a plant swap, a babysitting co-op, book club, or community yard sale.

38

Unleash Your Creative Spirit

When was the last time you created something other than dinner? What do you enjoy doing that nurtures your creative spirit? And don't say you don't have a creative spirit, because it's in there somewhere. It's very easy to let our own hobbies get lost in boxes in the back of the closet while we raise our kids and attend to the real world. But remember when you were a kid and you had hours that stretched out in front of you unencumbered by responsibilities? What did you do then?

Every January I find myself in a ballroom at a cheesy resort in Gettysburg with over 200 other women. We gather there to work on our scrapbooks. There are moments when I look around at these women of all ages, dressed in their jammies (I kid you not!) trading stickers and stories, and think, "What am I doing here?" Lots of these ladies are part of the polyester set and get pretty worked up over a trip to Cracker Barrel. I would never have dreamed I'd have anything in common with them. But there I sit listening to their tales of trips to the Grand Canyon or the local dirt track. Pets figure in to many of their snapshots as well as babies smashing food and pretty little girls in pink ballet slippers or prom dresses. There are plenty of heirloom photos too - the kind with the crinkly edges, soft focus, and faces familiar even if the clothing and hair style isn't. Each year I spend 48 hours scrapbooking with 200 kindred spirits, many I have absolutely nothing in common with except the love of creating scrapbooks that tell stories, celebrate lives, and secure memories.

I don't have to tell many of you how hard it is to leave your husband in charge of his own children and home for a few days – all alone. I make lists and remind him all week long of who has to be where when. I write out the instructions for caring for the horses and chickens and he learns the hard way which horse to feed first. But he survives. I think it's important that we take time to pursue the things we enjoy. Not only does it set the example for our children, but it keeps us sane. And sanity is a good, if underappreciated, thing. Besides, our children need to know we have interests in life other than them.

We all need to nurture our creative, playful selves. What do you like to do for fun that you haven't done in ages because there isn't time, money, or opportunity? Did you collect butterflies? Build model cars? Paint watercolors? Maybe it seems nerdy or something only people who still live with their parents would do, but after spending a weekend with those women in that ballroom, I feel pretty good. I feel rested, content, happy.

The last time I was at my annual scrapbook weekend, one half of the resort was consumed by the scrapbookers, but the other half was host to a youth ministry conference of some kind. (Although I say resort, I must clarify that it is actually a sprawling, somewhat tired looking collection of low level buildings, with one "high rise" connected by a human habitrail, plunked down near the battlefields, serving up pressed turkey, powdered eggs, and lots of gravy in the *café*.) Late Friday night, a group of teens wandered through the habitrail over to our side of the complex. I can only imagine what they must have thought at the site of all those women surrounded by their scrapbooking gear gabbing away as the oddest assortment of music I've ever experienced warbled out of someone's iPod speakers. Obviously they felt they needed to shield the rest of the world from us, so they upended a few tables from the hallways and pushed them up against the ballroom doors, effectively barricading us in the room. We were so engrossed in our tasks and happy to be starting a weekend without children or responsibilities that no one even noticed. I think if someone from the hotel hadn't happened by, we might still be in that room happily ensconced in our tasks at hand. I'm not sure what happened to the good Christian youths when the incident was reported back to their leaders, but I appreciated their effort. It seemed like something I might have done if I'd found a bunch of *old women* quilting or canning or engaging in some other *old person* hobby when I was an invincible teenager.

I'm happy to find myself occasionally on the inside of those barricaded doors claiming time for me and my own hobbies, despite what it looks like to the busy, responsible people or the kids. It's good for my life. It's also good for my family. But mostly it is good for my soul. I hope you claim some time for your own hobbies this year. Make something, learn something, practice something, enjoy something – something just for you not for your family, not for your kids, not for your community. Just for you.

Challenges

Basic: Plan a day or an afternoon just for you. Do something you love.

Serious: Brainstorm or journal about the things you used to love to create when you were young. Take up one of your old hobbies again.

Extreme: Take a weekend away just for you and your creative self. Sign up for a class to learn something new or something you'd like to get better at doing.

39

Books, Books, Books, and Not a Moment to Read

In my fantasy life, I'd have a library with floor to ceiling wood bookshelves and that cool rolling ladder for fetching the books on the very top, but since I can't kick any kids out of the house yet, there isn't a room to spare. We have bookshelves in just about every room in our house, including two bathrooms. When my oldest son was in fourth grade, my husband built him bookshelves that covered an entire wall, floor to ceiling, just like his favorite place, the library. It only took him two years to fill it and then he began making stacks in all the corners of the room.

At this point, I'm sure you're imagining I'm a hoarder. But I would argue that I don't hoard anything (except maybe plants). I'm happy to get rid of things. Any book I won't ever need again moves out of my life. I keep the ones that still have things to teach me. The plethora of books on my shelves must mean I have much to learn.

There are just too many books in the world and I can't seem to resist them. Many of the books on my shelves are on my *To-be-read* list. I pick them up at yard sales, the Goodwill, and from those rare, but still operating independently owned bookstores (the kind with knowledgeable salespeople full of good recommendations and a cat roaming among the shelves). It does make me a little anxious when I see them piling up, but I remind myself that someday I'll have more time and when that day comes, I'll have plenty of good books to read.

My mother-in-law gave me a Kindle, so now I hoard books on the Kindle, too. I find free downloads and grab them up. I'm not certain when I will read these books. I'm sure if I did the math, I'd discover there aren't enough hours left in this lifetime, but I like to think there are. I rarely read on my Kindle. It was a fun novelty, but I missed the feel of a book in my hand.

I buy nearly all my books used. There are tales to be told simply in the way a book has been worn – the pages bent, the spine striped with creases, and sometimes I hit gold and discover hand-written notes in the margins. A pristine condition used book is probably not a good book. When I read a book, I underline phrases that astound me, profound thoughts, clever metaphors, and useful information. I write my own comments too, so I appreciate the thoughts of the previous reader. Finding an inscription and a date in a book leaves me to wonder about the gift giver and the receiver – what did this book mean to their relationship? Sadly, there is no history in an e-book. I appreciate the green-factor, though.

Kids' books present other challenges. My kids go through books like socks – constantly leaving them lying about, losing them, finding them, leaving them at their friends' houses, and always complaining that they need more. We do frequent the library, but with the overdue fines I pay, sometimes it seems cheaper to buy the books at the Goodwill, so I do. Books pile up at our house worse than dirty laundry. Our shelves are bursting with so many books it can be overwhelming. I accept some responsibility for this problem. My kids know I will rarely say no to their request for a book. And I double their allowance money if they're spending it on books.

Years ago, I came upon one small solution to the multitudes of books. We had so many, the kids couldn't possibly appreciate them all – at least not at the same time. So I bought twelve hard plastic magazine files and labeled each one with a month of the year. Then I sorted the picture books into the files, choosing themes for each month. Some were obvious, like Halloween books and scary books for October. August is water, beach, and ocean books, and April is anything to do with nature and the earth. Outer space books are in June because that's a great time to stargaze, and snow books are in January. Books about love fill the February file, and March is stuffed with Easter books. Over the years, the kids looked forward to pulling out the month's file. After not seeing them for a year, the books seem new to them.

This has been a great system for us as it lightens the load on our book shelves and creates Christmas moments each month as we look through the *new* books. The December file was replaced with a large plastic bin because we had too many Christmas books for the file to hold. Before we put the previous month's file away, we sort through it and pull out books that they've outgrown and pass them along.

Which brings me to the next dilemma – what do you do with books you don't want?

I sort the books into *keep* (to be read to the grandchildren) and *give away* piles. There are lots of deserving places for outgrown books. We generally divide them between the school, the preschool, friends with younger children, Goodwill, and the library book sale. I like to keep the books moving along. It seems a shame for any book to sit unread on a shelf. Books have the potential to open minds and foster creativity – they need to be read. I try to stay on top of our books, cleaning out the shelves on a regular basis. Books that aren't in the being-left-on-the-couch-or-in-the-car rotation might be ready for new owners.

My book club has another really nice way to pass along used books. We each pick out a book we've finished and wrap it up at Christmas time for our gift exchange. It's a fun tradition and a great way to pass along our books and our holiday wishes.

That tradition led me to try something new. All year I saved books I'd enjoyed but didn't need to keep, putting sticky notes on them with the name of the person I thought would most enjoy the book. At Christmas I gave people in my life a stack of gently used books with a note that said I'd donated to a cause in their name in lieu of new books. It was a great way to give a thoughtful gift and make a helpful contribution.

If your books are piling up, it's time to sort through them. Keep the ones that you need, but remember there are lots of opportunities to release their power on the world. Books can inspire, challenge, teach, and change us, but they can't do any of that collecting dust on a shelf.

Challenges

Basic: Sort out your books and give away the ones that have been outgrown.

Serious: Sort your kids' books into twelve sets, one for each month. Use boxes or magazine holders to store them. Pull the *new* books out each month and put the *old* ones away.

Extreme: Start saving books for the people on your gift-giving list. Write a note for each book explaining why you think a particular person will love this book. This holiday organize a book exchange.

Intentional

FAMILY

40

What are You Expecting?

Ask just about any parent of multiple children what drives them bonkers the most when it comes to kids and they'll say – the fighting. If it weren't so maddening, the things they can find to fight about would be funny. My main strategy in dealing with kids' fights is to duck and cover. I hear the voices escalating in the kitchen I head for the laundry room. The battle moves to the living room, I make a beeline for the garden. If they follow me outside I just keep moving. That's the key, never be a stationery target.

I wish something could be done, but I'm fairly certain there is no remedy. I remember fights with my little brother that got bloody. I think my own mother also employed the duck and cover strategy as I don't remember her officiating any of our battles.

My best strategy in the battle against sibling battles is to become their common enemy. When they're mad at mom they suddenly become the greatest of allies. They mutter under their breath, roll their eyes at each other, make faces at me behind my back (forgetting about the eyes in the back of my head), and run reconnaissance missions to keep tabs on my whereabouts. It's a beautiful thing siblings united against their mother.

A few years ago my husband, youngest son, and I were working outside tearing off an old deck while the older two huddled inside trying to figure out how to get beyond the list of chores that had accumulated all week leaving them with no computer time until they were accomplished. My husband ducked inside to grab a tool and overheard my son say to my daughter, "We can't do that! She's mean, but she's not stupid!" He managed to get back outside before doubling over in laughter. We howled for hours over that comment.

When I shared the exchange with a friend, she said, "That's awful that they think you're mean." I looked at her like she had three heads and said, "I'm fine with mean. Mean's relative; stupid's permanent." And this is true. I'm fine with my kids thinking I'm mean as long as they respect me. Compared to many of their friends, my kids live the good life when it comes to my attitude about chores, their appearance, the cleanliness of their rooms, their homework, and the number of pets I allow them to bring home. So while I might temporarily hold the title of "Meanest Mom," I know it's not forever. Someday, they'll appreciate me. At least I hope they do.

Expecting your children to do chores, act considerately of others (including their own family), be responsible for their own behaviors, and accept the consequences of their success or failure to do all those things, doesn't make you a mean parent. It makes you a real parent who understands she's raising not a child, but a future decent adult. And sometimes that can mean they won't like you. It's a price you pay, but it won't last and someday they'll be grateful. Someday.

If you are a parent, you've learned that children will live up or down to your expectations. Many times I have been floored to discover unknown abilities hidden in my children until another adult expected them to display it. Sometimes we parents are the last to see how much our kids have grown up. We expect them to behave the way they did yesterday, but today they are older, wiser, more mature. Believe it or not. Maybe it's time to think carefully about what you expect of your children.

Most of my expectations are in place simply because my children live here. They don't get paid for any of these jobs. I wish my list were longer and that my children felt compelled to do more in the way of housework. They are typical kids I suppose. I never wanted to participate in the cleaning or care of our home when I was their age. I did as little as possible. Most of the forced labor at my childhood home was in the way of yard work and gardening. Luring my children into the garden is only possible when the raspberries or cherry tomatoes are ripe.

I know that my kids learn best when they figure it out themselves. Natural consequences (and a few sort-of-natural consequences) are much more effective than me and my big mouth. If my kids don't follow through with the minimal expectations I have of them, they reap the natural consequences.

✓ *Clean up your belongings around the house* (or they get dumped in a box with other unclaimed belongings kept in the mudroom).

✓ *Bring your dirty clothes to the laundry* (or no clean clothes this week).

✓ *Turn your dirty clothes right-side-out* (or I'll simply wash and fold them inside-out).

✓ *Remove your sheets for washing and put them back on afterward* (or sleep on a bare mattress).

✓ *Bring your belongings in from the car* (or they may be thrown out at next car dumping).

✓ *Fix your own breakfast unless it requires the stove* (or go hungry).

✓ *Do your homework.* (This is an important expectation. A wise first-grade teacher once told me that if I sat with my child and made him do his homework, I would be sitting with him to get his homework done when he was a senior in high school. Taking that advice, I don't mention homework. I tell my kids I won't nag them about homework UNLESS a homework slip comes home. If that happens they are giving me carte blanche to nag and harass them about homework.)

✓ *Keep your room clean enough that I can run the vacuum cleaner without sucking up anything important* (or no one comes over to play until it's done).

✓ *Keep the computer/play room straightened up* (or it gets locked).

✓ *Put your shoes in the shoe cubbies* (or risk them being tossed outside or in the Goodwill box).

It is a bit of a battle to get kids to accept responsibilities around the house, but it's worth the effort. Their future spouse or roommate will thank you for it. Heck, your kids might even thank you for it. Take it from me – I'm mean, but I'm not stupid!

Challenges

Basic: Think about what you expect from your children. Consider the natural consequences of holding them to it.

Serious: Talk with your kids about expectations. Tell them what you expect of them and ask them what they expect of you.

Extreme: Post a list of expectations for your children. Talk to them about what will happen if they don't fulfill these expectations. Let natural consequences happen.

41

Mom Bucks

First off, I don't do allowance. My reason is that nobody gets money for just existing. We all have to earn it and the sooner my kids learn this, the better. Instead, my kids earn *Mom Bucks*. Mom Bucks are worth 25 cents each, but they double in value to 50 cents if the money is used to buy books, deposited in a savings account, or donated to charity. Yes, I am blatantly bribing them to read more, save more, and be more compassionate.

All three kids (ages 7, 10, and 12 when I wrote this) are expected to help with dinner chores on weekdays. Their father and I handle the dinner chores on the weekends and holidays. They earn a Mom Buck for each job. If they fail to do their job, their Mom Buck can be earned by another sibling who takes over the job. If I have to do it, they pay me a Mom Buck. They can be excused without penalty if they have practice, too much homework, another commitment, or I don't feel like dealing with their whining. They can lose Mom Bucks for using the words – *stupid, hate, dummy*, or any other truly disrespectful word.

We do offer potential to earn more money and find that the kids only take us up on these tasks if they have a need. My daughter will come to me and say, "I saw this great shirt online, what can I do to earn it?" We then negotiate a few tasks to earn enough Mom Bucks for the shirt. This system makes the money they spend – theirs. My kids are significantly more frugal when they spend their own money than they would be if I simply handed them an allowance they didn't have to earn.

Mom Bucks can also be earned at my discretion. If it's raining and the chicken coop door needs to be closed, I might offer a Mom Buck to anyone who runs up to close the door. I've been known to pay 2 Mom Bucks to someone who takes the puppy out to run for at least 10 minutes. If I catch them doing something nice for a sibling, I might award a Mom Buck or two.

Once a week, each child is assigned a "big chore". This can be vacuuming and dusting the living room, cleaning the kids' bathroom, or putting away all the stuff that accumulates on the stairs and then vacuuming them. They get up to ten Mom Bucks for these jobs, but are paid on a sliding scale depending on the effort exerted. I also keep a list of chores they can choose to do if they'd like to earn more Mom Bucks - clean the kitchen, straighten up the playroom, stack wood, sweep the porch, etc. The harder the job, the more Mom Bucks they earn.

We keep track of everyone's Mom Bucks, chore assignments, and activities on a chalk board in the kitchen and update it each week. It also lists the running tally of Mom Bucks each child has earned. I tried paying them weekly in the beginning, but inevitably I didn't have the cash or I forgot altogether. Now we keep the running tally and actual money doesn't go out until it's requested.

Some people say that you shouldn't pay kids to do household chores. They should do them simply because they are members of the household. I couldn't agree more. However, unless you start that practice while your children are toddling, it's very difficult to throw it at them later. I've chosen a middle ground with our Mom Bucks system. The dinner chores are not optional. Kids can wind up owing me money if they don't do them. The BIG chore each week is also not optional. It can result in loss of screen time, play dates, or curtailed activities.

Our system has evolved over many years and works for us. Find one that works for you. Intentionally teaching your children how to earn, manage, and spend their money responsibly can set them up for a lifetime of success.

Challenges

Basic: Give your kids a list of jobs for which they can earn some form of payment.

Serious: Develop a chore system for daily jobs.

Extreme: Develop your own Chore/Allowance system. Have a family meeting and explain the system you've developed. Hang a chalk board up in a prominent place and assign daily and weekly jobs. You could even come up with your own currency system using pennies or bottlecaps if your kids are too young to understand a running tally on the chalkboard.

42

Teach Your Children to Cook

When my first child encountered Home Ec in Middle School (now Family and Consumer Science), he came home each day and proudly announced his latest culinary masterpiece! Smoothies! Coffee drinks! Cake Pops! Cookies! Pancakes! If it contained sugar, it was on the menu. By the end of the semester I felt confident that my son could hold his own behind the counter at Starbucks.

When my daughter worked her way through the same classes, she took pride in correcting me as to the proper names of the cooking instruments. "It's not a *spatula,* it's a *turner*, Mom," she said in a tone that implied I was too ignorant to be trusted with lifting the cookies off the sheet. When I lamented that she wasn't learning to cook any real food, she protested, "But tomorrow we're making Cherry Crisp!" Ten to one the cherries came out of a can, loaded with sugar and food dye, and there were no cherry pitters involved in the lesson.

Home Ec has changed since I was a kid toiling away in the *Kumquat Kitchen*. The kitchens in my middle school Home Ec classroom were named for the color of their counters. There was the *Red Kitchen*, the *Yellow Kitchen*, the *Orange Kitchen*, and the *Kumquat Kitchen*. Hearing our elderly teacher say *kumquat* never failed to elicit giggles and snickers. We didn't know what it meant, but it sure sounded dirty and worked its way into the vocabulary heard in the back of the bus.

As I said before, Home Ec has changed. You can't teach a child to cook in 8 weeks when there are 30 or more kids in the class, and you have no budget for fresh ingredients.

Quiz a young adult on their cooking abilities; 9 out of 10 will tell you frankly, they don't cook. And really, they don't. They reheat; they unwrap; they order out. Many of them don't know much about cooking beyond boiling a pot of pasta, and that's being generous.

While on vacation recently, we employed a lovely young woman to house and horse sit for us. She is a former honor roll student, very bright and articulate. When we arrived home from our trip, she had forgotten to remove her groceries from her stay. Every single item she left required no more than a microwave to prepare. I don't think she's outside the norm.

Much attention is focused on children in this time of the *Obesity Epidemic* in the US, but take a look around and you'll see those same children growing into adults who do not know how to eat healthy. The schools aren't teaching them. Nutrition rears its important head during health class and occasionally science, but I would wager to bet it's not a vital cog in the home economics curriculum where they make such great use of a blender.

If we want to stem the tide of this epidemic, we must equip our children not only with the knowledge of what foods they should eat to be healthy, but how to cook those foods. What I wouldn't give for my daughter to come home and announce, "We learned how to cook broccoli today without letting it get mushy!" Sadly, I'm guessing those words will never pass her lips.

To that end, I instituted a new policy in my house for my two Home Ec grads. One night a week they each are responsible for planning and preparing dinner. My only guidelines are – it needs to be balanced and it needs to include at least two vegetables or fruits. My son took the news of our new policy in stride planning a steady menu revolving around hamburgers. My daughter sighed and slumped and warned that I had to eat what she cooked. Touché!

My husband assisted my son on his night. Being boys, the meals frequently involved the grill. I assisted my daughter and she produced delicious meals that almost always included her favorite food group - pasta. The first was fettuccini alfredo and chicken fingers. I watched from the other side of the counter as she dipped and breaded the chicken, wiping her hands on a towel after each piece. I said nothing. They were delicious. One summer she made homemade pesto with the basil from our yard. It was magnificent!

Cooking has a way of transforming kids. It gives them confidence and skills so that when the time comes they will be able to cook a real meal for themselves and not subsist on frozen dinners. My husband calls my daughter the "apathetic chef" doing a funny imitation of her attitude each week when we inform her it's her turn. "*Whatever*," she says and pretends she doesn't care. When we ask what she would like to cook, she again replies, "*Whatever*." But once she gets started, her interest piques and she creates delicious meals. I doubt she would ever have volunteered to cook a meal before this trial began. Now I'm certain that she will be cooking circles around me in no time.

My youngest son asked me recently if he could cook dinner. I said, sure, and his eyes lit up. Whatever his older siblings do, he wants to do. More than that, he hears us having fun together in the kitchen and he wants in on it.

Challenges

Basic: Let your kids help you plan a healthy menu for the week. Have your kids assist you in the kitchen. Give them real jobs like grating cheese and chopping vegetables.

Serious: Ask your kids to prepare one element of dinner – salad, rice, dessert, or at the very least, let them make their own sandwiches for lunch.

Extreme: Turn your kids loose to create an entire meal.

43

The Family That Eats Together...

"What time is dinner?" My kids had grown accustomed to a 6pm dinner hour every night if they were home. Some days all five of us ate together, but most days we ate in shifts. Whoever was home at 6pm ate then, and everyone else warmed up something later. But then I messed everything up. At least for my daughter who prefers we eat between 5pm and 7pm (when her computer is shut down by the computer gods). Now dinner might be at 5:30pm or it might be at 7:30pm. Sometimes it's not until 8pm ("Think of it as European..."). Now we eat together. Except for Thursdays. Thursdays are *Fend-for-yourself-nights*. Thursday evenings are just too complicated to find a common dinner hour.

What's brought on this change? Possibly my middle-age panic that I'm missing out on what's left of my kids' time at my table. And possibly the fact that there are too many people going in too many directions every afternoon and it's become difficult to figure out what I can cook in 15 minutes between car pools.

Studies show what I must have instinctively known all along - *family meals make your family healthier*. Rutgers University evaluated nearly 70 studies to gather information about the benefits of families eating together at home. The studies revealed that families who eat together have a healthier diet and consume less junk food. Teens who eat at home with their families show fewer signs of depression. And all family members are more likely to have a healthy weight.

Forty percent of the typical American food budget is spent on eating out which makes me wonder how many of us are eating together as a family around the dinner table. This is a no-brainer. You can save money, be healthier, and help your kids by cooking and eating at home. Okay, I hear you now. But how do we get a healthy meal on the table when we're busy with work, volunteer commitments, and shuttling kids to and from all of their activities?

I don't have an easy answer, but I have a few helpful suggestions.

Create a family meal book. Half the time, it's the challenge of thinking of something to serve that slows me down. Our family meal book is a loose-leaf binder with menus and recipes that most everyone likes. Two of my kids prepare a meal each week, so they consult this book when they do their meal planning. I regularly add new recipes I discover to prevent it from getting too boring.

Keep staples in stock. Our freezer and pantry are almost always stocked with the ingredients the kids and I need to make the meals we eat often. You will also find casseroles, soups, and flour tortillas for nights when dinner has to be quick and easy. Because I know these things are there, I can cook confidently and the kids have what they need when it's their turn to cook.

Keep a shopping list posted where everyone can add to it. Our system is *if you open the last one, add it to the shopping list*. That goes for anything –can of beans, bottle of ketchup, jar of jelly, clove of garlic, paper towel roll. This system makes my life easier. I don't have to try to remember everything we need. The only time it fails is when I go to the store without the list.

Keep meals simple. Your meals don't need to be fancy to be healthy and tasty. Our meals usually contain some kind of protein, one carbohydrate, and two veggies or fruit. Done. I can get a healthy meal on the table in five minutes or two hours, depending on my day's options. Cheese & bean quesadillas, corn, and applesauce is a five-minute meal. Keep it simple and don't let unwritten rules get in the way of your meal planning. You can have carrots or apple slices as a side dish. Eggs, beans or cheese work fine as a main dish. And crackers can be just as nutritious as rice. Soup can be a meal in itself.

Utilize your slow cooker. Everyone's got one. Crock-Pots are the go-to gift for first homes, new babies, and weddings. I got three for my wedding. If you've dodged the slow-cooker gift, check your Goodwill. They almost always have a selection. Nothing reduces stress like knowing dinner is ready to go the moment you walk in the door. The internet is loaded with Crock-Pot recipes, blogs, even websites dedicated to crock cooking, so get your pot on!

Get everyone involved in making the meal happen. Each day my kids are assigned, *Table Set, Table Clear*, or *Dishes*. This makes getting a meal on the table quickly much more feasible. It also underscores their investment in our meal. We have a chalkboard mounted on the wall listing the jobs. I recreate the board each week based on who will be home to set the table and whose schedule would make dishes a better option.

Make eating together a priority. My kids fussed when I initiated this new practice. I ignored them. If they were hungry and dinner wasn't for two hours, I pointed them towards the baby carrots and dip or I opened a jar of applesauce. I did not cave. It only took a few weeks for them to get the message. Remember —you're the adult here. You get to make the rules.

Turn off the TV and leave the electronic habits elsewhere. When you gather for a family meal, focus on being together.

Encourage the conversation. Once you have them all gathered around the table, make a point of getting everyone talking. I have a friend who asks her kids to share one good and one bad thing that happened that day. My kids like to ask if anyone has new jokes (there seems to be an endless supply if you attend a middle or high school). I like to ask them one thing they learned each day. Sometimes it garners sarcastic comments like, "The corn dogs in the cafeteria are gross," but sometimes I learn something myself.

Like any change, it takes a while to make this happen. But it's worth it. One study conducted by the National Center on Addiction and Substance Abuse at Columbia University showed that teens who eat regular family meals are less likely to smoke, drink alcohol, or use marijuana and other drugs.

The study also showed that children and teenagers tend to get better grades when their families eat dinners together at least five times a week. Frequent family dinners were associated with better school performance, with teens forty percent more likely to get As and Bs.

Miriam Weinstein, author of *The Surprising Power of Family Meals,* reflects that, "Family supper is important because it gives children reliable access to their parents. It provides anchoring for everyone's day. It emphasizes the importance of the family."

I think that last comment is the one that most resonates with me. Our family meal anchors our day. All five of us are going in many directions all day. We're encountering people, teachings, and media that offer conflicting messages about life, values, and the choices we make. It's good to come together near the end of each day to process what we've heard, seen, and experienced with people who love us and support us no matter what. After being disconnected all day, a meal is a few precious minutes to reconnect.

Challenges

Basic: Plan one family meal together each week.

Serious: Plan to eat together several times a week. Talk to your kids about how they can help make this happen.

Extreme: Find a way to make family meals happen every day. Get kids involved in preparation, cooking, and clean up. If dinner gets impossible, consider having breakfast or lunch together. Make it a priority and stick to it.

44

Bathroom Etiquette for Selective Listeners

Do your children listen to you and do what you tell them to do? They do? Wow. Great for you. You can stop reading now.

My children, on the other hand, tune me out when I give them any direction other than, "Time to eat!" Recently, I found myself grumping around my house muttering about the ungrateful residents who can't be bothered to pick up their rooms or put their dirty dishes in the dishwasher. I retrieved yet another abandoned sock from the center of the living room floor and in a fit of frustration, flung it with all my strength. The dog cowered in her bed as I spewed obscenities and fetched the offending sock (which is not very aeronautically astute), before tromping up the stairs to the laundry room.

I'd grown tired of my angry, ranting self, as had my children. (Or they would have if they heard me, but all three seem to have grown permanent ear buds.) When the stench of rotting towels drew me to their bathroom, I reached my bitter end. The floor was strewn with slowly mildewing towels and clothes lying in the flood left by the last bather. The toilet had not been flushed (ew), the toilet paper holder hung empty, and toothpaste frosted nearly every square inch of the counter that was visible beneath the plethora of hair care products, abandoned flossers, wet washcloths, tubes of skin creams, and make up.

As I maniacally cleaned the bathroom, flinging dirty laundry and empty bottles of shampoo, I searched for a solution. Withhold privileges? Sit them down and explain my expectations and their responsibilities? Remind them that they are not part of the royal family? *But they don't listen to anything I say,* I reminded myself. Finally as I sat on the edge of the tub, scrubbing at the moldy grout, I was struck with a moment of brilliance. They don't *listen* to anything I say, but they *read* anything they see!

My children are all addicted to reading. They read while they eat, while they watch TV or listen to music, while they travel in any kind of vehicle (which is why my 16-year-old had no idea how to get to the school or the library when he started driving), even while swinging on the swing set. My youngest loves to read while bathing. They each have several bookshelves full-to-bursting and live amongst books scattered beneath their feet and stacked in the corners of their rooms.

I raced to my computer and typed up *Directions for Bathroom Use,* slipped the pages into sheet protectors, and hurried back upstairs to post them before the beasts appeared from their lairs. I hung one set of directions regarding the sink area on the mirror, and one about the tub/toilet area above the toilet.

The results of my effort have been mixed. For several weeks after I hung the signs, conditions improved. It seemed they really didn't know what I expected. After about a month, my daughter asked me if I could take down the signs. She was embarrassed when friends came to visit. I took them down because I'm not in the business of embarrassing my kids, just teaching them how to clean up after themselves.

Since then, the condition of the bathroom is vastly improved. That's not to say that it's perfect, but I never expected that. But now when it gets really bad and I complain, at least they know what needs to be done. Now they know about bathroom etiquette which leaves them with no excuse.

I'm sure you have your own rules for the bathroom, but just for reference, I'll share mine.

Directions for Bathroom Use

If you use a **washcloth** – wring it out and hang it over the edge of the sink or on a towel bar. If it is beginning to smell or is dirty, take it to the laundry room and hang it over the edge of the marked bin for towels. (If you leave it balled up and lying around it will mildew and smell.)

If you use a **hand towel,** hang it up on the ring to the right of the sink. Only one hand towel should be in use at a time. If it gets smelly, dirty, or used up, place it in the towel bin and hang a fresh towel on the ring.

Use the **bath towels** hanging behind the door. When you are finished, hang your towel back on the hook where you found it. When it is in need of washing, put it on the washing machine.

When you finish brushing your teeth or washing your face, put the things you've used away and clear off the counter for the next person. If you want extra points in heaven, wipe out the sink and counter with your washcloth and hang it on the rim of the towel bin in the laundry.

If your bathroom cup begins to look gross, put it in the dishwasher.

Put away your personal care products on the shelves provided so that the counter stays clear.

If you are running out of personal care products (deodorant, skin creams, toothpaste, etc.), let management know ASAP. Expect at least 3 days for replacements to arrive.

More Directions for Bathroom Use (hangs over the toilet)

When you have finished using the toilet, **FLUSH it every time.** If you accidentally miss the pot, please use toilet paper or a rag and wipe it up so the bathroom doesn't begin to stink! (Flush toilet paper. Put rag on the washing machine so I know it's priority laundry.)

If the toilet paper has run out, **remove the empty roll and replace it** with a new one (extra rolls are in the closet or under the sink).

If you use up a bottle of shampoo or conditioner, first fill it with water and use the dregs one more time. Then, take the empty bottle downstairs and place it in the recycling.

If you get undressed by the shower, remember to **put your clothes in the correct receptacle** in the laundry room when you exit the bathroom.

If you run out of shampoo/shaving cream/soap, etc., please be sure to let management know ASAP. Expect about three days to receive replacements.

Challenges

Basic: Create your own rules of bathroom etiquette.

Serious: Sit down with your kids and discuss the rules together. Then post the rules and hold them to it.

Extreme: Post the rules of bathroom etiquette and a cleaning schedule rotating the cleaning duties between your kids. It's their bathroom, why should you clean it?

Note: if your kids are little, you'll have to take this in stages. Your directions might need pictures or drawings. You might need to walk them through the tasks the first few times, but training them from an early age is infinitely better than reforming a teen!

45

Turn off the TV

How can you live without TV? I've had this question posed to me by friends, family, and even the plumber. I'm tempted to point out how unnecessary the television is in fulfilling the necessary bodily functions of breathing, eating, and drinking, but generally I simply smile and say, "We just do." In actuality, we do have TV. What we don't have is cable, satellite, or any other means of expanding our channel selection past the major networks.

When my husband and I married and bought our first house, we didn't have TV because it didn't fit in our budget. It has never really fit in my lifestyle. There are too many other things I'd rather be doing. On the rare moments when I do sit down and watch the TV, I'm almost always doing something else simultaneously, at the very least a Sudoku puzzle. Maybe I'm weird. Judging by the number of shows my friends regularly discuss, I'd say I am a bit out of step. I can't tell you how many times I have entered a conversation already in progress and been horrified by the actions of the subject of the discussion, only to find out the people being discussed are actually TV characters. I'm sure I'm missing something. Only I don't really want to find out what.

Whenever we stay in hotels, I eagerly turn on the remote to see all these great TV shows I'm missing. Inevitably, I end up clicking into the triple digits only to discover that there truly isn't anything worth watching. I'm amazed at the number of channels. It makes me appreciate how big and varied our population is if there are audiences for all these shows.

My children face the same scrutiny that I do concerning our lack of viewing options. Their friends feel sorry for them, or so I'm told. My two oldest have accepted their lot without too much fuss. They've found other ways to entertain themselves and are amazingly creative souls. (I'm fairly certain there's a correlation here.)

My youngest child begs for television. He whines, he bargains, he guilts. Most people don't think of *guilt* as a verb, but in the case of my son, it is. He knows how to lay it on. We have thrown in the towel on Saturday morning television. For those of you out there who have many more options than the major networks, you might be surprised to know that most of the popular cable kids programs are regurgitated on the major networks on Saturday mornings. My child rises early and languishes on the couch for nearly four hours each weekend. I see traces of bliss on his face and there is quiet all morning.

But then the television goes off and I remember why we don't have it in the first place. He is grumpy. He is surly. He *hates the outside.* There is *nothing to do.* He is convinced that his day is ruined. Each weekend, he goes through withdrawal from television. It pains me to see this. But the next weekend arrives and he lands happily back in TV land, and the cycle repeats.

The American Academy of Child and Adolescent Psychiatry states that children who watch a lot of television (more than 2 hours a day) have lower grades, read fewer books, exercise less and are more likely to be overweight. Even without their evidence, that seems obvious to me. I know when the screens are off (ALL of them) because that's when I hear music wafting from my daughter's room, hear tennis balls whacking against the garage, or find my youngest swaying in the hammock with a book and the cat.

When my TV beliefs are challenged, I stand firm. I say, "We don't watch TV in our house on weekdays," and then walk away as quickly as I can. I could recite all the reasons why I don't believe in TV, but they've heard it before. Sometimes as a parent you have to take a stand. This one's mine. It's non-negotiable.

I don't think we're missing out on that much by not having cable. I've heard the argument for the History Channel and I'm tempted. Each football season, my husband's commitment to our cable-less life is reexamined. But those two possibilities are outweighed by pressures, expectations, and examples that I would prefer my kids not be exposed to. Does this mean I'm overprotective? Am I shielding my kids from reality? Perhaps. I realize that lots of kids grow up just fine on a steady diet of these programs. I'm glad for them. I just know that when the television is off, there is more time to play, more time to explore, more time to talk, and more time to be a kid.

Computers are an entire other ball game. Who needs TV when there's YouTube? I'm horrified by the crap (and I use this word intentionally) that my children watch on YouTube. I worry that they are watching unhealthy videos. I know they are being exposed to all manner of nasty language and suggestive actions. And yet I haven't figured out a way to control this. What I've settled for is keeping the computers in a central location where other people can see and hear what they're watching. I try to pay attention to what they're watching, but confess that I miss a lot. At some point I have to trust their judgment and their sibling's power to tattle.

I have two other weapons in my war on screens. The first is utilizing a program on our computer that allows us to give our computers curfews. By networking the computers in our home, we have the ability to turn computers on and off at will. We determine how many hours each user has available. The negotiations over this tool can be endless. We do lift restrictions for each child as they get older and demonstrate the ability to manage their online time well.

The other weapon, is one of last resort. It's the master switch on the wifi. Sometimes we all need a break. When chores are not being done or the sibling meanness quota has been reached, it's time for a shut down. Sometimes it's announced and sometimes it's a surprise. In the summer, we have a "screen-free" day when none of us (me included) use any screens. I worried the first time we tried this, but the kids adapted quickly. My daughter even told me she liked the screen-free day because it gave her time for her other projects and her music. (I didn't point out that those things are always available to her.)

I'm sure this is not the end of my battle with screens. My youngest is clever and persistent. We will have this discussion repeatedly. And when he is 18, he may move out and watch TV 24 hours a day. I just trust by that time, he will be able to figure out for himself that he hasn't missed out on anything.

Challenges

Basic: Limit the amount of time you and your children watch television.

Serious: Consider declaring a no TV (or no-screen) day and see what happens in its absence.

Extreme: Cut the cable TV. Use the money to do something fun as a family.

46

Raise Competent Kids

How capable are your kids? I'm not talking about their math ability or how well they throw a baseball. Can they operate a vacuum cleaner? Can they cook a meal? Can they handle an overflowing toilet? Can they change a light bulb?

Many kids today live a life of entitlement. Very little is asked of them in terms of responsibilities at home. I know, at least in my house, this is mainly due to parental laziness. It's much easier to do a job myself, especially if I want it done right (interpretation – the way I think it should be done). I get tired of nagging, demanding, and threatening. I accept half-hearted efforts because *at least they did something.* My kids have very few responsibilities in the real scheme of things, yet they claim that kids at other houses aren't enslaved as they are in our home. Hmmm.

In her book, *Cleaning House: one mom's 12-month experiment in ridding her home of YOUTH ENTITLEMENT,* Kay Wills Wyma cites the frequency of young adults who quit jobs because they don't like them and throw away educations because they've changed their minds. They move home and freeload expecting their parents to take care of them. They don't feel responsible for paying the bills, especially if it means taking a job that is hard and doesn't pay well.

Why should they? Isn't the world here to serve them? Aren't they entitled to a strife-free happy life? She makes a point. I know my own kids are indignant when I ask them to do a chore not on their assigned list.

Wyma takes the argument another step. She says that when we do the work and problem solve for our kids, essentially we're saying they aren't capable of doing it themselves. When their rooms get beyond messy, we barge in and clean up for them, sending the message that they can't do it themselves. When we do all the laundry, housework, and cooking, we continue to assert that they're not capable of doing their part. We treat them like long-term guests in our homes. When they spill something and shed tears of frustration or embarrassment, we rush in to rescue, teaching them that they aren't responsible for cleaning up their own messes. And when a homework project overwhelms and they're exhausted after practice, we offer our assistance, instead of allowing them to learn that sometimes life is hard and you have to deal with it.

Wyma begins her experiment with a list of *Life Skills* she believes her children need to be competent adults. I loved this idea and decided to come up with a list of life skills of my own. I'm down to less than a two year countdown on one of my kiddos, so it's time to cut to the chase. If my first-born leaves the nest with the following skills firmly mastered, not only will it mean fewer calls home for help, but it will bolster his own confidence in his God-given ability to take care of himself.

Here's our current **Life Skills List:**

Write and cash a check plus balance a checkbook.

Operate a lawn mower – push and ride. Operate a weed whacker.

Ride a bike safely on a road with traffic.

Run a vacuum cleaner and dust a room.

Do laundry, using washer, dryer, and hang-drying.

Drive a car safely, fill it up with gas, and check the oil.

Write a letter and mail it.

Operate a drill, jigsaw, and hammer (plus how to remove a nail).

Paint a room.

Make pancakes. Bake cookies. Pop popcorn on a stove.

Put up a tent. Build a campfire.

Safely operate a woodstove and fireplace. Collect and stack firewood.

Change sheets. Make a bed.

Take and leave phone messages.

Sew on a button.

Unstop a toilet and clear a clogged drain.

Clean a bathroom.

Plan, cook, serve, and clean up a real meal.

Change a light bulb. Replace a battery. Test a smoke detector.

Register a complaint for a defective product, bad service, or problem.

Order correctly and leave a tip at a nice restaurant.

My list is still evolving, but already it's changing our parental behavior. When my youngest discovered a black banana peel petrified to the carpet in his room, instead of flipping out and giving him a lecture about food taken out of the kitchen, clean bedrooms, and how no-one ever listens to me, except the dog and she's deaf, I took a different tack. I explained to my little cherub that he would need to figure out how to get the banana peel out of the carpet. At first, he was shocked at this expectation and tried the stalling tactic to see if we would break first. He placed books over the spot to hide its unsightliness. But I knew he was a smart, resourceful, creative kid. He would solve this problem. And he did, more or less (there really is no way to completely remove the marks left by a petrified banana peel). And someday when he has his first apartment, he won't lose his security deposit because he now knows how to get nasty things out of the carpet.

I purposefully left planting and weeding a garden off my list figuring that gardens are optional, but I hope my kids will be launched with those skills, as well as, baking bread, making peanut butter, and canning tomatoes. I did not possess many of these skills when I left home and had to figure them out on my own. I'm sure my kids could do that also, but as I said to them when we began this discussion - I'm doing this for their future roommate, boss, co-workers, and spouse.

Challenges

Basic: Make a life skills list. Look for opportunities to check them off.

Serious: Using your list, begin assigning your kids chores/assignments. Aim for one new skill each month, or if your kids are very little - one per year.

Extreme: Work with your kids to develop a life skills list. Ask them which skills they'd like to learn first and begin assigning weekly and monthly jobs using the list as a guideline.

47

Get Moving

Running keeps me sane. It makes me a better mother. It makes me a reasonable wife. It keeps me from going nuts and gives me time to let my mind loose. It makes it possible for me to eat chocolate on a regular basis without becoming the size of a small ocean liner. Mostly, it makes me happy. But there are some other benefits from running or any aerobic exercise.

Did you know that exercise not only reduces your risk of cancer, Alzheimer's, heart disease, stroke, and diabetes, but it can actually create new brain cells? Me neither. I'm all for adding brain cells. Charles Hillman, director of the Neurocognitive Kinesiology Laboratory at the University of Illinois at Urbana-Champaign, says, *"Aerobic exercise increases the supply of a protein called brain-derived neurotrophic factor, or BDNF, which protects brain neurons and promotes the growth of new nerve cells and synapses that are related to learning and memory."* Which in English means exercise makes your brain work better. And this was true regardless of age. The protein BDNF is active in the area of the brain related to relational memory – the ability to make logical connections among pieces of information.

The Illinois researchers also found that aerobic exercise improves the brain's ability to plan and make decisions, correct mistakes and react to new situations. All I know is that after a long run, I can think clearly. I thought it was just me, but turns out exercise makes everyone's brain think better.

All of this is well and good for those of us who appreciate improved executive function and relational memory, but what about our kids? The best way to teach kids to do anything is to model it for them. We all know our children are much more likely to do what we do, than what we say (no matter how many times or how loudly we say it). If you aren't already a regular at the gym, then it's time to get off the couch. If not for you, and your improved brain function, then for your kids.

This is where the sneaker rubber needs to hit the road (or the treadmill or the gym). It's not really optional. You need to exercise, and your kids need to exercise. This is not something to put off until you have more free time. Find a way now. This is so much cheaper than medical bills and so much less painful than heart attacks, cancer, and premature death. If you don't teach your kids the importance of exercise, they may never know. This is a total win-win. When you exercise, you feel better mentally and physically and you model a behavior that could save your child's life. Plus, it makes you smarter – and who doesn't need a few more brain cells?

Here's another interesting tidbit – *sitting can kill you.* Peter Katzmarzyk, an epidemiologist at the Pennington Biomedical Research Center in Baton Rouge, Louisiana, says, *"People who sit for the majority of their day have much higher mortality rates than people who don't, even if they're physically active during another part of the day."*

How can this be? Sitting for prolonged periods suppresses the immune system. Your blood stops circulating normally and can create the perfect scenario for blood clots and heart disease, not to mention raising your resting blood pressure and increasing your cholesterol. Long hours spent sitting may cause large muscle groups to shut down which can lead to damaging metabolic changes.

Another obvious factor could be the junk food consumed by people sitting for long periods of time in front of screens. Given the opportunity, my children will mindlessly eat in front of any kind of screen. As long as the food is within arm's reach, I think they would eat without ceasing. We keep the feed bins in the barn shut tight because I know if my horses got loose and found their feed, they would eat themselves to death. They don't know better. Do we?

If growing new brain cells and not dying aren't enough motivation for you, how about this - active people are less likely to be diagnosed with depression than inactive people. Our bodies were designed to move.

Here's a few ideas to get you and your kids moving.

✓ **Enter a 5K**. I know from personal experience that even very young kids can run (or walk) a 5K. I get beaten in races by runners half my height on a regular basis. Pick a cause you care about. Bring along the family dog if rules allow. If running the entire time is too daunting, make a plan. You can run at the start and finish and walk in between (everyone will think you ran the whole way!) or choose a pattern like running a minute and then walking a minute. I have a running watch that times intervals. On days when I don't have energy for a run, it helps me by sounding an alarm that reminds me to walk (one minute) and then run (4 minutes). I've discovered I can run much farther and much longer with intervals.

✓ **Go for a hike.** Invite some friends. Make it a scavenger hunt and give your kids a list of things to find. Make it a family goal to hike all the parks in your area. Or all the parks in the country. Geocaching is another great way to get your family moving (check out *geocaching.com* for information on this fun treasure hunting hobby).

✓ **Walk the dog.** Don't have one? This is a great excuse to get one. They need exercise several times a day. Having a dog forces *you* to get out and exercise, too.

✓ **Join a team.** Swimming, soccer, baseball, basketball, and lacrosse all require you to move and have the added bonus of the camaraderie of being on a team. I aim for allowing my kids two extracurricular activities each season – one that gets their body moving and one that gets their mind moving.

- ✓ **Ride bikes.** Ride skateboards or scooters. Jump rope. Rollerblade.

- ✓ **Take a spin in a skating rink**. As a kid, this was a regular event in my social life. These days they are a little harder to find and maybe they no longer feature a disco ball, but they're out there.

- ✓ **Play games.** Remember the neighborhood games like Capture the Flag, Kick the Can, hide & seek, kickball, wiffleball, ultimate Frisbee? Play with your kids.

- ✓ **Do an exercise video** together.

- ✓ **Create a weightlifting center** in your basement. You don't need anything fancy, just a clear space and a few weights to start. A bench and a mat help too. Take a personal training session together with your kids and learn how to do exercises safely.

- ✓ **Set a goal.** Aim for a number of miles or a number of hours and track your progress. Plan a celebration when you're finished.

- ✓ **Try something new.** How about martial arts, gymnastics, dance, or fencing? Isn't there some sport you've always wished you could do? What's stopping you? Ask your kids to join you.

- ✓ **Buy a treadmill, stationery bike, or elliptical machine** if you've got the cash, so cold, dark, rain, or social humiliation don't stop you.

The bottom line is you have to make an intentional decision to exercise. It won't ever be convenient or easy. Some days it's really hard, but you need to do it *every* day. I mean that. A couple times a week is not enough. Our bodies were designed for real physical exercise every day. Now that we aren't out working in the fields or hunting down our supper, we have to find new ways to get daily exercise. Pick what works for you, but pick something. Your life just might depend on it. Not to mention your IQ.

Challenges

Basic: If you aren't an exerciser, make it a habit to take a walk several times a week. If you already exercise, try something new. Sign up for a class or join a team. Think about how much you and the members of your family sit still. Talk to them about the dangers of sitting still for long periods of time.

Serious: Join a gym and/or sign up for an exercise class or find an exercise buddy to train with you. Register to run or walk a 5K so that you have a goal to work towards. Bonus points if you get your family to join you. When you have the option of standing or sitting, choose to stand.

Extreme: Find a way to get 45-60 minutes of exercise EVERY day. Make a pledge, find a blank calendar and keep yourself accountable. Buy or borrow pedometers (or download an app) for everyone in the house. See who can move the most (bonus: include the dog!).

48

Cure Nature Deficit Disorder

In his book, *Last Child in the Woods: Saving Our Children From Nature-Deficit Disorder*, Richard Louv, expounds on the growing body of evidence linking the lack of nature in children's lives and the rise of obesity, attention disorders, and depression.

It makes sense. How much time does the average child spend outdoors? My childhood home was in the woods. I could walk out my back door and have access to miles of woodlands. A stream ran through our woods and my brothers and I spent hours building dams, catching crayfish, and stomping on skunk cabbage. Once we even dug an underground doghouse for a stray dog we planned to keep a secret from our parents. My best friend lived across the street and we liked to "cook" strawberry soup from the wild strawberries that grew in her yard and chew on green clover, cringing to keep from spitting out the sour leaves. Can you imagine what a parent would do if their child picked up a clover leaf and popped it in her mouth today? Most moms would fish it out, (me included since so many lawns and playgrounds are treated with chemical weed killers and fertilizers).

Our children know all about global warming and the deforestation of the rainforest. They have a hyper-intellectualized perception of animals thanks to Pixar. They are pros on recycling to save our resources. But can they tell an oak tree from a maple? Have they ever picked up a garter snake or discovered a bluebird's nest? Do they know what moss feels like? Have they seen a bat hunting mosquitoes at dusk? In their minds, they know all about the world, but they may not have discovered it with their hearts. Kids are open to learning all kinds of things, but as Louv points out we are in danger of raising a generation of kids indoors. I can't begin to imagine the implications of that.

Getting your kids outside can present a challenge. Sometimes its fear that keeps our children inside and I'm not talking about a child's fear. The media has hyped up our worry over the dangers lurking outside for unsupervised children. I hear myself saying, *It's not like when I was a kid. You can't just let them run wild.* But maybe we need to. And that might mean getting yourself outside. Children will follow. I know this for a fact.

Getting your kids outside is good for them for a multitude of reasons. Research confirms what I already know - open space, fresh air, dirt, plants, and animals are healing. Research cited by Louv says that kids who spend more time outside are more creative. They engage in imaginative, open-ended play. Nature can help relieve stress. A Cornell study found that "life's stressful events appear not to cause as much psychological distress in children who live in high-nature conditions compared with children who live in low-nature conditions."

When things get a little too hairy in my house and I find myself doing and saying things I never want to do or say as a parent, I head outside. I'll walk up to the barn and brush a horse or watch the chickens fuss at each other or I'll go study our fruit trees to see if any awful bug is assailing them. Sometimes I'll go for a walk in the woods. I do these things to calm down and get away from my kids, but not five minutes after I've made my escape I will hear footsteps behind me. My daughter is sure to become my shadow. And next I'll hear the kitchen door slam as my oldest heads for his fort in the woods or the swing set. The last one out will be the youngest who will trudge to the sandbox to stir up a new adventure (from which it will be nearly impossible to remove him an hour later). And peace will reign again. Nature can do that.

In 2001, Terry A. Hartig at Uppsala University in Gavle, Sweden, demonstrated that nature can help people recover from "normal psychological wear and tear" and nature also improves the capacity to pay attention, increases positive emotions, and reduces anger. I don't know about you, but I could use children who pay more attention, are happier, and yell at me less.

What do you do if you don't live on a farm or in a rural community? You seek out nature. It can be found anywhere. My dad can find birds in any setting just by listening quietly. Salamanders and really cool spiders hide under rocks even if there are a lot of tall buildings around. Find nature. It's still here underneath it all. And if you are blessed to live near it – get out of the house. You only have 18 years (at least that's the plan) to grow these little people and their brains – take advantage of the cheapest medication around for attention issues, depression, anger, and whatever else ails you. Get them outdoors. Get yourself outdoors.

Here are a few ideas:

✓ Check your newspaper. There are naturalist programs available through the national, state, and local parks. They are almost always inexpensive and sometimes free.

✓ Find out where the parks are in your area. Make it your mission to visit all of them this summer.

✓ Go fishing. At least in Pennsylvania, kids don't need a license (Dad's do).

✓ Take a walk and pick up the trash on your street. You're doing a good thing for your community and it's an excuse to get closer to nature. I promise you'll encounter some kind of wildlife (I'm not saying it won't have eight legs or more).

✓ Send your kids to camp. Find a camp that will get your kids outdoors for the day. Some kids need the encouragement of other kids and a structured environment to encounter nature on their own terms.

✓ Go geocaching or letter boxing.

✓ Have a picnic.

✓ Go camping.

✓ Plan a vacation to a state park. Many state parks rent relatively inexpensive camping cabins. Sometimes they have lodges that are still cheaper than a resort.

✓ Take the dog for a walk. A dog is great excuse to get outside every day. If you haven't got one, check with your local shelter, many will let you walk theirs!

Challenges:

Basic: Go for a hike in a local park. Sit outside and see how many insects, birds, and animals you can find just by watching and listening.

Serious: Train for a 5K run or walk that's held on a trail. Pick up trash on your street. Go for a streamhike. Find out if you can walk the local shelter's pets.

Extreme: Build a tree fort or a clubhouse in your backyard. Choose a hobby that will get you and your kids outside on a regular basis (collecting insects, birding, geocaching).

49

Surprise Somebody!

I love surprises. Well, maybe I should clarify that – I love good surprises. No one likes to be surprised by bad stuff. I once had a bad surprise that was actually a great surprise for my kids. We'd recently moved into our house and I was sorting through our accumulated life in boxes, when my oldest son burst out of the basement door yelling, "I need my bathing suit!" This alarmed me only slightly because my kids were big into dress-up at that time. As I continued sorting, curiosity got the better of me. It was early spring and definitely not bathing suit weather on our chilly hill.

Opening the basement door, I heard delighted squeals from my then 3-year-old daughter. Descending the stairs I got my awful surprise – the basement was under six inches of water. My daughter was happily splashing and the cat was floating on a "raft" made of the foam carpet squares we had just put down to create a play area for the kids. Sometimes a surprise can be good for one person and bad for another. (It turned out the sump-pump was jammed. It was easily fixed and helped us part with the ruined contents of too many boxes.)

My husband and I love to surprise our kids. Christmas morning is always filled with its share of surprises, but there are lots of other holiday and non-holiday surprises too. On St. Patrick's Day we hide tiny leprechaun hats, each with a clue tucked inside that leads to another hat and eventually a "pot of gold" (chocolate coins).

A few summers ago, we woke the kids up at 6am and said, "Get your suits on, we're going to the beach!" We fed them breakfast in the car as we drove 3 hours to the beach for the day. Never mind the fortunes we have spent renting beach houses, that day remains their favorite beach memory.

The cruise was our greatest surprise ever. We planned and prepared for it for six months without the kids knowing. On the day of the cruise, we waited for each one to get up and get dressed for school. When they found us in our room packing suitcases, they scratched their heads sleepily. And then we said, "How about instead of going to school today, we go on a cruise?!!" That was the best moment of the entire vacation!

What makes surprises so special is they are proof positive that someone was thinking about you. Which feels pretty good. I think surprising your kids is one of the greatest joys you can get as a parent. They don't have to be huge surprises. And they don't have to be that often. In fact, it's best to spread them out otherwise they cease being surprises and become expected. Need some ideas?

- ✓ Pick your child up at the bus stop for an impromptu movie date (the movies are cheaper before 5pm).
- ✓ Show up at school at lunchtime to pick up your child for an "appointment" (lunch with you at a favorite restaurant or a picnic at the park).
- ✓ Leave a small gift on their pillow.
- ✓ Write a note in their planner or leave one in the pocket of their jeans.
- ✓ Bring home a new outfit or a book for them "just because".
- ✓ Do a chore for them (mine love when I do their kitchen chore for them).
- ✓ Leave a love note on the bathroom mirror or the inside of the closet.
- ✓ Serve breakfast for dinner.
- ✓ Make a special dessert or hand out fortune cookies.
- ✓ Bring home a new pet (hermit crabs and beta fish count!).

Surprises don't have to cost a fortune. I find all kinds of treasures at the Goodwill and love to surprise the kids with them.

I think I picked up this habit from my husband. He surprises me regularly with small gifts or gestures. Sometimes it's messages in unexpected places (my to-do list, my calendar). Sometimes it's doing a chore for me, filling up my car with gas, or fixing something that's broken that I never mentioned to him. Every once in a while, it's even flowers. Little stuff, but it makes the ride more interesting. I just never know what might happen on a given day.

I hope my kids are developing this same belief that *anything could happen today*. Life is full of surprises. Sure, some of them stink. But the next one might be amazing. You might wake up thinking you have a science test and a few hours later find yourself on an airplane bound for warmer places. So much of the time I'm nagging my kids, driving them, reminding them, disciplining them, lecturing them, but every now and then I surprise them. That makes up for a lot of grumbling.

Challenges

Basic: Surprise your significant other or a dear friend with a small gesture or gift.

Serious: Surprise your kids or the mailman or coworker with a small gesture or gift (it can even be anonymous).

Extreme: Plan a big surprise for someone you love – a special evening or day or even a trip.

50

Road Trip!

Summer is all about letting things slip, like bedtimes, house cleaning, and diets. Summer is also about road trips. I've taken road trips with kids that lasted as long as 18 hours in a car and lived to tell, so here are a few ideas I have to make road trips as painless (and as fun) as possible.

A wise pediatrician once told me, it's not what they eat in a day or even a week. It's what they eat over a month. So don't stress a few, or even more than a few fat or chemical-laden meals. It won't kill them.

Pack lots of healthy food. We pack a cooler stuffed with fruits, veggies, cheese sticks, yogurts, and water bottles and keep it within reach so it's available whenever a tummy rumbles. That's not to say we don't stop for a few treats in more colorful packaging, but it keeps us from having to stop quite so often and hopefully takes the edge off so no one eats more than they really should when we do stop.

Pack lunch whenever possible. When you have a carload of kids, it's much easier to pull over at a rest area or park or even a church cemetery (that makes for a very interesting stop) to eat lunch and enjoy some fresh air. You'll save time, money, and know your kids got at least one decent meal.

Pack for the unexpected. Pack extra headphones, batteries, and books. Put a well-stocked emergency bag somewhere you can access it quickly.

> *Emergency Bag:*
>
> First Aid: *Benadryl cream (bee stings), Benadryl tablets, Band-Aids, Tylenol, instant ice pack*
>
> Spare Clothes: *Sweat shirt, T-shirt, shorts, socks and Flip-flops (in a size that will fit anyone in a pinch)*
>
> Just in Case: *Towel (serves as blanket, pillow, window shade, or clean-up), flashlight, sunscreen, insect repellent, sanitary pads/tampons, plastic bags, deck of cards, tennis ball*

We keep this pack in our trunk at all times because some road trips might just be to the soccer field but these things come in handy. I've used all of these things at some point or another for my kids or someone else's. Especially the Benadryl cream – don't forget that one. It takes the ow out of a bee sting.

Give everybody a map with the route clearly marked. This is easy to do since you can get them free from AAA or print out your own with MapQuest. The big paper maps provide an origami opportunity, too.

Don't be in a rush. I think the perfect philosophy for summer traveling is relax and enjoy what comes your way. Plan for pit stops and surprises. Traveling down I-95 in Virginia, we stopped at a place called Foamhenge. There was no admission or formal entrance, just a huge foam version of Stonehenge erected in a field. Do a little research before you take off and plan some fun detours.

Look out the window. We like to play a game we invented called, *The Weirdest Thing*. Everyone looks out the window and tries to spot the weirdest thing. We've seen peacocks in a parking lot, zebras in a backyard, all manner of interesting lawn ornaments, ground hogs in broad daylight, and laughed ourselves silly over the faces people make while driving (and how many of them pick their noses!). It's a great game because it gets us all looking out the window and appreciating the strangeness and entertainment this world has to offer.

Another favorite of ours is called, *Aardvark*. One person secretly chooses an object that can be seen out the window like street lamps or Exit signs or flowers. Then each time you pass the chosen object, that person says, *"Aardvark!"* until someone guesses what the aardvark is. There are lots of games involving license plates, road signs, and the color of cars. Find a way to get your kids' eyes off their screens and out the windows.

Enjoy a few road trips this year. Don't stress what your kids are eating (or you for that matter). There will be plenty of time for reading labels and counting calories when you get home. As long as you don't slip completely off the wagon, or at least you remember where you parked the wagon, it's all good. And don't worry about how fast you get there. Enjoy the time together away from your routines and chores. These days pass much too quickly. Plan an intentional adventure and the road trip will be twice the fun.

Challenges

Basic: Plan a trip to a park you've never visited that's at least 30 minutes away. Take a healthy picnic. Bonus points if you let the kids pick out the park.

Serious: Create your own emergency supply kit and be sure there is one in every car.

Extreme: Gather your family around and plan a real road trip – visit family or friends or pick a state you've never been to. This doesn't have to break the bank. Bring a list of games to play or research fun places to stop along the way.

51

Do-It-Yourself Summer Camp

July seems like the longest month of the year to me. I don't know if it's the long wait for ripe tomatoes, or the endless days of children brimming with energy and attitudes. Either way the month surely drags.

When my children were small I stockpiled all the camps for July. A few hours of peace were worth the price tag, besides Vacation Bible Schools ran back to back and cost nothing. But then the protests began. No one wanted to go to bible school. No one wanted to get out of bed for camp. It's too hot. None of my friends are going. Blah, blah, blah. And the costs of camps for bigger kids seemed to escalate with every year and every sport.

To avoid their rebellion, I rebelled. No more camps. Alright just one –CAMP ACHTERBERG!

CAMP ACHTERBERG is five days of homemade fun! When I first announced it, you could hear the groans for miles around. But ask them about it now, five years later, and they love to tell stories of CAMP ACHTERBERG. "Remember when that lady yelled at us for swimming in her driveway!" This was the stream hike that went a little too far and ended with threats from a distant neighbor when the kids were jumping off her driveway bridge into the creek that ran underneath. She was pretty worked up and it certainly didn't help that the kids cracked up when she stood on her porch and yelled, "No swimming in my driveway!"

CAMP ACHTERBERG is one week of planned events led by none other than mom. Here is a list of ideas we've used and/or considered:

- ✓ **Go on a stream hike.** You don't need a stream running down your street like we have, you can head over to a park or just pull over along the side of the road. Be sure to wear old shoes, sunscreen, and bug spray.

- ✓ **Visit a farm.** There are loads of farms out there that give tours. Check them out online or ask a farmer at your farmer's market if he would be game.

- ✓ **Visit an obscure museum.** Most of us never visit the museums in our town unless we have company visiting, and then we just hit the big ones. Look in your phone book or online and find a museum few people know about. Many times they're free or at least cheap.

- ✓ **Make a big, messy art project.** Go to your local arts & crafts store and buy something you've always wanted to do. Tie dye is fun. One year we painted tiles left from a rehab project as stepping stones for the garden (and grave markers when the fish we won at the carnival died).

- ✓ **Go to the movies.**

- ✓ **Have storytime.** No matter the age, kids still love to be read to. Fix a snack, get comfy and read.

- ✓ **Have a Taste Test.** Taste test all the ice cream stands in your town (get a pint to go from each and dig in blind folded!).

- ✓ **Go bowling or ice skating.**

- ✓ **Invite friends over**.

- ✓ **Take a hike.**

- ✓ **Get out on the water**. Go canoeing, tubing, kayaking, rafting, or paddleboarding.

- ✓ **Sleep in a tent** in the yard.

- ✓ **Have a bonfire** and make s'mores (or use your grill if it's too hot).

- ✓ **Swap bedrooms.**

- ✓ **Go berry picking.**

- ✓ **Take a factory tour.** (We loved the candy factory tour!)

- ✓ **Make a water slide in your yard.**

- ✓ **Put on a talent show**. (Pets are also invited to perform.)

- ✓ **Visit a kennel** with new puppies.

- ✓ **Volunteer** at a food bank.

- ✓ **Take a bike ride** somewhere other than your own street.

- ✓ **Build a collection** of bugs, rocks, shells, butterflies, or anything else you can find for free.

- ✓ **Go to the pool** from the minute it opens until the minute it closes.

- ✓ **Go geocaching or letterboxing.**

- ✓ **Have a picnic.**

- ✓ **Host a tournament.** How about ping pong, corn hole, Monopoly, or even Go Fish?

We brainstorm ideas and nothing is off the table. Sometimes a camp day is simply each kid inviting three friends to come play, which makes it feel like camp. Or it's a trip to the dollar store with all the money you can earn in one morning (great trick for getting your house picked up). It's doing anything you wouldn't do on a normal day. For us, going out to eat is rare, so a camp day might include a meal out somewhere new.

Some of the activities we do come with a price tag, but I figure I'm saving so much on camp fees I can afford to spend a little. I work out a budget for craft supplies and special treats. Sometimes bad weather means a trip to a book store, where my rubber arm is twisted into buying a few books. Even if we pay to visit museums and zoos, rent kayaks, and sometimes eat lunch out, I know our camp is still the best bargain in town.

If you haven't got a whole week to dedicate to camp, try one day a week. "Camp Tuesday" works just fine. Start your own camp this summer. I promise you'll make memories that last a lifetime and you'll never realize how much fun you can have in your own hometown.

Maybe it isn't *real camp* as one of my older campers lamented this past summer, but it is *real* time. It's time intentionally spent together exploring our town and our community. We experience nature, create art, go on adventures, learn a little, and have a lot of fun. Isn't that what camp is all about?

Challenges

Basic: Pick a day and do something touristy in your hometown.

Serious: Plan a week of camp for your kids.

Extreme: Invite a few friends and plan a week (to two!) of camp together.

52

Start School without Blowing the Budget

It had been my tradition to buy all new notebooks, lunch boxes, backpacks, and clothes for each school year. It felt good walking down the aisle tossing in fresh crayons, sets of highlighters in eight colors, and Sponge Bob book covers. It was fun to hit the young girls section and find new socks, a cute outfit, and maybe some hair accessories. Preparing my kids for the new school year always made me feel like a real parent. I pored over the list, labeled everything with permanent marker. So really, I'm in touch with the great urge to BUY STUFF, especially at the start of the school year.

For years I spent hundreds of dollars at the start of the school year. I lamented the expense every year until I finally realized I was wasting my money and stressing myself out unnecessarily. I decided to make a change. I would not get caught up in the frantic racing around from store to store finding all the school supplies and new clothes that herald the start of another year. It wasn't just budgetary considerations that kept me away from Wal-Mart that year. It was a sense that we were being swallowed alive by too much stuff. Whenever my 7-year-old heard I was headed to the store, he would grab his baggie of money and holler, "I wanna come, too!" When I asked him what he needed from the store he replied, "I just want to buy something." Sometimes I think we all succumb to this need.

With the exception of a few school supplies necessary for Middle School and two new lunch boxes (because the others smelled soooooo bad and even vinegar couldn't take the scent away), that year our budget escaped unscathed. There were no new clothes. My kids had plenty of clothes. More than they needed. I knew this because of the number of weeks they went before they finally brought their dirty clothes to the laundry room. Even then they were never naked, they had something to wear (they just might not like it so much).

As you get ready for school to start, consider what you already have. Are there notebooks that survived last year? Do you have as many colored pencils as I have? We bought a new set every year for all three kids for too many years to count and now literally have thousands. And really, who uses colored pencils? They aren't nearly as exciting as scented markers or twist up crayons. Now each year the kids sift through the thousands of colored pencils we've accumulated, crank up the pencil sharpener and create a custom set. We track down the highlighters from the junk drawer and write names on them (last names so they can be used again). Pencils seem to multiply at our house. It's just a matter of choosing the ones with the best working eraser and sharpening them to a surgical point.

The year I made the decision to reuse as many school supplies as possible, I planned to pay the kids a dime or a quarter for each supply they located and agreed to reuse. I figured they'd need incentive after years of consumer programming regarding the start of the school year and new stuff. Miraculously, I didn't have to pay them. They were fine with using the stuff we had (as long as they didn't have to use the same smelly lunch box!). There were some things on the list we couldn't avoid buying. (Why does a fifth grader need her own three-hole punch? Seems a little over the top to me, considering there's one in every classroom.) But if you need to bribe your kids, I think it would be money well spent and you'd still save hundreds of dollars.

Near the end of the summer we sort through all the clothes. We divide them between school clothes, play clothes, clothes that don't fit anymore and clothes they would never be caught dead wearing. We dig out some sneakers and make sure they still fit after a summer of bare feet. We pick out the perfect outfit to wear (or in the boys cases, I pick out the perfect outfit) and I lend my daughter some earrings or a lip gloss for the first day. I wait for the Labor Day sales to buy the new socks we need and make it a point to stop in the Goodwill a few times for a few unstained shirts for the boys.

It is possible to make it a special start of school without all the brand new clothes and fresh school supplies. On the first-day-of-school eve, we load the backpacks and bake cookies to pack in their lunches. We have a yummy dinner with food they love and we sometimes head out to the local ice cream stand for dessert to celebrate the start of school. And the next day, as always, I trail them to the bus stop, camera in hand, ready to start a whole new year.

Challenges:

Basic: Work with your kids to sort through their clothes – keep, give away, throw away – before you buy any new school clothes.

Serious: Challenge your kids to find the school supplies they need from what is littered around your house. Make a game of it. If necessary, offer to pay them if they need more incentive.

Extreme: Create a new ritual for the start of school – special dessert, silly picture in the same place, special packed lunch. Only buy what you absolutely have to in terms of school supplies and use the money saved to buy school supplies for kids who can't afford them. (Most schools can put you in touch with agencies that take these collections.)

53

Raise Responsible Voters

When I was growing up, Election Day meant a day off from school. The voting process itself was a mystery, done at the schools in secret, as far as I could tell. When we returned the next day there was no evidence that voters had been there, except for a few forgotten signs left on the lawn outside. I'm fairly sure my parents voted. It wasn't until I was an adult that I had an inkling of who they might have voted for. My father is a dedicated Republican and my mother a devoted Democrat, so in the name of peace, politics wasn't debated at my house. Once I was old enough to vote and broached the subject, my mother told me, "It's my patriotic duty to cancel out your father's vote every election."

I remember the first time I voted. I was young and living on my own and I drove to the local elementary school building to vote. I worried that one of the crazy people with the signs out front would accost me and want to know for whom I was voting. I was certain of my choice, but I wasn't about to tell anyone. I signed in and handed the election official my driver's license and voter's registration card. As she scrutinized my ID, I remember feeling like a high schooler in a liquor store. I felt true relief when she motioned me on to the next election official who led me to a little booth with a black curtain and handed me a ballot. Behind the curtain, my mind felt fuzzy with nerves. I stared at the words and they made no sense. I was afraid to ask for help, because then everyone would know that I was an idiot and worse than that, they would know who I was voting for! Eventually, I committed my pencil to filling in the little ovals – confidently to the names I knew and then randomly voting for people I didn't know based on how much I liked their names. Sort of like how I bet on horses at the race track.

I'm happy to report that I got better at voting, and more outspoken about my choices. As young as 2, my children could certainly tell you who I was voting for. In our home we talk politics as much as my husband can stand it. I want my children to know who I'm voting for and why. They don't have to agree with me, but I want them to know that I've learned about the candidates and I've chosen mine for good reasons.

Many children grow up in homes where politics are not discussed. If they're discussed at all, it's only to lament, "All politicians lie, they're just a bunch of crooks." Sometimes the mention of politics elicits broad generalizations about entire political parties such as, "Democrats are soft on crime," or "Republicans don't care about the poor."

How will today's children turn into tomorrow's informed voters, if they hear adults making blanket statements about entire political parties, or worse, not talking at all? We have to talk to our children about politics. We have to teach them the importance of elections. We have to make it clear that voting may be a right – but it's also a duty. If you don't vote, you don't get to complain. If you don't vote, you have no right to say boo about how your country or your county is being run. If you don't vote, you can just sit down now.

Here are my suggestions for how parents can help their children grow up to be voters:

Learn. Learn all you can about everyone who is running. Read their platforms. Decide for yourself who you support. If you haven't voted for a while check with the Office of Elections to be sure you're registered. Smartvoter.org is a non-partisan website that can connect you to your county's voter registration, give you information about the candidates, and even show you a sample ballot.

Talk. Talk to your children about politics. Explain how the system works (or as much as you know about how it's supposed to work). Tell them about the offices, the candidates, the political parties. Do your best to be objective. Sure, tell them who you are voting for and why, but try not to completely slam the other parties or candidates (or you risk sounding like the partisan commercials that assault our airwaves). If your children are interested, watch the debates together. It's fun to let them stay up late with a bowl of popcorn to see history happen – it's a great memory and a great example.

Answer. Encourage them to ask questions. Answer when you can, but find the answers if you don't know them. You'll learn lots in the process. Look up the candidates' websites and read what they say about themselves (as opposed to what they say about the other candidate). There are also good kids' books on democracy that can help you both. Head to the library and check out books written especially for children about the election process and the privilege of voting.

Evaluate. It's obvious when a commercial is just a slam filled with exaggerations. Talk about what you know and analyze whether the ad is trying to mislead you. Teach your children to think for themselves and not buy everything they see on a screen or in print. Always remember to ask my mother-in-law's favorite question, "What's your source?"

And here's my best suggestion - **Take your child to the voting booth with you.** Really. You're allowed to take kids in with you. They can even push the buttons for you. Taking my kids with me helps relax my nerves about voting (I still get crazy nervous – don't ask me why!), but it also helps them to become comfortable with the process. When kids see lots of people voting, it will make an impression. Magically, you will have created a future voter. Plus, kids are way more adept when it comes to using the computerized voting machines! Try to pick times when it's less likely to be crowded. Right after school is a great time to hit the voting booths. If you do have to stand in line, bring something for them to do. Even though the people-watching is great, you don't want to risk them being turned off of voting because the lines are longer than Disney.

Teaching your children about voting teaches them something about who you are, and about who they are, but mostly it teaches them something about what this country is. I managed to turn into an informed voter despite my parents' silence, but not everyone may be as motivated to voice their vote. As parents, we have an opportunity to impact the future. We can raise an educated voter and that is a powerful thing.

Challenges:

Basic: Read a book about democracy, the election process, or voting and talk to your kids about it. If there is an election coming up, explain why you're voting for your candidate.

Serious: Take your kids with you to the voting booth and let him/her push the buttons. Watch debates, speeches, conventions, and returns with your child. Make them special events.

Extreme: Take your kid along to a political meeting or volunteer for a campaign and take your child with you door-to-door. Better yet, volunteer for a voter registration drive and register voters. Keep Voter Registration forms in your car to offer to anyone who needs one.

Intentional

GARDENING

54

Make Compost Happen

Compost happens. Good bumper sticker. Compost does just happen. There's not much work involved other than gathering the right stuff and dumping it in a container. We've had lots of different compost set ups over the years; currently we've got two composts going. One is specifically for the high rent plants (tomatoes, peppers, new perennials) and one for everything else. The high rent compost is kept in a fancy composter that I purchased from Gardener's Supply catalog in a fit of this-is-an-investment-so-it's-okay-to-spend-a-fortune. Really, it's not necessary. I have a friend who got her composter free from the extension service by attending a seminar on composting. You can easily build your own and there are lots of plans out there. You can also simply designate an area and start piling. Depends on how seriously you take your composting (and maybe what your Home Owners Association will allow).

We began our composting journey by reading the book, *Compost This Book!* by Tom Christopher and Marty Asher. Considering the topic, it's eminently readable and entertaining. If you don't have the time or the inclination to read a book, there are plenty of websites to help you out.

Here's the basic recipe for compost – green stuff (nitrogen), brown stuff (carbon), water, and air. No two compost piles are alike, but they all get the job done.

Green stuff is fruit and vegetables scraps, eggshells (crush them), coffee grounds and filters, tea leaves and tea bags. It's pretty much any food leftover that doesn't have animal fat or meat in it. Think: *the stuff we put down the garbage disposal.*

When we designed our kitchen we added a compost collector to our pull-out garbage bin. Before that we kept a fancy compost collector on our counter. It was porcelain and had a lid with a built-in filter. Any upscale garden catalog will have versions of these. Prior to that, we had a plastic bucket under the sink. Anything will work, but if you don't want to run out to the compost pile/bin several times a day, I'd encourage you to use something inconspicuous but large, with a lid. When compost begins breaking down, it does smell a little, but it's not a bad smell. If it starts to stink badly, think carefully about what you've been putting in your compost. It can attract fruit flies, so a lid is a good thing.

Beyond food leftovers, green stuff is also manure of any animal that isn't a meat eater. In other words don't try to compost your dog or cat poop. Not good. But horse, cow, and chicken manure are all good. In fact, chicken manure is especially good, and rabbit manure is even better. If you haven't got any of these animals yourself, make friends with a farmer. They will usually gladly give you whatever you'll pick up. (We LOVE to give away our horse manure; we advertise on Craig's List and give it away to grateful strangers.) Grass and flower clippings are also green stuff, as long as they're chemical free. You can even throw in weeds if you're sure they haven't gone to seed. Otherwise you'll be only creating problems.

You need 2 parts brown stuff for each 1 part green stuff. Brown stuff is generally dryer to begin with. It's things like dead leaves (preferably chipped up so they break down quicker), newspaper (don't use the glossy circulars), shredded cardboard, egg cartons, corn cobs & stalks (chopped up), wood chips, sawdust, wood ash (lightly), pine needles (go easy – they're very acidic), straw, and shrub prunings (chopped up). I'm sure I'm forgetting something, but basically it's anything that is organic and will break down. The more you can begin that process, by cutting up or chipping the brown stuff, the faster your compost will happen.

Your compost also needs air. This requires that you turn it occasionally. The fancy composter that I purchased is not supposed to need this turning because of its amazing design. Alas, that promise was too good to be true and getting a pitchfork into its fancy design turns out to be pretty difficult. But we paid way too much good money for the thing, so we persevere and find our ways. My husband sometimes uses my bulb-planting drill bit and his cordless drill. If you layer your compost steadily with brown-green, it shouldn't need too much turning.

The last thing your compost needs (besides time) is water. You can uncover it periodically and let the rain take care of that or you can manually water it yourself. Too much water and too little drainage will turn your compost into a murky, solid mess. So make sure there is a way for your compost to drain.

On the hill at the edge of our woods, is a compost pile that is basically a free-for-all: yard clippings, horse manure, leaves, straw, miscellaneous paper, and cut-up worn out cotton clothing (anything that is so gross it can't be donated). It's a long term investment. It's not covered, but because it's on the top of a hill it has plenty of drainage. Turning it requires our neighbor's front end loader, so that doesn't happen often.

So compost happens and then what do you do with it? We use up nearly all of our high-rent compost each summer when we transplant the new babies. We will dig a hole much bigger than necessary for the transplant and then work lots of compost into the bottom of the hole before planting. Our tomato plants grow over six feet high and produce wheel barrows full of tomatoes. You can work compost into your garden in the fall and also in early spring. If you haven't got a garden, you could even donate it to a CSA or nonprofit garden.

Compost doesn't just work for your garden. It also works for our world. It reduces waste and adds nutrients back to the soil. Start composting today – drill some holes in the bottom of a garbage can and get started. Teach your children about composting. There's a great science lesson in all this nitrogen and carbon. It's also a lesson in life. Everything is useful – even garbage and when you add in all the right garbage, you can make gold. Pass it on. Compost happens.

Challenges

Basic: Stop bagging your grass clippings and let them compost right on your yard

Serious: Start composting! Just do it.

Extreme: Start composting for your garden and start a long-term compost pile, too. Teach your kids about composting. Locate free manure to add to your compost. Shred your old cotton clothing and newspapers for the compost.

55

Start a Garden Inside and Out

Do you ever say to yourself, *If I had all the money in the world, I'd hire a landscaper and turn my entire lawn into a garden?* Maybe that's just me. But if you didn't have to dig up all that grass and till the heck out of it, wouldn't you like more garden space? If for no other reason than it's less grass to mow? Organic fruits and vegetables are expensive – new gardens are not.

Everyone needs a garden, even if it's just a pot on your porch. If you own a home or have access to some open space – cultivate a garden. Nothing will save you more money or make you happier (of course, I'm biased). If your home is limited – be creative. You'd be surprised what you can grow with very little space. You can build a raised bed on your deck or attach window boxes to not just windows, but railings. There are lots of books on growing vertically. Potatoes will grow in a garbage can and tomatoes can grow in hanging pots. Herbs will grow in a sunny window or under fluorescent lights on a bookshelf.

I find little use for flower beds, but most houses have them. You can plant all kinds of herbs and vegetables alongside your flowers. Tuck some basil or better yet, a perennial herb like oregano or sage or chives alongside your azaleas. Lettuce likes a partly sunny garden and even grows well in the heat of the summer in deflected sun. You can plant it under a porch or in a flower box that you move out of the sun and heat when it gets too hot. Cherry tomatoes thrive in hanging baskets and climbing beans will crawl up a trellis alongside your house. Look around you – the possibilities are endless.

If there is absolutely no way you can have a garden at home, do you have friends who have the space but haven't put in a garden? Maybe they're intimidated by the work or worried about having time to care for it. Together you could grow some wonderful stuff. You won't just share the work – you'll share the rewards!

If you have a suitable spot that would make a nice garden, *lasagna gardening* is the easiest garden starting method I know. It begins with any patch of ground. It can be an old garden, an underachieving garden, or an absolutely unadulterated lawn. (I'm generally in favor of staking your claim on the useless lawn, but that's just me.) It's easiest to start a lasagna garden in the fall, but truly you can start one anytime.

After envisioning the size and shape of your garden, cover the desired area with a thick layer of newspaper. Yep, newspaper. Be sure to leave out the shiny colored circulars. It's best if the newspaper you choose uses vegetable inks (most do). Try to choose a day when the wind is not whipping around, or if you do find someone to videotape your efforts – it's comical. After you lay out the newspaper, wet it thoroughly and then begin your lasagna.

Lasagna consists of layers of "green" (compost, manure, grass clippings, basically anything rotting) and "brown" (leaves, straw, peat moss, mulch, pine needles, wood ash). Wet down your lasagna occasionally, especially if you have a dry spell. Continue adding layers for a month or two and then leave the whole thing to *cook* over the winter.

It may not look pretty (until the first snow hides it), but by spring you'll have rich luscious soil, ready to garden. And you didn't have to lift a spade because you turned your lovely lawn into compost for your new garden! If you want more detailed, technical directions, I highly recommend the book *Lasagna Gardening* by Patricia Lanza.

When it comes to gardens – where there's a will there's a way. Find yours. We are really not that far removed from our ancestors who grew all their food. There is no magic or mystery. Anybody can do it. *You* can do it.

Another option for people truly unable to garden (or even those who do, but would love even more veggies!) is to join a CSA (Community Supported Agriculture). Most CSAs let you sign up for weekly whole or half shares of produce. At a CSA you'll meet lots of great people who will share their wisdom and you'll get a larger variety of plants than you could ever grow on your own. Some CSAs operate year round and some have dairy and meat products, in addition to vegetables and fruit. Check out *localharvest.org/csa* to find a CSA near you.

Once you've created a perfect gardening space, what will you put in it? There are plenty of plants that do just fine starting out in the wilds of a freshly dug bed, but the most expensive ones – the peppers, tomatoes, fancy herbs, and perennial flowers need a protected start. Starting your own seeds inside, as opposed to loading up on seedlings later in the season will save you enormous amounts of money, allow you to choose from literally thousands of varieties, and give your garden a substantial head start. I start seeds in late February so I can set them out in early April or May.

Planting Medium. Look for a seed starter mix that is organic or at the very least, doesn't have chemical fertilizer added to the medium. Seed starter is exactly what it says it is – a medium for starting seeds. Typically, it has very little nutrients in it because seeds don't need nutrients to germinate. Once they have their first true leaves, however, they need some food. That's when it's recommended that you transplant your baby seedlings to potting soil. I'm a lazy gardener in a hurry, so I create a mix that is seed starter and soil all in one and skip the whole transplanting step.

My mix is made up of screened compost (4 parts), vermiculite (1 part), perlite (1 part), and sphagnum peat moss (2 parts). If I'm in a crunch (or can't get to my compost because the snow is too deep), I'll mix peat moss with vermiculite, and water my seedlings with organic seaweed fertilizer.

Pots. I start my seeds in recycled yogurt containers, but you can buy seed flats or pots. If you're using yogurt containers, put holes in the bottom to allow for drainage and watering from the bottom. I fill the pots up with seed starter, water them well, and then line them up in plastic under-the-bed boxes so I can water from the bottom once they start to grow. Follow the directions on the seed packet to know when to start your seeds.

Lights. There's no need to purchase expensive plant growing lights, a regular fluorescent bulb will do. Grow lights can be set up anywhere. An easy way is to utilize a bookshelf you already have. Clear off the books and suspend grow lights from the underside of each shelf. Investing in a timer for your grow lights is also a wise move unless you're more reliable than I am about turning the lights on and off at the correct time each day. Seeds can also be started in a sunny window, but they will be slower growing and must be kept warm when temperatures dip outside.

Watering. You'll need a spray bottle with a mist setting to water your seeds as they emerge. Once they pop out and sprout a few leaves, you can water from the bottom. Popsicle sticks make inexpensive markers so you don't forget what you planted.

Moving Outdoors. Once your seedlings are grown, it's important that they are "hardened off" before you plant them outside. If you don't, you'll end up with stressed out, or possibly dead seedlings. Hardening off means moving them outdoors in a gradual way so they get used to the wind, temperature, and strong sun which are all much harsher than the fluorescent lights and warm house. Even store bought seedlings need to be hardened off.

If I had a sunny window I would start by letting them spend some time there. Alas, the only sunny window I have is in my youngest son's room directly behind his drum set and that might not be the safest of surroundings. So I move them outside to the shade on my porch on a warm day for an afternoon. From there I increase their time outside and their exposure to real sunlight a little each day. Eventually graduating them to sitting in the very spot where I plan to plant them. If the temperature threatens to dip low, I bring them in for the night. This process takes 7-10 days.

Planting. At this point I watch the weather. Ideal conditions for planting your seedlings would be daytime temps around 70, not too sunny with some light rain. But life is not ideal, now is it?

Dig the hole larger than the seedling pot and water the hole before planting the seedling. If you have compost to add, work the compost into the hole also. Getting the seedling out of its pot and into the soil seems simple, but that isn't always the case. If you use plastic containers (like the used yogurt cups I use), tap the bottom to loosen the plant. If there are roots growing out of the bottom of the cup, tear them off. Then carefully shake the entire plant out of the container into your palm and set the plant in the hole, firming soil around it. I bury seedlings deeper in the ground than they were in the pot, especially tomato plants.

Planting seedlings is careful work. Like so many other things that look great at home, once you get them out of their element they seem incredibly small and fragile. Clearly mark their new digs or surround them with a string fence for protection so that other folks who traverse your garden won't trample them.

Creating and tending a garden is incredibly satisfying. For as many years as I've been doing this, I'm still humbled by the miracle of creating food for my family from tiny seeds and my own efforts. Yes, creating gardens, starting seeds, and tending to them is work; but it's well worth it.

Challenges

Basic: Buy some herb seedlings or zinnia seeds and grow them in a sunny window. Join a CSA. Assess the possibilities for adding herbs or vegetables alongside the plants you already have.

Serious: Set up a small area to start seeds and grow a few tomatoes from seed. You can use a book shelf or even the under the cabinet lights on your counter. Re-claim present flower garden for a vegetable garden and/or purchase/build window boxes and pots.

Extreme: Create a lasagna garden or do it the old fashioned way and dig up a garden plot. Set up an indoor growing area for starting seeds. Read the next chapter and then order seeds early enough to get a good start. Teach your kids how to care for the seedlings. Let them plant a few seeds of their own.

56

Plan a Garden and Order Seeds

One of my winter rituals used to be sitting down with a hot mug of tea, sharp pencils, graph paper, and a stack of glossy seed catalogs to sketch out the gardens for the coming year. I loved the powerful, albeit delusional, feeling of control as I assigned each square foot its allotted vegetables for the year. My plans were usually grand, and I was proud of my neat little diagrams, confident the fantasy would play out come June. It never did. Really. Never. As much as I would like to be organized and as much as I would like my garden to replicate those neat graph paper creations. It didn't happen. Oh, the seeds wasted, the money gone, the hope denied. But now I'm much smarter and my gardens, while still pretty much a free-for-all-plant-on-today's-whim-or-whichever-seed-packet-I-remembered-to-bring-with-me kind of thing, are bounteous.

Before you start marking up the seed catalogs and planning the garden of your dreams, let me share a few lessons learned.

Plant what you eat. It doesn't matter how beautiful the purple radishes look in the glossy catalog, no one in my house will eat them. Waste of space. Think about what you actually eat and plant that.

Plant more of what your family eats and less of what sounds like a good idea.

Check the seeds you have before placing your order. A lot of seed companies sell seed packets with hundreds of seeds in them – more than you can possibly use. If they're stored properly, seeds keep for years. Any seeds left from the previous year are fine to use this year. Just sow them a bit heavier.

If it doesn't freeze well, only plant what you can eat. I love sugar snap peas. Love them. I devote ridiculous amounts of garden space to them. This is silly because *a)* we can never eat all of them and *b)* they don't freeze or can well. Much is wasted. Same goes for carrots. I always plant several big rows and they are a HUGE pain to weed. And in the end a good number of them rot in the ground before we can eat them. The horses are the beneficiaries of this mistake each year.

Buy seeds strategically to save money. Plant expensive vegetables, the kind that cost the most when you buy them at the store. Fancy red peppers cost an arm and a leg – plant lots of them. Many heirloom tomatoes can't be purchased at the store – plant them. As much as I love broccoli, it's a space hog and locally grown broccoli is plentiful and cheap. Besides, my kids will only eat so much broccoli.

A few definitions that may be helpful:

Hybrid. This is a seed that has been developed by cross-breeding several plants in the interest of developing things like "disease resistance", "early harvest", and "high yield" which are all good things. However, when commercial seed companies design these seeds, they are focused on performance features sometimes at the expense of taste. You can't save seeds from hybrids because they can't reproduce themselves, what you wind up with is a shadow of the former plant or basically one of the strains used to create it.

GMO or GE. These are genetically modified or genetically engineered seeds which means they were altered using molecular genetics techniques. For example, corn seeds are developed with a pesticide as part of their genetic makeup which will help the plants kill certain pests. When you are planting hundreds of thousands of acres this can be financially beneficial. It is a little frightening though, as seeds become more and more genetically identical we put ourselves at risk for disaster should some type of challenge prove too much for that particular seed. Of course, it also means we eat a lot of pesticide.

Heirloom. Heirlooms are seeds that have been saved and passed down by individual gardeners. These seeds must be "open pollinated" meaning they can reproduce themselves. They provide the most variety and security. Heirlooms will vary in their ability to thrive in certain climates, so choose heirlooms that grow in your area. If you plant heirlooms and save seeds from only your best plants, you're doing your own genetic modification on a much smaller scale and developing your own heirloom seeds!

Organic. Most seed companies carry a line of organic seeds these days. Regulation can be spotty, so if you're serious about organics, you may want to look for the USDA seal. You'll pay dearly though. Organic seeds are produced entirely through organic practices by a certified organic operation.

There are lots of seed companies out there. When selecting yours, pay attention to where the seeds are coming from. If you're growing in upstate New York, you might not do so well with seeds developed in southern California. If you're buying non-local seeds pay attention to the zones specified for each seed. You can find your zone at the National Gardening Association's site *garden.org/zipzone.*

Also, if you've never ordered from a company before, you might not want to order *all* your seeds from them. Be sure you can trust them before you trust them with your entire garden. Seeds are relatively cheap, so it's fun to try out a few newfangled plants and a new company or two each year. Keeps the gardening exciting. Of course, excitement is relative.

Challenges

Basic: Mark up a seed catalog for fun. Let your kids circle the stuff they like. Order some easy to grow seeds like beans and lettuce.

Serious: Make a list of the plants you'd like to grow. Determine which you have space for and which most people at your table will eat. Order the seeds that you can start outside unless you have the means to start seeds indoors.

Extreme: Draw up your garden plan. Measure or estimate the square footage and designate the proper space for each vegetable. Order seeds from several seed companies (read reviews online). Order your seeds early enough to start them inside. (Read the next chapter on starting seeds!)

57

Get Your Kids in the Garden

Some kids naturally love to garden and some don't. Don't let the experts tell you otherwise. It's not always easy to get kids in your garden for purposes other than building roads in the dirt for their hot wheels. I got my daughter in the garden on dreams.

One spring, while planting all alone on a beautiful afternoon, I grabbed a plant marker (recycled paint stirrer) and wrote "cooperation" on the opposite side of the label I'd so meticulously prepared. It had been a rough morning. As I worked, I thought about the qualities I hoped I had planted in my kids. Soon, I was turning over all my plant markers. I dreamed up all the things I wanted to plant in my family's life besides sugar snap peas and early spinach - humility, honesty, laughter, and kindness. My husband was helping me with my pea fence and although I know he noticed the signs, he didn't say anything. Perhaps he knew better or maybe he was as frazzled as me and hoped it would be as easy to plant those things as it is to plant seeds.

My daughter, on the other hand, is a kindred spirit. She spied my new stakes and decided she would name my plants, too. As we worked, we talked about the scientific studies that say plants do better when you talk to them. This was her kind of world. When I finally looked to see what she was planting, I saw that the rows were now marked with her favorite names – Ariel and Polly (as in Pocket). She named two similar sounding seeds Rhonda and Wanda. She named our plum purple radishes Cinderella. But my favorite was the name she gave my Lolla Rosa lettuce. She named it Layla. Layla Lolla Rosa. It was just fun to say. Even without the plants, the garden looked pretty colorful and it made me smile all season.

Getting kids involved in your garden is always a good idea, but sometimes you have to lure them into it subtly. Give them their own row or patch. The rows may be crooked and a few seeds may be sacrificed, but that's a small price to pay for their interest. If they invest some of themselves in the garden, they just might eat some of the results.

You can involve your kids in choosing seeds, laying out the garden, planting the seeds, and certainly making the seed markers. My seed markers are paint stirrers and wood shims inexpensively purchased in packs at the hardware store. Once upon a time, I used Popsicle sticks, but they got lost once the plants start coming up. My fancy metal markers wound up bent or lost. I like my big wooden markers. Big markers expect big things.

Ask your kids what they'd like to grow and then find a way to make it happen. Don't let space or sunlight limit you. One summer I even grew peanuts (in an old manure bucket). When my daughter was little, she loved purple so we spent an afternoon at the nursery buying purple plants and planted them near the play set. She's grown now, and more inclined to black than purple in terms of fashion, but we still call that garden "Addie's Garden."

Challenges

Basic: Give your kids a colorful pair of gardening gloves, some seed packets and a shovel with their name painted on it. (Paint pens, nail polish, or permanent marker will work.) Invite them to decorate a pot or window box to plant their garden.

Serious: Invite your kids to get in on the garden planning. Ask what they'd like to plant. Invite them to make big plant labels and signs. Create a walking path through the garden and maybe a spot to sit. Let them give the plants names.

Extreme: Give your kids their own garden. Help them create it and plan it, but let them truly be responsible for it. If you don't have room for an entire garden, give them a few rows or window boxes. Encourage them to name their garden and invite others to tour it. If you have lots of room and ambitious kids, you can also set up a self-serve veggie stand and let them make some money!

Intentional

CELEBRATING

58

Have a Homemade Party

June is party time at our house. It's full of birthdays (five!), Father's Day, and end of year activities, not to mention an anniversary. It is followed by our biggest party of the year – our annual Fourth of July party.

When it comes to parties, it's time to loosen the food rules. It's a party, after all! But there's no reason to go overboard on junk or expenses. As tempting as it is to farm children's birthday parties out to Chuck-E-Cheese or Laserdome, there's no need. You can have even better parties at home.

I don't even try to substitute on the junk food. I take the kid-to-be-honored to the store, walk down the snack aisle and let them have at it. But I also serve healthy food dressed up as much as possible. Presentation is everything when you want kids to eat something healthy. Carve out a watermelon and fill it with fruit. Make the punch from 100% juices and freeze an ice ring with fruit. Carrot sticks and dip, strawberries, and orange slices are other offerings that can tempt the junior palate. When it comes to serving healthy food at kids parties, split the difference. Let them have the snacks they beg for, but counter that with appealing healthy options.

The kids at our latest event, *The Feast of the Oblong Table* (celebrating the birthday of a Monty Python fan) ate more watermelon balls than Doritos. When they'd had enough of jousting on scooters, duels on hippity hop balls (using pool noodles), and Capture the Flag, they swarmed the food table. I gave them toothpicks as utensils and they gorged on fruit before using the toothpicks as swords. Then we brought out the chips and pizza. After eating all that fruit, seven kids only made a small dent in the bag of Doritos. Their bellies were full with fiber rich fruit.

Here are some ideas for keeping parties kid-friendly, earth-conscious, and semi-healthy.

Buy sturdy plastic plates, bowls, and cups you can re-use. We bought ours in blue, yellow, pink, and green. At a one dollar for 10 plates, we now have service for eighty if necessary and I always have a color to match the theme of whatever party we're throwing, whether it's a princess party (yellow and pink) or a race car party (blue and green). No one misses the theme decorated paper plates that cost $4.50 for eight. It's much nicer to eat on sturdy plastic than flimsy paper. We've discovered that we can even wash our plasticware in the dishwasher if we set it on the "fine china" setting and use "energy-saver dry". I know I've saved literally hundreds of dollars on unbought paper goods, plus this is much better for the environment.

Buy utensils specifically for parties. We found inexpensive metal utensils and bought service for forty. These utensils also get packed in kids' lunches when necessary so Mom won't freak out if they slip up and toss them in the trash barrel.

Have your party at home. I know it's easier to go to Chuck-E-Cheese, but it's definitely more expensive and much harder to truly celebrate your kid. Sure, the big mouse sings to them, but after that the kids are scattered all over celebrating the token-bound games and might not even see your kid until the end when their parent forces them to track you down to say thank you. Consider having a smaller party at your house. There are endless ideas to be found on the internet. Winter birthdays can be harder, but get creative and keep the numbers down. No one needs that many presents anyway. Ask a relative with a bigger house to host the party. Just like presents - it's the thought that counts. You don't need to blow the bank on a birthday party for a six year old. Keep it simple and get creative.

You don't need prizes for games. I have never given prizes at birthday parties and kids don't miss them. It's just fun to play the games. We almost always have a piñata so they go home with candy no matter what. Prizes seem to make one kid happy, but other kids sad. Skip the cost and stress altogether.

Give a real gift instead of a goodie bag full of junk. Instead of a bag full of candy and plastic jumble, pick out something nice the kids can use. We've given away Beach Balls (signed by all the kids), shovel and pail (decorate the pail), Flashlights (bonfire party), and for the latest party – pool noodles (their "swords"). None of those gifts cost more than two or three dollars, so I saved money and the kids had something useful to take home.

The younger the kids, the more planned activities you need. Once they get older (say 7), you need to build in some free play too, but when they are young remember the best defense is a good offense. Have a plan with more activities than you think you'll need. There are lots of people with too much time on their hands posting a gazillion birthday party, game, cake, and theme ideas online. Check out Pinterest or google "kids birthday party ideas" - you'll be amazed and grateful that people actually post this stuff!

Take a picture of each guest (actually take 2 or 3 because someone's always got his eyes closed or a finger up his nose) and use the picture to make a thank you note. I take random pictures throughout the party, but when it's time to open presents I sit the giver next to the birthday boy/girl and take a picture of them together as the present is opened. Not only does it give me another potential picture for the thank you note, it also gives me a record of what each kid gave the birthday child which is critical information when writing thank you notes.

Bake your kid's birthday cake. Now this one might make you groan, but hear me out. I don't have to say you'll save money, that's obvious by the price of decorated cakes these days. And I probably don't have to tell you that homemade cakes taste WAY, WAY, WAY better than store bought cake. And you can probably figure out that if you bake it yourself you can use some healthy ingredients. No, the real reason to bake a cake for your kid instead of buying one is that *it's a gift*. When my husband asks why I'm once again spending too much time trying to figure out how to craft a cake that resembles a race car or Tinkerbell or a s'more, I tell him, "This is my gift to them. I make their cake. I make exactly what they want." Sometimes the birthday child has a vision or even a picture of the cake they want which can be helpful or not. Expectations are hard to live up to. But no matter what, they know I'm going to try my best to make them a really special cake. As they get older they even like to help me which makes it even more special.

When I was cleaning up *The Feast of the Oblong Table* and the kids were outside having a loud game of capture the castle supervised by my kid-at-heart hubby, my mom commented that I was really good to give my kids all these parties. She said she let me and my brothers have a party every other year. I only remember one or two parties, but they are good memories. Maybe I'm over the top with the parties for my kids. Possibly, but I love the opportunity to celebrate my kids. You can never say – "You're special and I'm glad you were born" too many times or in too many ways. So I'll keep throwing these crazy parties and making one-of-a-kind, by-request cakes, because by doing that not only am I making it clear how much I love these kids, I'm making memories. And someday when they're negotiating the birthday party plan with their own spouse, they'll say, "My mom used to throw the best birthday parties..."

Challenges

Basic: Bake your child's birthday cake.

Serious: Host a party, bake the cake, and buy a useful favor for each kid

Extreme: Buy permanent plastic place settings and metal utensils to re-use for all your parties. Remember to take pictures of each guest with the birthday boy at present opening time. (*Really extreme*: make cloth napkins for parties.)

59

What are You Going to be this Year?

Americans spend 5 billion dollars on Halloween. Does that seem a little crazy to you, too? And what is it spent on? Costumes and candy – two items that have little meaning the next day. Now, contrary to what my children would have you believe, I like Halloween. It's a wonderful opportunity for creativity and play. Unless you work at Disneyworld, it's the only chance you have to dress up once you become an adult. And dressing up is fun. Even people who say it isn't, secretly enjoy it. I have a great flapper costume, but it's not entirely appropriate for trick or treating, so on Halloween I am traditionally a witch. But not this year because my daughter has appropriated my witch hat, the one with a spider dangling from the rim.

Halloween costumes can break the bank. I admit I've spent my share of fortune on the perfect costumes for my children, painstakingly choosing from the elaborate catalogs that start arriving in late July. I justified this expense because my kids used the costumes year round. They liked to dress up on an almost daily basis. Now that they're older they still occasionally indulge their alter egos with a pirate patch or Egyptian head covering. The costumes are getting a bit long in the tooth, but they can still inspire an adventure or two.

My oldest has been crafting his own costumes since he was old enough to explain his plans to me. He's been Harry Potter playing Quidditch, a crazy scientist, a winged dragon with *real bird wings*, and a faceless ghost. Last year he was an *enigma*, which looks strangely like a bank robber to me. (Sweatshirt hood pulled tight to hide face, dark clothes, dark shoes, dark gloves, and a colorful scarf. Okay, that last detail might be the one that gives you away on the police tape, but still.)

The younger two have been a little harder to convince. They think the store bought costumes will truly transform them. And many years I've been too weak to fight the onslaught. But after all those years of wimping out, we've accumulated literally dozens of costumes. Certainly there are plenty of options in our costume bins.

The last few years I've insisted that we not be like most Americans and spend too much on Halloween, so I recycled (and then canceled) the catalogs before the kids got home from school. I told the kids we would make their costumes. The first year, my youngest was relentless in his wish to BUY a costume and my talk of the crowded landfills and working conditions in China fell on deaf ears. I caved and agreed to take him to the store. But only to *look for ideas*. I stressed to the kids that we weren't there to buy a costume per se, just to *look*. What we needed was inspiration, not a polyester masterpiece for $29.99.

We headed to the store to see all the new costumes on display. Many of the costumes seemed very adult. We cruised the aisles admiring and wondering over all that we saw. In the end we left with a pair of fake eyelashes which inspired a fancy witch with big orange lashes and a plastic sword for the "knight-deatheater-with-a-sword" my youngest envisioned. I was happy because I only spent $10.

If my kids hadn't been agreeable and then excited about the idea of creating their own costumes, I was prepared to bribe them. I'd rather spend money on something of value, like a trip to the book store, than more over-packaged, fake looking costumes from China. In the end, that wasn't necessary because my children believed in their own creative capabilities.

Most kids can come up with their own costumes from what you have. Purchasing a prop or two is fine, but try to stay away from the all-in-one bag costumes. Homemade costumes always win at the costume contests anyway. Plus this is a wonderful chance for your kids to use their imaginations and learn a great lesson about being resourceful.

Another idea for an ecologically responsible costume is to rent one. Local theaters typically rent costumes as a fund raiser. It's a great way to get an authentic costume and support the arts. These can be pricey and most are for adults, so this might only work for your older teens or your own fantasies, but it's a true win-win.

Children's magazines are full of homemade costumes. If you're crafty, this might be the way to go; although even these can get pricey depending on how particular you are about materials. The key is to not only be creative, but reasonable.

We live on a rural road and have never had a trick or treater dare our driveway, so I haven't got any great words of wisdom on healthy treats that won't make kids turn up their noses. As much as I believe in organic, healthy food, Halloween is a whole other ballgame. All bets are off. Kids want candy. They want the processed, colorful, additive-filled kind. And I'm not going to stand in their way. At least not for one night.

If you're feeling wealthy, there are a few organic treats out there. We've had organic lollipops and the flavors are unique and yummy. I wish it were still acceptable to make Halloween snacks, because homemade popcorn balls, caramel apples, and homemade cookies are so much better than store-bought concoctions.

Each year I wrestle with the question of – who controls the candy. I've asked more experienced moms than I and it seems that it's a fairly even split between *let-them-eat-it-all-and-get-sick* and *ration-it-out-and-steal-the-good-stuff*. Usually I allow them a hearty helping on Halloween night and then dole it out for lunch dessert and after school snack for a few days.

We store their candy on top of the fridge and I take it down for them when necessary. This keeps it out of sight and after a few days, when they've eaten all their favorites, they typically lose interest without the brightly colored plastic pumpkins staring them in the face. When they stop asking for the candy, I put the remains in labeled zip lock bags in a high cupboard and soon none of us remember it's there. The next summer I'll come across a hard lump of stale candy when I'm rooting around looking for my cheesecake pan, but by then I can throw it out with no one the wiser. It's not a very organized plan, but it works for us.

If you're ambitious, you can make homemade treats and sell them to your kids for the Halloween candy they come home with. For example, one caramel apple or popcorn ball could be traded for six pieces of candy. Our orthodontist buys back candy from the kids each year. I know my own kids would rather have the goods than the cash. And for one night, that's fine with me, especially since no one wants the Almond Joys.

Challenges

Basic: Design your own costumes using one or two store-bought props.

Serious: Find a pattern/plan in September and sew/make your own costumes.

Extreme: Let your kids dream up their own costumes and make them. Offer to make homemade treats that they can *pay* for with their processed candy.

60

Write a Holiday Letter

I need to say something in defense of Christmas Letters. It's not just because I write one (actually ours is a New Year's Letter because I just can't get it together before Christmas, so I've stopped trying). I hear a lot of Christmas Letter bashing – *it's too impersonal, they're boring, too long, no one really cares about all that stuff* (ahem...and I really want to know what you had for breakfast this morning via Facebook?), or the top complaint – *it's just bragging*.

Okay, if you can't brag to your friends and family about how great your kids are – who can you brag to? I absolutely want to hear about your kids – everyone should. Every kid needs to have people who brag about them! Is it worth telling us that your kid won third place in the 2nd heat of the Pinewood derby? Absolutely – I want to know! Should you tell us that your daughter was the little lamb in the school Christmas pageant? I can't get enough of this and there had better be pictures! And what about the pet's latest antics? Yes, yes, yes, this is good stuff. It gives me a window into your life.

People who criticize Christmas Letters just don't have enough to complain about. Or they're jealous that someone else is taking the time to write at length about their own family. Face it; no one has time to write personal notes in all their Christmas cards. A Christmas Letter fills me in on what you've been up to all year. For too many of my long lost friends, this is all the information I will get until the next Christmas Letter, so I'll take it and be grateful.

Some people are super creative and do things like Top Ten lists or poems about their year. Those are fun and quick to read. Some people send collages of pictures with comments – that's always good for a laugh. I have one friend who each year sends a collection of the funniest (or most poignant) things her children have said that year. Some people just use bullet points, but that works too. It gets the information across.

You can learn so much from the letters beyond the mere facts presented. The style can be self-effacing and make you laugh or it can be stiff and formal and make you realize the writer is a little embarrassed to be telling you all this but really wants you to know. Sometimes information about particular family members is conspicuously left out and then you have to wonder....is someone having a fight? Doing drugs? Living on a friends' couch? I'm telling you, I get a lot more out of these letters than the average bear.

The hard part is figuring out what voice to write in. Third person? That seems like you have a narrator for your life. This works for some people, but makes the letter read a little like a news report. First person makes it seem awkward to fully brag about your own accomplishments. And then there are the people who switch first persons throughout the letter which turns it into a bit of a mystery, which can be fun. Who's writing now?

If for no other reason, write for posterity. I've got annual letters that go back 20 years. That's a big chunk of my life history. Hopefully someday my descendants will want to read it, if only to gawk at how we lived *back in the days when we couldn't tele-transport and water was abundant and free*. There's important history in these letters. Something lasting. If I ever sat down to write my life story there's no way I would remember all the details of our life over the years. These letters are a clue. They celebrate the things that were important to us, the events that moved us, and the accomplishments we were proud of in any given year. I wish that my grandmothers had written letters for me to read. I would have loved to have known what their lives were like. So if you can't write for the rest of us, write for your future relatives.

I love Christmas Letters. I open the cards and make a stack of letters to savor over a cup of tea. After I read each letter, I think about the person who sent it and the people he/she wrote about. Sometimes there's a picture to study. Reading these letters is sacred time for me. For a few minutes my heart is connected to someone whose life has touched mine somewhere in this journey. There are lots of friends I haven't seen in years but who made an imprint on my life and heart, and I want to hold on to the fragile thread that connects us. These letters help me do that – much more than a beautiful card with professional greetings and a quick signature. I'm not complaining – if that's all you have time for than I'm just grateful I'm still on your list. The card lets me know I made the cut.

But for those of you who wonder whether you should write the Christmas Letter and are afraid of being boring or sounding silly or being one of those people – I'm here to tell you - write! Write the letter from your heart and brag all you want – there's nothing wrong with bragging about people you love to people you love. Nothing. And there's nothing wrong with photocopying your message to 100 of your closest friends and relatives. It's a celebration that you have so many people in your life who matter that you have to resort to mass mailings. This is a good problem! So please write that letter. The people who love you want to know what's happening in your life. They really do. Bring on the Christmas letters!

Challenges

Basic: Write a holiday letter. It doesn't have to be Christmas, it can be New Year's or Valentine's or any ole time.

Serious: Get your family involved in writing the holiday letter. Ask, "What was the best thing that happened this year?" Invite them to draw pictures or share their own thoughts.

Extreme: Make a video greeting. You could call it, "A Day in the Life of Our Family." Upload it and send the link and/or burn DVDs for everyone on your list.

61

Holiday Decorating on the Cheap

I am decidedly NOT a decorator. It's not simply that I don't have any knowledge of decorating and have never even perused a decorating magazine; it's that I have very little interest in the idea of decorating. Don't get me wrong – I completely appreciate someone else's ability to decorate a house or lawn or child. It's just that I take no joy from my own efforts.

Occasionally, I do get inspired to choose a new paint color or arrange a few flowers, but for the most part there is no theme, style, or strategy to the way my house, lawn, or children look. I do wish the lawn were decorated with a lot less garden jumble and child flotsam. The children prefer to decorate themselves without my assistance. And they each seem to have a unique "style" all their own. My oldest was a trend-setter in kindergarten when the zip off pants were all the rage. Each day at some point he would zip off the bottom portion of one of the legs of his pants. Not both, just one. This made him look like a pirate because his little white leg resembled a peg leg. It was cute until other children started doing the same and parents complained when pant legs were lost. That was the first call home from a teacher.

Most of the time I just don't see the need for holiday decorating. For a long time, I only put up Christmas decorations. Most of these decorations were wedding presents (which seemed an odd gift to me then and even more so now). A few years ago my youngest child visited a friend who decorates for the holidays as if her home is a finalist in *Extreme Makeover: Holiday Decorating Edition*. He came home incredibly disappointed in his mother's meager efforts. Since then, I've tried to step it up a bit.

Here are my guidelines for holiday decorating:

> *It has to be cheap (as in expense, not value).*
> *It can't take up much room in the off-season.*
> *If it's made of perishables, all the better.*
> *It has to be tasteful and/or meaningful.*

Supplies you'll need:

- ✓ *A big spool of wired red ribbon*
- ✓ *Evergreen branches* (Find a tree and cut some branches. If it doesn't live in your yard, you should probably ask first.)
- ✓ *A box of shiny ornaments* (Dollar store is an inexpensive source, although I found some at the Goodwill.)
- ✓ *Pinecones* (These need to be collected throughout the year. The ones lying around on the ground in December are undoubtedly mashed and moldy.)
- ✓ *Christmas Cards*
- ✓ *Children's Holiday Craft Projects* (What? You didn't save them?!)

With that in mind, I'll share my best tips.

Tie pretty red wired ribbon on anything and it becomes a holiday decoration (including the dog). I'm pretty horrible at the ribbon tying, but this much I know – start with one end longer if you want your bow to be even. Use wired ribbon because it's forgiving and anyone can make it look good (even me).

Utilize nature. It's free. Evergreen trees and bushes are everywhere and they forgive a little trim this time of year.

Pull the dead stuff leftover from summer out of the pots on your porch. (Unless you're the kind of person who has already cleaned them up. If so, dig the pots back out and fill them with dirt and/or rocks.) Arrange evergreen branches artfully in the pots, tie colorful ribbons on them, and arrange them on your front porch.

Add evergreens and ribbons to porch lights, mailboxes, and signs (be careful not to allow them to touch bulbs).

String white twinkly lights on anything – an old sled, a porch decoration you already have, a chair, a mirror, whatever happens to be lying around (not the dog).

Fill a glass bowl with bulbs, pine cones, candy canes or peppermints. (If you use mints, tell your children they are fake or that they're left over from five years ago so they won't beg you for them on a daily basis. If that doesn't work, tell them the dog had them in her mouth.) Add a ribbon if possible and it's instantly festive.

Hang up your children's Christmas crafts from years past. I love the finger-painted wreaths made from their tiny handprints and get a sentimental chuckle out of their signatures on the back.

Find a clever way to display your Christmas cards. We tape them around the kitchen doorway. You could also hang a string like a clothesline along a wall and clothespin them to the line. If you're really crafty, you can decoupage them on a hat box or similar item to create a pretty decoration.

Wrap the presents that aren't for children and place them in a decorative pile in a window, under the tree, or as a table centerpiece. This will not only decorate your house, but make you feel as though you've got Christmas under control.

Bottom line: Holiday decorations don't need to cost a fortune or take up half your basement. If I can do this, you can do this.

Challenges

Basic: Pull out your decorations early this year and reassess them. Donate what you don't want to Goodwill.

Serious: Locate evergreen trees/bushes and secure permission to cut branches. Find a holly bush if you can, too.

Extreme: Keep your holiday decoration budget under $15. Put your kids to work creating art or holiday chains. Devise a way to display cards. Cover something with lights. Dress up your front door with greens and ribbons.

62

Wrap Presents Without Paper

I've always loved Christmas morning – pretty much everything about it. The kids' faces, the grandparents searching for coffee, the big WAIT, then the rush down the stairs. I love being overcome by my children's happiness. I love the shouting and the guessing and the thank you hugs. I love the joy that registers on my daughter's face when she realizes she really did get the gift I told her Santa would never bring and the undeniable awe that overcomes my youngest son when he eyes the tree knee deep in presents. I even love the christening of the annual new hermit crab (We have no luck with hermit crabs. Every other living thing seems to thrive here, but not crabs.), the six thousand step instruction manual for the newest Lego creation, and my oldest with his nose in his new book. It's all wonderful.

Except the paper. It always bothered me that we ended up drowning in paper. The paper was beautiful one moment and trash the next. And I never knew what we should do with it. If I was a different woman I might have saved it and ironed it and used it again. But I really couldn't imagine doing that and besides, I don't iron. So we wadded it up and used it to start fires while I worried about all the toxins we were releasing into the air we breathe. Or we sent it to the recycling and I wondered if the people at the dump threw it out anyway since they don't like paper that is colorful and glossy. It truly bothered me, all this paper.

And then I made a decision. I would stop using wrapping paper. However, after surveying the options, not wrapping wasn't one of them. I realize it's very environmentally friendly and probably true to the real spirit of Santa to leave the presents bare, but I need the wrapping. I would miss the anticipation, which is possibly the best thing about a present. So I began wrapping our presents in fabric. I'd seen this idea in several magazines but I'd always assumed it took someone who knew her way around a fabric store, could operate a sewing machine, and speak the lingo ("Two yards will be plenty from that bolt."). I can now say that you truly don't have to be a whiz in home ec to handle wrapping your presents in fabric.

That first year, I set off for the fabric store with my daughter in tow. The Christmas fabrics were on sale for half price! We bought two yards of six different fabrics and a pair of pinking shears. Then we headed to the craft store where we used a coupon to buy ribbon also at half price. We picked out spools of different color ribbon - one color for each family member. In lieu of tags we would tie the appropriate color ribbon on each package.

Once home I chose a gift to wrap and carefully cut out enough fabric to cover the present just like I would if it was paper wrap. I used the pinking shears which made pretty edges on all four sides. Then I wrapped up the package like I would wrap it with paper, only I was using fabric which was soft and didn't tear or wrinkle. I folded the ends over and secured them with a tiny bit of tape. Then I looped a ribbon over the present which hid the tape and held the wrap job securely. It looked awesome! I have never been very good at wrapping presents neatly with paper. There always seem to be crinkles and gaps, but I'm a whiz with the fabric. Our presents are gorgeous! Another way to wrap with fabric is to place the gift in the center of the material, gather the ends and tie with ribbons – like a candy wrapper. It looks cute and even young kids can wrap like this. (It's my hubby's favorite method, too).

This system is not only better for the environment and my mental state, it makes wrapping a snap. Grab a present, grab a suitable already cut piece of material, wrap, tie on appropriate color ribbon – done! No rolls of paper, bows that cost a fortune, or frustration. And the best part is that on Christmas morning we simply fold up the material and ribbons and save them until next year.

The following year we got really fancy. We sewed bags out of fabric which made wrapping even easier. Now, before you stop reading, I must tell you that I don't sew either so if I could do this, you can too. I can barely operate the sewing machine and almost had a tantrum worthy of a toddler when I ran out of bobbin thread and had to figure out what to do. But I did it and in reality, it was super simple. The only thing you have to be able to do is sew a fairly straight line. I suppose you could even do it by hand, if you were so inclined.

You start by cutting out a piece of material about twice the size of what you want the bag to ultimately be. Fold it over with the back side of the material on the outside and sew along both sides, leaving the top open. When you're finished, trim off the excess thread, and flip the bag inside out. Instant gift bag! You can slip in the presents and tie the bag closed with a ribbon. I made assorted sizes to hold anything from a gift card to a Lego set.

When I told my cousin about our fabric bags, she shared her Santa bag idea with me. She sews a giant bag just like my smaller ones for each child. It is their "Santa bag". They leave the empty bag and a note for Santa with their cookies on Christmas Eve and Santa fills the bag with their special present. I snagged this idea immediately. It's environmentally friendly and makes Christmas Eve super simple. The kids like the tradition, too. Their Santa bag is the first thing they look for on Christmas morning.

I was so inspired by the success of this venture that I checked out the remnant bin at the fabric store and picked up material appropriate for birthday gifts. I'm finished with wrapping paper. I'll miss the long empty tubes that make such great swords, but not the expense or the waste.

Challenges

Basic: Buy fabric and experiment with wrapping some of your gifts with fabric this year.

Serious: Buy plenty of fabric and a different color ribbon for each person in your family. Wrap all your gifts in fabric this year.

Extreme: Watch for the holiday fabric sales (usually start around Thanksgiving) and stock up. Sew fabric bags and Santa bags. Buy fabric for birthday, wedding, baby shower, and other occasions.

63

Give Gifts That Matter

What to give? As I may have mentioned, I believe we already have plenty of stuff. Very few of us truly *need* anything, but many of us delight in giving gifts during the holiday. I would be one of those people. I love to see the faces of my loved ones when they open my gifts. I even love wrapping the gifts. I keep extensive lists on my smartphone of ideas I come across that would be perfect for certain people. I'm all about gift giving, but I'm fundamentally against stuff accumulating.

My gift giving guidelines:
- ✓ *The smaller the better (in size not substance).*
- ✓ *Perishables before permanence.*
- ✓ *Experiences are WAY better than anything you have to dust.*
- ✓ *You can never go wrong with books.*
- ✓ *It is ALWAYS the thought that counts.*

With those guidelines in mind, I'll share a few of my favorite gifts.

Charitable gifts are always a good idea. But as I've said, I love the wrapping of objects and a small piece of paper proclaiming that money was given in the recipient's name, just doesn't cut it. I've found ways to get around that.

Give used books along with a donation to any cause, one that promotes literacy if you like thematic gifts. I spent a year saving every book I read, underlining the parts I liked, making notes in it, and then affixing a note on it with the name of the person I thought would most enjoy it. At Christmas time, I bundled the books up with a pretty ribbon and tag saying I'd made a donation in their name instead of buying new books.

Give a gift of animals through the Heifer Project along with cookies in the shape of the animal given or a drawing or clay figure representing the animal.

Give a bundle of pencils or package of paper clips (or any school supply) to teachers with a donation to an organization that promotes education. I've done this with the *I Have A Dream Foundation,* and the teachers were truly touched. I did something similar for the music instructors with a charity that promoted the arts.

Family picture gifts work for relatives, particularly grandparents, who are happy to get updated pictures. Make a bookmark with pictures, notes, illustrations of the kids, yourself, whomever would delight the receiver. Laminate it, punch a hole in it and add a decorative ribbon (you can add beads or charms to the ribbons for extra flair)

Create a calendar of family photos. This can be simple using an online service or fancy if you have the time to scrapbook each page. I've been doing this for years and since it easily eats up multiple days, it's a gift of my time as much as the pictures. I enjoy the process. I reflect on the faces in the pictures and the people I'm making them for as I work.

My sister-in-law gave my kids a small spiral bound book filled with pictures of their cousins doing simple things like cooking, playing sports, and making funny faces. It was narrated and laminated. My kids enjoyed that book nearly every day for years. It is mashed and stained to near oblivion- evidence of their appreciation.

Food is an old standby, but people always appreciate it, especially single, young, or elderly people. *Granola* is a healthy alternative to cookies and it's easy to make. Fill pint jars and cut a small piece of fabric or decorative paper to dress up the lid.

Bread is a simple and much appreciated gift. I started giving bread instead of candy for a friend who is diabetic, but everyone who has received a fresh, homemade loaf of bread has loved it. It's easy to do, especially if you have a bread maker (but I take the dough out and bake it in a traditional bread pan so it's a normal shape and not that odd hat size loaf).

Infused Oils and Vinegars require a little preplanning. Recipes for simple infusions (rosemary olive oil, raspberry vinegar) are all over the internet, but most require only that you leave the additive in the oil or vinegar for a period of time. You'll need to start early if you want to give infused treats!

White Wine Balsamic Lemon Infused Vinegar

1 bottle white wine balsamic vinegar

1 lemon

1. Pour vinegar into an airtight container. (I used a quart mason jar.)

2. Cut lemon in to pieces and place in jar. I only use ½ a lemon in each jar and the flavor is fine, but an entire lemon would make it more intense.

3. Seal and store for three weeks in a dark place that doesn't get too hot or too cold.

4. Strain vinegar and fill gift jars. You can put some fresh lemon peel in the jar to make it more decorative or add a gift tag with serving suggestions.

Experiences are my favorite gifts because they take up no space and force us to go do something, sometimes things we'd never do if someone else didn't pay for it. I like to give (and get!) tickets to see plays, musicals, concerts given with a flyer for the venue or a small trinket that goes with the theme or a bag of popcorn (white-chocolate covered is my favorite!). Passes to a museum along with a little cash for the gift shop is an excellent idea.

Give gift certificates for bowling, ice skating, laser tag, mini golf, whatever floats your boat with a box of Twizzlers, mittens, golf tee or something useful that is in keeping with the activity. Prepaid lessons are a gift that keeps giving - guitar, sailing, archery, drawing, painting along with a guitar pick, sunscreen, or pencils. Subscriptions to magazines, wine-of-the-month club, flowers-of-the-month club, or better yet a CSA membership will last all year long.

I'll add homemade gift certificates a bit cautiously because I am aware that many of these well-meaning certificates or coupons don't ever actually come to fruition. I am in possession of coupons for clean rooms, dishes done, etc. which I've never been able to use because there always seems to be fine print involved (*I'm too tired, I have homework, Can I do it a different time?*). Still, these are great stocking stuffers. Here's a few I've used in our Advent boxes (25 little boxes they open each day of advent).

Get-out-of-kitchen chores free for one night

Ride to the movies for you and three of your friends (notice this is only a free ride, not a free movie)

Choose your own dinner coupon (must be redeemed at least 48 hours in advance of said dinner)

Challenges

Basic: Give someone on your list something that can't be dusted.

Serious: Make or bake something for the people on your list.

Extreme: Give only gifts that follow my five rules this year. Or make your own rules.

64

Calm and Peaceful Holidays

Being calm and peaceful during the holidays may be an unrealistic goal, but I do believe it's a worthy one. We want to create a perfect holiday, but most of the pressure we feel at the holidays comes from expectations we put on ourselves. Sometimes we're so busy pursuing that perfect holiday that we never get to enjoy it. How can you make this year more calm and peaceful?

Don't feel the need to bake every holiday treat your mother did. I pursued this at one point in our family history. I collected every recipe for Christmas cookies I remembered my own mother making. And you know what? I'm the one who ended up eating all those cookies and then berating myself for it. The kids don't like the ones with nuts on them anyway. Pick a couple everyone likes and stick with that. Or better yet – let your kids do the baking (and cleaning up). Or – don't make any at all!

Don't put up every holiday decoration you own, every year. Tone down the chaos and pressure a little. If someone misses a particular decoration, direct them to the appropriate storage bin or shelf. At the end of the holidays fill a box with all the decorations you don't really like. Mark it *Goodwill Holidays*. Next year, without opening it, take it directly to Goodwill. I finally remembered to do that last year and this year it felt awesome to show up at Goodwill with the box of Christmas decorations right after Halloween.

Cut down on presents. No one needs all the stuff we give them. A few good gifts are much better than a ton of meaningless ones. Anything you run out to buy the day before Christmas is likely not something anyone will want. I remember sending my husband on such a mission many Christmas Eves ago when I had finally finished wrapping and realized one of the kids had far fewer presents than the others. It was Rite Aid or the grocery store – everything else was closed. These days that's probably not the case, but it's still best to avoid the last minute panic shop.

Give presents that don't need to be wrapped. Experiences and gift certificates can go in a nice card. If it comes down to the wire and you haven't got a gift ready to go, create a coupon for an experience like a hike + lunch (for a friend) or a movie night with five friends at your house (for your kids).

Use reusable wrap if you need to wrap. It has truly revolutionized wrapping in this household. Fabric, real ribbon, and paper bags can be used year after year.

Make time for quiet. I know you're busy. I know your kids are noisy. I know you're exhausted. But find five minutes of quiet to reflect each day. A great place to do this is in a dark room with a lighted Christmas tree. Or outside. Or with an animal in your lap. Or standing in your children's room while they're sleeping. It will make the holiday feel like a holiday.

Make time for your kids. Read a holiday book together (even if they're big kids). Ask them what holiday activity happened at school today. Go for a walk, shoot baskets, play music with them. Just be with them. Kids have more down time at the holidays. Take advantage of this. Your presence is the best present.

Enjoy your holiday food. Put a moratorium on stressing over calories or artificial ingredients. Enjoy a Christmas cookie – slowly, savoring it. Don't do anything else except eat that cookie. Or sip some eggnog. Yeah, I know it has six zillion calories, but this is the only time of year you drink it. Even better – warm it up and add Bailey's! Focus on the taste, the extravagance, and the sheer pleasure. Let go of the guilt.

Sleep more. Go to bed earlier. Take a nap. Close your eyes for five minutes (not while you're driving). Rest your soul. This is the darkest time of the year. If you were a bear, you'd be burrowed in your cave, so give in to your body's natural inclination to sleep more and – sleep more!

Exercise every day. I know, I know. But do something. It'll relieve stress, keep your guilt in check (remember those cookies?), and give you energy. You need this. Make it a priority, even if it's only ten minutes. Can't find a parking place at the mall – perfect opportunity to get some exercise. Kids making you nuts? Take a time out on the treadmill or put on your sneakers and go for a hike. If nothing else, make more trips up and down the stairs.

Go to a holiday concert. One of my favorite holiday memories is singing in a Messiah Sing-a-long in a candle-lit church. The Hallelujah Chorus brought me to tears of joy. Even if you can't sing, find a concert to attend. Many holiday concerts performed by community chorus' and church choirs are free. Close your eyes and listen to the music. Remember what you are celebrating.

The holidays are a rich time of year. But it can also be a stressful time of year. Let go of some of that stress this year. Don't worry so much about how the house or the kids look. Don't worry about the number of presents or the perfect holiday. Enjoy the holiday you've got. Instead of wishing everyone a happy holiday, *actually have one.*

Challenges

Basic: Make a pledge to yourself to find some alone time and be quiet for five minutes each day.

Serious: Think through your holiday rituals and habits. Drop a few. Use the time saved to exercise.

Extreme: Gather your family together and decide what's important about this holiday. Focus your activities, expenses, and time on what's most important. Ask for help with the holiday chores.

65

Garfield, Augustus, Obituaries, and Resolutions

As my then 7-year-old son, Ian, sat down to breakfast, he asked in all seriousness, "Who would win - Garfield or Augustus?" He'd obviously been in the middle of this scenario when I'd called him to breakfast, and he paused over his plate for my answer.

Playing my well-worn role of the clueless parent, I asked, "Who's Augustus?" I knew that Garfield was obviously the fat orange cat found in the funny pages, but I hadn't a clue who Augustus might be or what he might be trying to win.

Ian sighed at my slowness, and said, "You know, Augustus." Cue the *you're-not-really-that-stupid-are-you?* look. When I registered no recognition, he shook his head in disgust and said, "From Willy Wonka?" He took a bite of french toast and watched me, waiting for my answer.

I scanned my brain for some recall of any kind of recent battle between Garfield and Augustus and came up empty. "What are Garfield and Augustus trying to win?" I asked.

Again, the sigh and now a roll of the eyes thrown in to express his exasperation with my ineptness. "An eating contest!" Duh, like I should have known this!

My child hasn't discovered the hot dog eating contests on TV yet, but the last time my husband's best childhood pal was here, he and Ian had a pizza eating contest (which Ian won, I'm not proud to say), so I know this is a sport he is destined to aspire to, no matter how much I hammer home the idea of eating only what you need. As another of our friends said when Ian challenged him to an eating contest, "The person who wins an eating contest isn't always the winner."

I asked for more information, stalling for time to make my decision. "Why are they having an eating contest?"

Ian shook his head at my silly question and took another bite of his French toast. "Who would win?" he asked again between bitefuls. "I picked them because they're the biggest eaters I know."

"I'd have to go with Garfield," I decided, picturing my own fat orange cat the time he got the lid off the cat food canister. Ian nodded his head at my wise choice.

I think one of the primary functions of children is to remind us that we should never let reality get in the way of our thought processes, especially our dreams. Reality can really hamper possibilities. This conversation was a good reminder for me as I contemplated my New Year's Resolution. I'm all about New Year's Resolutions. Using your imagination to dream up an amazing life is a wonderful exercise. Each resolution should move you another step towards that amazing life. I usually do my dreaming and scheming during a run, but at least once a year I ponder my resolutions on paper.

I once did an exercise for a class in college in which we had to write our obituary. We had to write what we hoped we would be remembered for and how we would be described. When we finished the essay, the professor told us that we had just written our life's mission statement. Mine was pretty lofty at the time, but I've held on to it and edited it as my values and my world view have shifted. Every morning when I read the newspaper, I always scan the obituaries. I'm not looking for anyone I know (although from time to time a familiar face does appear). I'm just curious. I look at the faces and I read some of the write-ups and I think about who those people were. I wonder why that particular picture was chosen. I wonder what kind of life the person had. I wonder if they were happy. I look for a good mission statement. As I read the mission statements revealed in the obituaries, I think I'm unconsciously comparing them to what my own obituary will say. I would like to be better at living out my mission statement.

New Year's resolutions call us back to our mission. They can help us stay on the track we want to follow. I keep a copy of the mission statement I first wrote twenty years ago in my wallet. I rarely look at it and am always surprised when I come across it as I'm searching for whatever store bonus card the cashier happens to be demanding. But at the start of the year, I pull up my mission statement on my computer and look it over. I decide if it's still my mission and whether I'm making any progress towards fulfilling it. I imagine my life the way I want it to be and then I sit down and write out some New Year's resolutions to help me get there.

New Year's resolutions aren't just for adults. It's a great idea to have your kids come up with their own resolutions. Teach them now that we are all under construction. We can all be healthier, happier, life contributors. My family has a memory book that we started at the new millennium. Each New Year's Eve we all answer five questions in the book.

1) **What do I want to be when I grow up?** It's funny how my husband's and my answers keep changing, too. Growing up is truly relative.

2) **What's the best thing that happened this year?** The answers from the kids when they were toddlers and preschoolers are telling. They say a lot about what's memorable for children.

3) **What's important to you?** This is my favorite question. I love seeing how my kids' values are developing. They always make me catch my breath.

4) **What have you learned this year?** This one causes all of us to be grateful and takes the most thought.

5) **What do you think will happen in the next year?** Sometimes this gets pretty wild as in, "Chickens will rule the world!" from my preteen. Sometimes it's very simple as in, "Santa Claus will come," from my then two- year-old.

A brand new year is the perfect time to take stock, but you can do it anytime. What's important to you? What do you want to be when you grow up? And most importantly, what have you learned? Ask yourself, and ask your family. If nothing else, it will give you a chance to hit the pause button on your crazy life and consider what your mission is.

Challenges

Basic: Think about the five questions listed. Write your new year's resolutions.

Serious: Ask your family to answer the five questions and write them down in a notebook to save for next year.

Extreme: Write your obituary and your mission statement. Keep a copy somewhere you can read it on a regular basis.

Final Thoughts

"There is no passion to be found in playing small - in settling for of a life that is less than you are capable of living." Nelson Mandela

One of the beta readers for this project said to me early on after reading the book, "I love the ideas, but making any change in my household is like turning a tanker in the ocean." What a perfect analogy! That's exactly what you're doing when you decide to live an Intentional Life. You are making small changes every day in the way you eat, think, and live. Those little changes may feel insignificant at first, but they add up and soon you'll see that your ship is headed in an entirely new direction.

The simple fact that you are holding this book in your hands means that you are already on course for a new kind of life. You have the power to feel better physically and emotionally by challenging yourself and your family to make better decisions in terms of diet, lifestyle, and priorities. You have the power to draw your family closer by making an intentional effort to infuse meaning not just in your holidays, but in your daily life. You have the power to change.

When Ian was first diagnosed with alopecia areata and lost his hair, I was distraught. But in the months that followed I began to see something special happening to the people around him. They acted more intentionally. They went out of their way to help him. I realize that their behaviors were motivated by the fact that they thought he had cancer, but no matter the reason, it was beautiful to watch. In the years since, I've seen this play out time and again. Strangers gave him their giant stuffed bear at the boardwalk Skeeball games after witnessing his happy, but unproductive efforts. A father I'd never met shadowed him down the long ladder at an indoor maze. Store clerks regularly chat Ian up and adults we don't remember meeting greet him on the sidewalk. People remember his name and just about everyone smiles at him. They go out of their way to be kind and considerate to him.

The collective actions of all these random people have had an interesting effect on Ian. Having only experienced exceptional kindness from strangers since he was a preschooler, he has grown to assume that people will be kind. He looks for their good sides. He loves people. This humbles me on a near daily basis. But I have to wonder – what if we all acted intentionally toward each other, our planet, ourselves? Wouldn't the world look different? Wouldn't the world *be* different? Wouldn't *we* be different?

There is nothing miraculous, difficult, or complicated about living intentionally. It's very simple. Living intentionally means thinking about your actions and choosing to do what is right for your body, your family, your community, and this earth. I'm not going to promise that it will be easy. Sometimes it isn't. But the part that *is* easy, is deciding that you want to live the life you are capable of living.

You can do this. It starts with a few little changes and the ripples begin, sending your tanker in a whole new direction.

Blessings,

Cara

Group Guide to *Live Intentionally*

Opening – Open the group and focus them by reading something motivational or inspiring. It can be a quote, story, poem, or even a prayer if you're so inclined.

Introductions – Maybe you know each other already, but even if you do, you don't know everything about each other. Each person should give their name and finish one of these thoughts:

> This week I'm worried about....

> Today I'm feeling......because.....

> I'm glad I'm here because........

> This week I learned/accomplished......

> Today I hope we'll talk about....

Follow Up From Last Meeting – If the group took on any of the challenges at the last meeting, share experiences.

Topic/Discussion – This is where the leader for the week takes over. You can introduce the topic, or simply read from the chapter. You can share other information you've gathered. If there is a recipe included in this week's chapter, you might want to make it ahead of time and share it (and tell what went right and wrong with your efforts). This is a good time to ask everyone to share what they know and what they'd like to know about this topic. It's a great chance to teach each other.

If you're planning to get through the entire book and don't have 65 weeks to accomplish the task, you may want to invite several people to select topics to cover each week. Or you can simply focus on the areas that are most important to your group.

Challenges – Go around your group again and share which challenge you are choosing to accept. If this week's topic is not one you want to tackle (which is a perfectly fine choice), consider choosing one of the extra 75 challenges from back of the back.

Closing - Leader can read another inspiring message and/or close with prayer.

Homework – Decide which chapters you will cover at the next meeting. Assign leadership.

Optional Field Trips!

Consider taking your group on an outing. Here are a few ideas, but you can probably come up with better ones local to you.

Visit a pick-your-own farm.

Gather for a group canning session.

Travel to a natural grocery store – look for one that sells food in bulk.

Visit a CSA and take the tour.

Host a Yard Sale together.

Take a hike. (Bring your kids and/or dogs!)

Visit the Goodwill.

Swap books, clothes, toys, recipes, unwanted housewares.

75 Extra Challenges

1. Write a real letter.
2. Look up an old friend on Facebook.
3. Write a thank you note to your mother/father.
4. Organize family photos – in a scrapbook, online book, or just print out and file.
5. Write a letter to each of your children.
6. Choose a guardian for your children.
7. Give your children's teachers a thank you gift/note.
8. Remove ten things you don't wear from your closet.
9. Take a box of stuff to Goodwill.
10. Organize your bookshelves.
11. Make something from scratch you've never made before.
12. Cook in your crockpot every night for a week.
13. Figure out how to make one of your kids' store-bought treats from scratch.
14. Invent or modify a recipe.
15. Make pretzels.
16. Clean out the fridge and wipe down shelves.
17. Clean out a drawer/shelf/closet.
18. Draw up a garden.
19. Give something away on Freecycle.
20. Make a donation of time or money.
21. Write to an author you admire.
22. Invite someone to lunch you haven't seen in a while.
23. Invite someone to lunch you'd like to get to know better.
24. Help your kids make/bake/create something.
25. Volunteer to help somewhere.
26. Clean up a road.
27. Take a hike somewhere new.
28. Visit a farmers market.
29. Go geocaching.
30. Turn off your screens for a week.
31. Leave your phone in your purse when you're home.

32. Go Letterboxing.
33. Text something sexy to your spouse.
34. Learn something new.
35. Make music (or at least organize new play lists).
36. See live theater.
37. Go a day or a week without social media.
38. Draw/paint something.
39. Visit a museum
40. Write a Letter to the Editor for the newspaper.
41. Organize your jewelry and get rid of what you don't wear.
42. Patronize a locally owned store and get to know the owner.
43. Visit a pick-your-own farm and pick!
44. Visit a local winery/brewery.
45. Take a class at your library.
46. Organize your kindle, computer files, phone apps and get rid of what you don't need.
47. Read a poem out loud.
48. Write a poem.
49. Make at least one new recipe a week for a year.
50. Try a vegetable you never liked as a kid.
51. Create your own cookbook of favorite recipes– either in a loose ring binder or on your computer.
52. Put your kids in charge of the menu for a week.
53. Let your kids paint/redecorate a room.
54. Eat out of your cupboards instead of going to the store.
55. Drink a glass of water when you wake up and before you go to bed every day for a week.
56. Plant something you've never grown before.
57. Plant a fruit tree.
58. Save seeds.
59. Take your kids to Goodwill or a thrift store and tell them to pick out an outfit for themselves for less than $10.
60. Have a yard sale where everything is free!
61. Read up on all the candidates running for office – even the ones running for offices you've never heard of.
62. Don't renew any magazines this year.
63. Discover a new locally owned shop.
64. Take a tour in your own hometown.
65. Invite another family over for "game night."

66. Match up all your plasticware and throw out the single lids/bottoms with no match.
67. Match up your socks and throw out/compost/repurpose the onlies.
68. Give blood as many times as you're allowed to this year.
69. Run or walk a 5K.
70. Visit the animals at the shelter; walk them if you're allowed.
71. Write a letter to the President.
72. Write a letter to your children when they are the age you are now.
73. Say something positive to every person you meet for a day (or a week!).
74. Make homemade valentines for the people you love.
75. Take a vow of silence for a day.

Resources cited

Agency for Toxic Substances and Disease Registry (ATSDR). 1999. "Toxicological profile for *n*-hexane." Atlanta, GA: U.S. Department of Health and Human Services, Public Health Service.

American Academy of Child and Adolescent Psychiatry. "Children and Watching TV." *Facts for Families Pages*. Washington DC: AACAP, December 2011.

American Association for Cancer Research. "How Diet, Obesity and Even Gum Disease May Affect Immune System and Cancer." *Science Daily*. 15 November 2006.

Bittman, Mark. *Food Matters*. New York: Simon & Schuster, 2008.

Bittman, Mark. *How to Cook Everything*. Hoboken, NJ: Doubleday, 2008.

Bureau of Labor Statistics. "Consumer Expenditures 2013". *US Department of Labor*. 9 Sept 2014. http://www.bls.gov/news.release/cesan.nro.htm

Centers for Disease Control and Prevention. "Nutrition for Everyone: Protein." October 2012. cdc.gov/nutrition/everyone/basics/protein.html.

Christopher, Tom, and Asher, Marty. *Compost This Book!* San Francisco: Sierra Club, 1994.

Daley CA, Harrison K, Doyle P, Abbott A, Nader G, Larson S. "A review of fatty acid profiles and antioxidant content in grass-fed and grain-fed beef." *Nutrition Journal*. 10 Sept 2010.

Dhiman TR, et al. "Conjugated Linoleic Acid (CLA) content of milk from cows offered diets rich in linoleic and linolenic acid." *Journal of Dairy Science*. 2000;83:1016-1027.

Fallon, Sally. *Nourishing Traditions*. Washington, DC: New Trends, 2001.

Govindan M, Gurm R, Mohan S, Kline-Rogers E, Corriveau N, Goldberg C, DuRussel-Weston J, Eagle KA, Jackson EA. "Gender Differences in Physiologic "Markers and Health Behaviors Associated With Childhood Obesity." *Pediatrics*. August 12, 2013.

Gomez-Pinilla F, Hillman CH. "The Influence of Exercise on Cognitive Abilities." *Comprehensive Physiology*, 3, 403-428.

Graham, Tyler, and Ramsey, Drew. *The Happiness Diet*. New York: Rodale, 2012.

Hartig, Terry. "Psychological Restoration in Nature as a Positive Motivation for Ecological Behavior." *Environment and Behavior*, Vol 33, No. 4, July 2001.

Harvard Public Health Review. "Vitamin D: How Much is Enough?" Spring/Summer 07. www.hsph.harvard.edu/review/spring07/spr07vitaminD.html.

Hyman, Mark. *Ultrametabolism*. New York: Atria Books, 2006.

Kingry, Judy and Devine, Lauren. *Ball Complete Book of Home Preserving*. Ontario, Canada: Robert Rose Inc., 2006.

Larsson SC, Bergkvist L, Wolk A. "Consumption of sugar and sugar-sweetened foods and the risk of pancreatic cancer in a prospective study." *American Journal of Clinical Nutrition*. November 2006 84: 1171-1176.

Louv, Richard. *Last Child in the Woods: Saving Our Children from Nature-Deficit Disorder*. Chapel Hill, NC: Algonquin Books, 2008.

Lustig, Dr. Robert. *Sugar: the Bitter Truth*. YouTube, posted by University of California Television. 27 July 2009. http://uctv.tv/shows/Sugar-The-Bitter-Truth-16717.

Martin-Biggers, Jennifer. "Benefits of Family Mealtime Across the Growing Years: A Conceptual Model." *Rutgers University Study*. 2012.

Mozaffarian D, Pischon T, Hankinson SE, et al. "Dietary intake of trans fatty acids and systemic inflammation in women." *American Journal of Clinical Nutrition*. 2004; 79:606-12.

Mozaffarian D, Katan MB, Ascherio A, Stampfer MJ, Willett WC. "Trans fatty acids and cardiovascular disease." *New England Journal of Medi*cine. 2006 Apr 13;354(15):1601-13.

Pollan, Michael. *Omnivores Dilemma*. New York: Penguin Press, 2006.

Ponnampalam EN, Mann NJ, Sinclair AJ. "Effect of Feeding Systems on Omega-3 fatty acids, conjugated lineoleic acid and trans fatty acids in Australian beef cuts: potential impact on human health." *Asia Pacific Journal of clinical Nutrition*. 2006;15(1)21-9.

Rampersaud GC, Pereira MA, Girard BL, Adams J, Metzi JD. Breakfast Habits, Nutritional Status, "Body Weight, and Academic Performance in Children and Adolescents." *Journal of the Academy of Nutrition and Dietetics*. May 2005.

Reese, Jennifer. *Make the Bread, Buy the Butter*. New York: Free Press, 2011.

Roach, Mary. *Stiff*. New York: Norton, 2003.

Sacks, F. "Ask the Expert: Omega-3 Fatty Acids." *The Nutrition Source*. Harvard School of Public Health. http://www.hsph.harvard.edu/nutritionsource/omega-3/.

Sandbeck, Ellen. *Organic Housekeeping*. New York: Scribner, 2007.

Scanlan, Richard A. "Nitrosamines and Cancer." *The Linus Pauling Institute*. http://lpi.oregonstate.edu/f-w00/nitrosamine.html.

Shane, Vic. "Too Much Protein is No Good." *Nutrition Research Center*. 8 May 2008.

Sinha R, Cross AJ, Graubard BI, Leitzmann MF, Schatzkin A. "Meat intake and mortality: a prospective study of over half a million people." Archives of Internal Medicine. *National Institutes of Health.* 23 March 2009.

Staiano AE, Harrington DM, Barreira TV, Katzmarzyk PT. "Sitting time and cardio metabolic risk in US adults." *British Journal of Sports Medicine.* August 2013. http://bjsm.bmj.com/content/48/3/213.

The Humane Society of the United States. "*A Brief Guide to Egg Carton Labels and Their Relevance to Animal Welfare.* "March 2007.

http://humanesociety.org/issues/confinement_farm/facts/guide_egg_labels.html

Voss M, Nagamatsu LS, Liu-Ambrose T, and Kramer AF. "Exercise, brain and Cognition Across the Lifespan." *Journal of Applied Physiology.* July 25, 2011. online addition, http://jap.physiology.org/content/jap/111/5/1505.full.pdf.

Weinstein, Miriam. *The Surprising Power of Family Meals.* Hanover, New Hampshire: Steerforth Press, 2006.

Weir, K. "The Exercise Effect." *American Psychological Association.* Dec 2011. http://www.apa.org/monitor/2011/12/exercise.aspx

Wells, N. "How Natural and Built Environments Impact Human Health." *Department of Design & Environmental Analysis.* Cornell University College of Human Ecology, 2010.

Wills Wyma, Kay. *Cleaning House: one Mom's 12-month experiment in ridding her home of YOUTH ENTITLEMENT.* Colorado: Waterbrook Press, 2012.

Movies Mentioned (and recommended)

Craig's List Joe. Dir Joseph Garner. CLJ Films, 2012. DVD. *(This is a movie about a guy who lived off of Craig's List for a month. It actually made me cry.)*

Food, Inc., Dir Robert Kenner. Magnolia Pictures, Participant Media, and River Road Entertainment, 2009. DVD.

No Impact Man. Dir Laura Gabbert and Justin Schein. Eden Wurmfeld Films and Shadowbox Films, Inc., 2009. DVD. *(The whole family watched this one and its impact was felt for months. We still talk about it!)*

Super Size Me. Morgan Spurlock. Kathbur Pictures, 2004. DVD.

Websites Mentioned (and recommended)

AppleValleyCreamery.com – *home delivery of milk products in South Central PA.*

Catalogchoice.org – *remove your name from catalog mailing lists.*

Eartheasy.com - *website explains composting.*

Earthhour.org

EatWild.org – *resource for finding grass-fed products.*

Freecycle.org – *find and give away free items.*

Garden.org/zipzone - *find your gardening zone.*

Geocaching.com

Heifer.org. - *Heifer Project International – nonprofit working to eradicate poverty and hunger through sustainable, values-based holistic community development.*

Ihaveadreamfoundation.org. - *a nonprofit that works to ensure that all children have the opportunity to pursue higher education.*

Letterboxing.org

LocalHarvest.org – *resource for finding locally grown products.*

Optoutprescreen.com –*remove your name from mailing lists.*

Organicgardening.com

Smartvoter.org - *non-partisan website with information about voter registration, the candidates, and even sample ballots.*

Thewaterproject.org

Recommended Reading

Ban Breathnach, Sarah. *Simple Abundance*. New York: Warner Books, Inc., 1995.

Bittman, Mark. *The Food Matters Cook Book: 500 Revolutionary Recipes for Better Living*. New York: Simon & Schuster, 2010.

Bittman, Mark. *Food Matters*. New York: Simon & Schuster, 2008.

Bittman, Mark. *How to Cook Everything*. Hoboken, NJ: Doubleday, 2008.

Carpenter, Novella. *Farm City: The Education of an Urban Farmer*. New York: Penguin, 2009.

Christopher, Tom, and Asher, Marty. *Compost This Book!* San Francisco: Sierra Club, 1994.

Damrosch, Barabara. *The Garden Primer*. New York: Workman Publishing, 1988.

Fallon, Sally. *Nourishing Traditions*. Washington, DC: New Trends, 2001

Graham, Tyler, and Ramsey, Drew. *The Happiness Diet*. New York: Rodale, 2012.

Kingsolver, Barbara. *Animal, Vegetable, Miracle*. New York: Harper Perennial, 2007.

Kingry, Judy and Devine. Lauren. *Ball Complete Book of Home Preserving*. Ontario, Canada: Robert Rose Inc., 2006.

Lanza, Patricia. *Lasagna Gardening*. Emmaus, PA: Rodale, 1998.

Louv, Richard. *Last Child in the Woods: Saving Our Children from Nature-Deficit Disorder*. Chapel Hill, NC: Algonquin Books, 2008.

Nestle, Marion. *What to Eat*. New York: North Point Press, 2006.

Pollan, Michael. *Food Rules*. New York: Penguin, 2009.

Pollan, Michael. *Omnivores Dilemma*. New York: Penguin Press, 2006

Reese, Jennifer. *Make the Bread, Buy the Butter*. New York: Free Press, 2011.

Roach, Mary. *Stiff*. New York: Norton, 2003.

Rubin, Gretchen. *The Happiness Project*. New York: Harper, 2009.

Sandbeck, Ellen. *Organic Housekeeping*. New York: Scribner, 2007.

Schofield, Deniece. *Confessions of an Organized Homemaker: The secrets of uncluttering your home and taking control of your life*. Cincinnati, OH: Betterway Books, 1994.

INDEX

Acknowledgments

This book has been shaped by so many people it would be impossible to name them all, but I'll attempt it anyway. My humble thanks to:

My Beta Readers: Lisa Weigard (my relentless cheerleader and dear friend who recruited and led the merry band), Susan Robinson, Donna Gilmore, Jana Phillips, Gina Moltz, Leslie Johnson, Doreen DiMeglio, Amy Moffitt, Eunice Minick, and Jen Savin.

The faithful readers to my original blog, Kid Friendly Organic Life, who gave me the courage to pull this together.

Demi Stevens, who held my hand through the lay out and publishing jungle.

My parents, Patricia and Dave Hazlebeck who offered a lifetime of lessons, constant encouragement, and last minute proofreading.

My mother-in-law and friend, Margot Tillitson who has read all of this book in parts over the course of the last eight years, sent her good karma, and given her expert editing services whenever asked.

Linda Soper, who lives too far away but is always near in my heart, for her endless enthusiasm and hours-long phone consults.

My husband Nick who is almost always game for every crazy new project I come up with and creates plenty of his own. His unconditional support and underappreciated IT help make my writing possible. You are my better half in so many ways.

And of course, my kiddos. Forgive me for spending too many hours at the keyboard and not enough playing Monopoly. You are my inspiration.

About the Author

Cara Sue Achterberg lives on a hillside in South Central, Pennsylvania with her three kids, three horses, one dog with compromised impulse control (but a sunny outlook), a frequently changing number of cats, too many chickens to count and her endlessly patient husband. When not toiling at her keyboard or in her gardens, Cara enjoys running, hiking, teaching workshops on Intentional Life, visiting Virginia wineries, and trying not to fall off her favorite horse, True. She is currently in the process of publishing a young adult novel and writing a memoir about her experiences breaking a difficult horse and raising children (you can imagine the crossover I'm sure). You can find links to her blogs and inspiration for teen writers on her website CaraWrites.com.

21183091R00186

Made in the USA
Middletown, DE
20 June 2015